SOME FAMOUS MEDICAL TRIALS

SOME FAMOUS MEDICAL TRIALS

LEONARD A. PARRY M.D., B.S., F.R.C.S.

BeardBooks
Washington, D.C.

Copyright 1928 by Charles Scribner's Sons
Reprinted 2000 by Beard Books, Washington, D.C.
ISBN 1-58798-031-2

Printed in the United States of America

INTRODUCTION

THE perennial popularity of crime as a vicarious indulgence among the great masses of humanity is so obvious a fact that the most casuistic social optimist is unable to predict a utopian world in which readers will turn instinctively from the details of a thrilling murder to the less exciting, but undoubtedly more edifying, chronicles of ennobling deeds. Moreover, the average reader's rapt concern in the derelictions of his fellows is not only increasing and spreading, but also taking on a shrewdly cultivated and technically exacting spirit of criticism. The art of murder, of which De Quincey wrote so eloquently, even if extravagantly, has become a part of our modern æsthetic curriculum.

Psychologists have sought to trace this general absorption in crime to some fundamental lesion in the imperfect human being of to-day; and a vast library of speculation has resulted. But the explanation, I believe, lies—like that of so many other behavioristic predilections and *penchants*—in a complication of reasons. We are undeniably primitive, despite all our noble gropings toward an unworldly idealism; and there are in nearly all of us latent criminal tendencies which seek an outlet in the imagination. The various safeguards of modern life have sapped us of the courage and daring necessary to the fulfilment of our savage impulses; and consequently we give vent to these impulses through the medium of criminalistic literature. Subconsciously, perhaps, we admire the criminals and murderers of history. Do they not represent an adventuresome, if perverted, freedom, and carry to a climactic actualization certain suppressed urgings in our own natures? Murderers appeal to us very much as do great actors, great generals, and great rulers.

Again, a spirit of sportsmanship enters into our attitude when reading of the intrepid acts of malefactors. Any gambling for high stakes is a fascinating spectacle; and the criminal—especially the murderer—plays for the highest stakes—to wit, his freedom and his very existence on earth. Nearly every crime is a sporting event—a game of chance compared with which the most reckless wagers at Monte Carlo are but simulacra. Also, the element of primitive curiosity, which has been developed in man by the necessity of understanding the world he has had to conquer, plays a part in our thirst for the history of anti-social acts. In addition, the various taboos laid down by the moralists have created a morbid fascination for us in the forbidden phases of life.

Nor can we overlook the appeal of the intellectual problem that forces itself upon the reader of criminological books. Marlowe's *Doctor Faustus*, when he bemoaned the fact that analytics had ravished him, voiced the complaint of all thinking humanity; and the puzzle-makers, the problemists, the mathematicians, and the inventors of parlor games have been pandering to this analytic instinct in man from time immemorial. The accounts of all deliberated crimes present a problem to the reader: they stimulate his mind to speculation; they launch him upon a sea of intricate conjecture, and call upon him to solve, by logic and a knowledge of human nature, the mysteries of motive, technic, and legal evasion.

While Doctor Parry in this present record of famous medical trials satisfies one's longing for the morbid and

INTRODUCTION v

thrilling, and also appeals strongly to one's sporting instincts, he nevertheless emphasizes, by a judiciously legalistic approach to his subject-matter, the problematic and intellectual aspect of the cases he has chosen, and thereby makes a direct claim upon the attention of the analytic reader. By this method of treatment he has presented his subject in the most satisfying manner possible. Indeed, his book is a model of what crime literature should be. My one regret is that this eminent expert in legal jurisprudence has never turned his hand to the detective story, for I feel certain such a work would set a new and much needed standard in that exacting field of literary art. It is no mere coincidence that Doctor Parry's former book is entitled "Risks and Dangers of Various Occupations."

The present work is not a mere collection of haphazardly chosen legal cases, but a well-planned and well-balanced record of original sources, which will prove as valuable to the student of legal medicine and to the amateur criminologist as it will prove irresistible to the casual lover of grim and gruesome melodrama. By segregating thirty-two cases that deal directly with medical evidence, not only has Doctor Parry succeeded in unifying his material and maintaining a single mood throughout, but he has brought to light many interesting cases which have been passed over by the more general chronicler. Moreover, he has chosen his cases with a view to their historical and legal significance. Three of the first four cases of aconite poisoning are recorded here—those of Doctor Warder, Doctor Pritchard, and Doctor Lamson—as well as the first case of murder by morphine poisoning—that of the young Paris doctor, Edme Castaing, in 1823. And there are also included a summary of the first trial in which medical privilege was pleaded, and an account of the trial which resulted in the last public execution in Scotland.

In this connection it should be stated that, in reading these cases, one gets an excellent idea of the evolution of criminal jurisprudence in England; and it is possible to make comparisons between the legal procedure of the early and the late nineteenth century, as well as between that of the nineteenth and the twentieth century.

Perhaps the outstanding feature of Doctor Parry's book is the vast fund of information it contains. Each case has been boiled down to the essentials: all speculation and irrelevancies have been eliminated. Nor is there either romancing or moralizing in these stark records. Every statement is based on authentic data, and reveals not only wide research but a profound familiarity with criminal history. In six or eight pages Doctor Parry achieves what the average writer on criminology takes 10,000 words to set forth. The account of the Crippen case—to name but one instance—is a model of condensed information. Only one other account with which I am familiar is as satisfactory, and that is the 211-page volume on Crippen in the Notable British Trials Series.

But Doctor Parry's vignette of the Crippen trial is no exception. Many current errors and superstitions relating to famous cases are done away with in this book. Many mooted points are clarified; and many misstatements made by less careful writers are scotched. Doctor Parry possesses an impartial, historical attitude; and his records are as authentic as they are scholarly. Being a physician, a Fellow of the Royal College of Surgeons, he has naturally accentuated the medical evidence in the cases treated. But since he has carefully chosen only those

INTRODUCTION vii

trials whose outcome depended largely on medico-legal testimony, he has been able to render each of his documents wholly satisfying.

This limitation of theme has in no wise curtailed the general appeal of his book. Twice as many cases are included as in the average treatise of its kind; and more actual ground is covered than in three or four ordinary volumes of criminal exposition. This fulness of text and subject-matter is, in large measure, the result of Doctor Parry's terse and compact style. The records of each case have been painstakingly studied, and the salients carefully selected and set down with the precision and vividness of thoroughly assimilated knowledge. Especially is the account of the notorious Lamson case an example of straightforward dramatic narrative, stark in projection yet with full and arresting information.

The field of research covered by Doctor Parry is unusually extensive. For his first chapter he has gone back to the historic case of Sir Thomas Overbury in 1615; and he has included cases as recent as 1910. Many famous trials are recorded—among them Doctor Pritchard's, Doctor Webster's, Neil Cream's, Doctor Palmer's, and the Resurrectionists'. But the book is by no means a mere restatement of *causes célèbres*. There are at least a dozen cases here which will be unfamiliar even to the avid reader of criminal literature; and, in addition, there are accounts of many important trials which, while known by name, have had no popular chronicler.

Not all the trials set down are those of murder. There are cases of treason, medical forgery, abortion, rebellion, torture, libel, and assault. Nor do all the chapters deal with proven felons and murderers. Many of the cases ended with acquittal—such as Doctor Watson's, John

Long's, Doctor Sheridan's, and Doctor Hadwen's. Doctor Parry is primarily interested in the medico-legal aspect of his subject, and he views all the trials he relates through the eyes of a doctor. In this very concentration of vision he seems to have touched the very mainsprings of interest in his cases, and thrown upon his subject a new and fascinating light.

WILLARD HUNTINGTON WRIGHT.

PREFACE

I HAVE had considerable difficulty in choosing a title which will accurately describe my book, and even now I have not succeeded, for in some of the instances selected medical men were not on trial, though they were concerned with the cases reported. However, the title is not of vast importance. To interest those who read the book is much more to the point.

I have recorded many cases of major crimes committed by doctors, but I would not have it imagined for one moment that my profession is addicted to lawlessness. Far from it. The instances of serious criminal lapses by medical men are few and far between. Mr. Kingston, who has written so many works on the subject of offenders against the law, characterises as a dismal procession of degenerates those doctors who have earned notoriety for themselves. Fortunate it is that comparatively few medical men have waged war on the public. Sherlock Holmes says that when a doctor goes wrong, he is the first of criminals. He has nerve and knowledge. Is this true? I doubt it. For example, nearly all of those who have indulged in poisoning have made the most egregious blunders, which have brought them to the gallows. Sir James Crichton Browne has called them the scum of the profession. He is right. They are both in intellect and morals.

PREFACE

The cases described are not intended to be a complete list of famous medical trials. They are selected mostly from this country. They are not arranged in any particular order, either alphabetically or chronologically. They contain no example of the trial of a woman doctor.

My best thanks are due to Mr. Lister, Librarian of the Hove Library, and his assistants, for much valuable help in the preparation of this work.

L. A. PARRY.

CONTENTS

	PAGE

CHAPTER I. The Murder of Sir Thomas Overbury .   1

Early life of Overbury and Essex. Overbury poisoned. Weston charged. His trial, verdict, and sentence. Sir John Hollis and Sir John Wentworth accused of attempting to interfere with justice. Sir James Stephen's comments on the Star Chamber. Earl and Countess of Somerset tried for murder. *Peine forte et dure.* Spiggot and Phillips stand mute. Case of Major Strangeways. Development of medical jurisprudence and toxicology. Mary Blandy tried for poisoning her father with arsenic.

CHAPTER II. A Queen's Physician Charged with Treason   17

Sir George Wakeman accused of plotting to murder the King. Titus Oates and his perjury. His early life. Trial. Wakeman tried for treason. Oates the chief witness. Wakeman's defence. Found not guilty. *Rôles* reversed. Oates accused of perjury. Wakeman testifies against him. Well-deserved punishment of the perjurer.

CHAPTER III. Dr. Cross, his Wife and his Governess .   31

Dr. Cross and his relations with Miss Skinner. Mrs. Cross dies under remarkable circumstances. Suspicious conduct of the doctor. Exhumation of the body. Arrest of Dr. Cross. Trial and execution.

CHAPTER IV. Two Medical Forgers . . .   36

The financial transactions of Daniel and Robert Perreau. Their connection with Mrs. Rudd. Her fascinating personality. The trial of the brothers for forgery. Mrs. Rudd acquitted. Petition for pardon of the condemned men. Their execution.

CHAPTER V. Collins, the Abortionist . . .   40

The brilliant career of Collins. His association with Mrs. Uzielli. Her death. Dr. Collins charged with murder. Trial at Central Criminal Court. Evidence of Sir John Williams. Mr. Justice Grantham's summing

CONTENTS

up. Collins convicted of manslaughter and sentenced to seven years' penal servitude. The professional abortionist.

CHAPTER VI. A Medical Firebrand . . . 54

Dr. Watson's politics. The Spafields meeting. Dr. Watson leads the rioters to the Tower. Failure of the outbreak. Arrest and trial. Charged with treason. Mr. Wetherell's brilliant defence. Acquittal of his client.

CHAPTER VII. The Trial of Dr. Pritchard . . 64

Death of Dr. Pritchard's wife and mother-in-law. Aconite the cause of death. Trial and conviction of Dr. Pritchard. His confession. The last public execution in Scotland.

CHAPTER VIII. A Nineteenth Century Fashionable Quack 70

Long attends Miss Cashin. Her death. The quack arrested and accused of manslaughter. Convicted and fined. Resumes practice. Death of Mrs. Colin Campbell Lloyd. Long again accused of manslaughter. Trial and acquittal. His death four years later.

CHAPTER IX. Levi Weil, Thief and Murderer . 77

Weil's career. Murder of Mrs. Hutchings. Search for the criminal. Betrayal of Weil by one of his band. Trial and sentence. Execution at Tyburn.

CHAPTER X. The Trial of Florence Hensey, M.D., for High Treason at Westminster Hall, June, 1758 . 80

Dr. Hensey accused of treasonable correspondence with the French. Trial at bar. Lord Mansfield's summing up. Sentence of death. Reprieve and liberation of Dr. Hensey.

CHAPTER XI. Dr. Lamson 88

Lamson accused of the murder by poison of his brother-in-law, Percy John. Aconite the cause of death. Evidence against the prisoner. Mr. Justice Hawkins on the facility with which deadly poisons can be obtained. Dr. Stevenson on his analysis of the viscera. Mr. Montagu Williams' speech for the defence. Reply of the Solicitor-General. Jury convict. Execution at Wandsworth. Mr. Justice Hawkins' view of the case.

CONTENTS

PAGE

CHAPTER XII. Dr. Hunter and the "Pall Mall Gazette" 104
Dr. Hunter sues the *Pall Mall Gazette* for libel. Mr. Coleridge appears for the doctor. "Impostors and dupes." Lord Chief Justice Cockburn sums up. His views on quacks. Dr. Hunter wins his action and obtains one farthing damages.

CHAPTER XIII. Dr. Spreull and the Torture . . 110
Dr. Spreull's connection with the Covenanters. Tortured by order of the Privy Council. Trial for rebellion. Acquittal. Further charge and sentence. The question of the legality of torture in England. Instruments used. *Peine forte et dure.* The case of Felton. The Master of Orkney. Elizabeth Cellier. Ravillac the parricide brutally tortured in France. Mr. Thomas Picton, Governor of Trinidad, and his torture of Luisa Calderon. Lord Coke on torture.

CHAPTER XIV. The First Case of Murder by Morphia 122
Dr. Castaing and the Ballet brothers. Castaing tried for murder by morphia. Evidence of M. Orfila, the celebrated toxicologist, and other experts. Medical evidence for the defence. Castaing convicted and executed.

CHAPTER XV. The Murder of Doctor by Doctor . 131
Disappearance of Dr. Parkman. Discovery of remains. Dr. Webster suspected. Arrest. Evidence of a dentist. Dr. Webster found guilty of murder. Execution.

CHAPTER XVI. The Case of Dr. Edward Sheridan . 135
Irish grievances in the nineteenth century. The Catholic Committee. Irish Convention Act. Dr. Sheridan charged with misdemeanour. The speech of the Attorney-General. Brilliant defence by Mr. Burrowes. Lord Justice Downes sums up. Dr. Sheridan acquitted.

CHAPTER XVII. Dr. Neil Cream, Wholesale Poisoner 147
Mysterious deaths of several girls. Cream's peculiar conduct. Suspicions of Detective Sergeant M'Intyre aroused. Cream's attempt to blackmail Dr. Harper. Arrest and trial. His letter to Dr. Broadbent. Evidence of Dr. Stevenson. Mr. Geoghegan's defence. Mr. Justice Hawkins' summing up. Sentence of death. Cream's mentality.

CHAPTER XVIII. The Murder of M'Donald by Dr. Smith, of Aberdeenshire 164
The finding of the body of M'Donald. Dr. Smith and

CONTENTS

his life insurance transactions. The usual conflict of
medical evidence. The Lord Justice Clerk sums up.
Verdict of not proven. Public indignation.

CHAPTER XIX. Dr. Crippen's Trial . . . 170

Crippen's career. Disappearance of Belle Elmore.
Crippen's suspicious conduct. Discovery of the remains
of Belle Elmore by Inspector Dew. Crippen's flight.
Arrest by means of wireless. Trial. Evidence of Mr.
Pepper, Dr. Spilsbury and Dr. Willcox. Crippen in the
box. His cross-examination. Medical evidence for the
prisoner. Mr. Tobin's speech for the defence. Mr.
Muir replies. Lord Chief Justice sums up. Conviction.
Appeal of Crippen to Court of Criminal Appeal.
Failure. Petition for reprieve. Trial of Ethel Le Neve.

CHAPTER XX. A Medical Libel 186

The relations of Dr. Field and Dr. Austin. The
anonymous letter. Action for libel. Evidence of
colleagues. Sir Benjamin Brodie. Verdict for plaintiff for £100.

CHAPTER XXI. Dr. Smethurst's Lucky Escape . 193

Dr. and Mrs. Smethurst. The meeting with Miss
Bankes. The mock marriage. Illness and death of Miss
Bankes. Suspicions of Dr. Julius. Cause of death of
Miss Bankes found to be irritant poison. Trial of Dr.
Smethurst. Professor Taylor's mistake. Remarkable
medical evidence for the defence. Verdict of guilty.
Curious procedure of Home Secretary. Sir Benjamin
Brodie's report. Pardon of Smethurst. His letter to the
Lancet. His action to obtain the property of the woman
he had murdered.

**CHAPTER XXII. The Trial of Charles Bateman,
Surgeon, of London, at the Old Bailey for High
Treason, 1685** 208

Dr. Bateman's connection with the Rye House Plot.
Law of trials for treason in Stuart times. Trial and
execution of the doctor. Remarks of Sir John Hawles,
Solicitor-General in the reign of William III., on the
whole procedure.

CHAPTER XXIII. The Brighton Murder . . 216

The life of Dr. Warder. His marriage to Miss Branwell. Her strange illness and death. Suspicion

CONTENTS

aroused. Inquest on Mrs. Warder. Verdict of murder against her husband. His suicide. Inquest. Felo de se. His burial.

CHAPTER XXIV. **Miscellaneous Cases** . . . 223

Penruddock and his examiners. Assault on Mr. Hardy. Sentence of twelve months' imprisonment. Dr. Willobycki. His criminal career. Sentenced to fourteen years' penal servitude. Commonwealth regulations. A doctor's attempt to save a man from the gallows. First case in which medical privilege was pleaded.

CHAPTER XXV. **The Case of Dr. Joseph Collier** . 229

Religious feeling in the reign of George III. The Reformation Society. Dr. Collier charged with conspiracy. Mr. Erskine's defence. Failure of the prosecution. Chief witness for the Crown tried for perjury and sentenced to two years' imprisonment.

CHAPTER XXVI. **Palmer the Poisoner** . . . 235

Palmer arrested for murder by strychnine of his friend Cook. Trial of Offences Act passed to enable the venue of the trial to be changed. Careless conduct of autopsy. Medical witnesses for the prosecution. Fantastic views of doctors called for the defence. Conviction of prisoner. Views of Sir James Stephen. Sir Henry Hawkins on Palmer. Dr. Swayne Taylor on the subject of medical evidence.

CHAPTER XXVII. **The Resurrection Men** . 259

Body-stealing. Trial of Holmes and Williams. The Burke and Hare crimes. Many brutal murders. Trial of Burke. Hare accepted as King's evidence. Conviction of Burke. End of Hare. Other examples of murder by the gang. Execution of Burke. Amendment of the law and passing of the Anatomy Act.

CHAPTER XXVIII. **Dr. Bastwick and the Star Chamber** 277

Star Chamber procedure. Its abolition. Dr. Bastwick charged with seditious libel. Convicted. Terrible punishment. Review of sentence by Committee of House. Lord Clarendon's views on the case.

CHAPTER XXIX. **The Case of Dr. Archibald Cameron** 280

Early life. He joins rebel army. Flees to France after Culloden. Betrayed on his return to Scotland.

Tried under Act of Attainder. Death sentence and execution. Trial of Deacon. Criminal law under the Hanoverians. Reforms. Views of Justice Hawkins. Sir James Stephen. Methods of execution. Accidents during process. Cases of Patrick Ledmond and of George Foster.

CHAPTER XXX. **Court-martial on a Naval Surgeon** . 293

Exile of Napoleon. Fears of British Government. Act of Parliament to regulate his captivity. Death of Napoleon. Post-mortem. Letter of Sir Alexander Simpson. Mr. Stokoe sent to attend Napoleon in his illness. Tried by court-martial for partiality in his dealings with Napoleon. Sentence.

CHAPTER XXXI. **The Case of Henry Harrison** . 299

Harrison and Mrs. Vanwicke. Dr. Clenche's mortgage. Harrison accused of murder of the doctor. Chief witness disappears. Harrison found guilty. Executed.

CHAPTER XXXII. **The Prosecution of Dr. Hadwen** . 310

Views of *Truth*. Events leading up to the charge of manslaughter. The trial. Mr. Vachell appears for the prosecution. Medical evidence. Sir Edward Marshall Hall's defence. Dr. Hadwen in the box. Mr. Justice Lush sums up. Verdict of not guilty. Universal approval.

SOME FAMOUS MEDICAL TRIALS

THE MURDER OF SIR THOMAS OVERBURY

THE TRIALS OF RICHARD WESTON AT THE GUILDHALL, LONDON, AND OF JAMES FRANKLIN AT THE KING'S BENCH, IN 1615 FOR THE MURDER BY POISON OF SIR THOMAS OVERBURY

THE first trial of any medical man for a serious crime in this country, of which there is any record, is that of James Franklin for the murder of Sir Thomas Overbury in the reign of James I. Franklin and his assistant, Weston, were both connected with the medical profession, but it must be remembered that in the seventeenth century the doctor was not so clearly differentiated from the laity as he is now. There was no Medical Act (the first was passed in 1858) and no General Medical Council to regulate medical education and qualification. Each guild or college made its own provisions as to granting degrees or diplomas, and there was no standard of rules to which each had to conform.

The murder of Sir Thomas Overbury, the poet and essayist, born in 1581, was one of the most sensational crimes recorded in history. Overbury, when a young man, and a youth named Robert Carr, then page to Lord Dunbar, had struck up a great friendship, and they determined to come to London together to seek their fortunes. They both secured appointments at the Court of James I., and, for Carr especially, promotion was rapid. He was soon created Lord Rochester, and (this was after the murder of Overbury) finally Lord Somerset. He became infatuated with the youthful and infamous Countess of Essex, and this intrigue bade fair to spoil his life. His devoted friend Overbury used every argument and inducement of which he was capable to save Rochester from the wiles of this woman. She had been married at thirteen, following what was an ordinary family custom at that time, to the Earl of Essex, a boy only one year older. He at once went abroad, and when he returned his wife, then seventeen years old, had fallen in love with Lord Rochester. The intrigue between Rochester and the Countess was so well staged by the latter that she made it appear she was a most unfortunate woman. A divorce was secured without much difficulty, and she married Rochester. A deadly enmity had sprung up between the Countess and Sir Thomas Overbury on account of his efforts to save his friend Rochester from the base intrigues of this woman. She laid a series of traps for the overthrow of Sir Thomas.

Rochester, infatuated with the Countess, had become a false friend to his old comrade, and, after getting the King to offer Overbury the Russian Embassy, suggested to Sir Thomas that he should refuse the appointment as he would better himself by staying in England. The King, James I., was then made to believe that he had been grossly affronted by the refusal, and a warrant was issued to consign Sir Thomas to the Tower.

The Countess determined Overbury should give no further trouble. She obtained for her friend Sir Gervis Elwes the appointment of Governor of the prison, and with others of her *protégés*, including Franklin, the apothecary, and Weston, she found little difficulty in getting rid of Sir Thomas by a brutal process of slow poisoning.

Two months after Rochester, now Earl of Somerset, married Lady Essex. It was not till a year later that any suspicion of her guilt arose. In the celebrated trial which followed, the whole plot was disclosed. There were

THE MURDER OF SIR THOMAS OVERBURY

indicted Somerset and his wife, Sir Gervis Elwes, and four others, including Franklin and Weston.

The trial of Weston, who had been an "apothecary's man," but at the time of the murder was under-keeper of the Tower, took place before the Lord Chief Justice of England, Lord Coke, the Lord Mayor of London, and other judges, at the Guildhall.

Lord Coke, in his charge to the Grand Jury, said he desired to express the pious inclination and command of the King that all who were in any way concerned in the murder of Sir Thomas Overbury should be punished. (This excellent sentiment was with King James I. a mere matter of frothy words. He allowed the wretched underlings to be hanged, but respited the titled principals.) The Lord Chief Justice expressed to the jury his feeling that " of all felonies murder was the most horrible, of all murders poisoning the most detestable, and of all poisonings the lingering was the worst." By an Act of Parliament the punishment for this offence was boiling to death ; he quoted the case of Richard Rowse, who, for the murder by poison of a man and a woman, had actually been scalded to death. The use of poison in England was fortunately rare, and was against the feeling of our people. He finished his charge by begging the jury to do justice in the trial, no matter how great the position of the guilty.

The case, as outlined against Weston, was that he had been guilty of murdering, by a process of slow poisoning, Sir Thomas Overbury whilst a prisoner in the Tower. He was accused of using rosalgar (this is a compound of arsenic), sublimate of mercury, and white arsenic, which he mixed with food and gave to Sir Thomas. He poisoned broth, tarts and jellies which Sir Thomas consumed. He and Franklin also administered an enema containing mercury sublimate to the deceased. After these various procedures had been carried out Sir Thomas became very ill and eventually died.

The prisoner refused to plead in the form the law required, saying he referred himself to God. The Judges spent one hour in trying to persuade Weston to comply with the law, pointing out to him that unless he did so a very terrible punishment, would have to be ordered namely, that of *onere, frigore, et fame* (by weight, by cold, and by hunger). For the first he was to be stretched out and have weights placed on him, but to stop short of being crushed to death; for the second he was to stand naked in the open air; and for the third he was to be fed on the coarsest bread on one day, followed the next day by nothing but water out of the nearest puddle or sink, this treatment to be continued till he died.

The Lord Chief Justice intimated that it was plain that Weston had been persuaded not to plead by some persons of high position, in case he might give evidence which might incriminate them.

The prisoner still remained mute, but finally, after an adjournment of some days, he thought better of it, and pleaded not guilty.

The Attorney-General in his opening statement charged the Earl and Countess of Somerset as the prime movers in this cruel murder. The Countess was a dead and rotten branch of a noble family, which would be all the better were that branch lopped off. The motive for the murder was the malice of the Countess against Sir Thomas Overbury for his part in attempting to dissuade the Earl of Rochester (at that time he had not been created Earl of Somerset) from the adulterous marriage with Lady Somerset (then Countess of Essex). Sir Thomas, seeing the infatuation of Lord Rochester for the Countess, did all he could to persuade him not to have anything to do with the lady. On one occasion, at Whitehall, he said, " Well, my lord, if you do marry that filthy, base woman, you will utterly ruin your honour and yourself; you shall never do it by my advice or consent; and if you do, you had best look to stand fast." Lord Rochester, bewitched by the charms of the youthful Countess, replied, "My own legs are straight and strong enough to bear me up; but, in faith, I will be even with you for this." He parted from Sir Thomas in a great temper.

Overbury, not doubting Somerset's devotion, thought this was but an exhibition of peevishness, and still trusted implicitly his friend.

The King shortly after this offered Sir Thomas the post of Russian Ambassador, which he most gratefully accepted, but Rochester later persuaded him to decline the appointment, saying it was much to his advantage to remain in England. Every action of the Countess and her lover was the result of plotting and intrigue to injure Overbury. By strategy they got him sent prisoner to the Tower. The Countess used every influence she possessed, and obtained the dismissal of the chief officers of the Tower and the appointment of creatures of her own in their place. Weston was one of these, and now, as the keeper of Sir Thomas, was in a position to carry out the desires of the Countess. He was heavily bribed to administer poison to the prisoner, and made a commencement by giving some yellow poison called rosalgar (an arsenical preparation) mixed with Sir Thomas' supper. This produced excessive vomiting and diarrhœa. For some weeks this sort of thing went on, Sir Thomas growing weaker and weaker from day to day. Rochester wrote to him, promising to secure his release as soon as possible. This was certainly his intention, but not in the way the wretched prisoner understood. The months passed on, and in September (Sir Thomas had been in the Tower since May) Weston administered an enema with poison in it, and this resulted in the death of the victim. The effect of the various poisons produced a large number of blains and blisters on the body, so the rumour was spread that syphilis was the cause of death.

The statement of the Attorney-General was borne out in evidence. Weston still averred his innocence, although he had practically confessed his guilt in the testimony he gave.

The Judge, after the evidence had been heard, summed up. He exhorted the jury to take God before their eyes, and with equal balance to weigh as well the answers of the prisoner as the proofs against him. As a matter of law, the judge instructed the jury that though the poisoning in the indictment be said to be with rosalgar, white arsenic and mercuric sublimate, yet they were not to expect precise proof on that point, warning the jury how impossible it was to convict a poisoner " who useth not to take any witnesses to the composing of his cibber sauces." He declared the law to be the same as if a man were indicted for murder with a dagger, and the evidence proved the crime to be committed with a sword or with a rapier. " In this case, the instrument skilleth " (*i.e.*, " signifies ") " not so that the jury find the murder." And so in this poisoner's case, if they were satisfied poison had been used, it was immaterial what the poison was. (It is to be noted that Lord Campbell in the trial of Palmer used just such reasoning, pointing out to the jury that whether the murder were committed by aconite or strychnine was quite unimportant ; whatever poison caused the fatal result, it was murder.)

The jury found the prisoner guilty, and he was sentenced to be hanged by the neck till he was dead.

Franklin, the apothecary who supplied the poison, was tried at the King's Bench. He confessed his crime. He stated that in a house near to Doctors' Commons he was approached by a Mrs. Turner, who asked him for material to slowly poison a man. She gave him four angels (about two pounds), whereupon he brought a water called *aqua fortis* (weak nitric acid) and gave it to Mrs. Turner, who tried it upon a cat, which died after languishing for two days. Later the Countess sent for Franklin, and told him *aqua fortis* was too powerful. " What think you of white arsenick ? " He told her it was too violent. " What say you to powder of diamonds?" He answered, "I know not the nature of that." She said he was a fool, and gave him pieces of gold and told him to buy some of that powder for her.

A little before the death of Sir Thomas the Countess sent for Franklin and showed him a letter from Rochester with these words in it: "I marvel at these delays, that the business is not yet despatched." There was also another letter from the same source, in which it was hinted that the prisoner would be released in two days, and it would then be too late. Weston told the Countess that he had given enough poison to kill twenty men. It was not long after this that the poisoned enema which killed Sir Thomas was administered.

A fortnight after the arrest of Weston the Countess sent for Franklin and told him Weston had confessed everything and that they would all be hanged. She besought him to remain silent about his connection with the murder. If he talked, " you shall be hanged, for I will not hang for you," said the Countess. Mrs. Turner added, " I will not hang for you both." They were not very loyal comrades.

Franklin at his trial acknowledged he had procured the poison for the Countess and Mrs. Turner, but that he had no idea for what purpose it was required. He was found guilty, and the Lord Chief Justice, after a short exhortation, added these words: "that knowing as much as he knew, if this had not been found out, neither the Court, city, nor any particular family had escaped the malice of this wicked cruelty." Franklin was one of the four hanged for this cold-blooded murder.

When Weston was on his way to the scaffold, two friends of Lord Somerset, Sir John Hollis and Sir John Wentworth, rode by the prisoner's side and entreated him to deny the confession he had made, hoping thus to influence for good the trial of the Somersets, but Weston, being prepared for death, refused to perjure himself in his last moments, and maintained the truth of his state-

ments. For this offence Hollis and Wentworth were
tried in the Star Chamber, being accused of traducing
public justice, and were each fined and given imprisonment for one year.

A totally different version of this incident is given by Sir
James Fitzjames Stephen in his " History of the Criminal
Law of England."

The following is his account of the matter: " The Star
Chamber proceedings reported in the 'State Trials' leave
a singular impression on my mind. As far as the mere
management in court of the different cases went, it cannot
be denied that they are for the most part calm and dig-
nified, though the strange taste and violent passions of
the time give them occasionally a grotesque appearance;
but the severity of the ' censures ' or sentences is in these
days astonishing. A few instances may be mentioned.
In 1615 Sir John Hollis and Sir John Wentworth were
prosecuted for 'traducing the public justice.' Weston
had been hanged for the murder of Sir Thomas Overbury,
to whom he had administered poison. Wentworth and
Hollis went to Weston's execution, where Wentworth
asked Weston whether he really did poison Overbury,
and pressed him to answer, saying ' he desired to know,
that he might pray with him.' Hollis ' was not so much
of a questioner,' but, ' like a kind of confessor, wished him
to discharge his conscience and satisfy the world.' Hollis,
moreover, when the jury gave their verdict, said, ' if he
were on the jury, he would doubt what to do.' It is
difficult to see how this could be regarded as in any
sense criminal conduct; but it seems to have been thought
that Wentworth's question and Hollis's remark remotely
implied that Weston's guilt might perhaps be not absolutely certain, notwithstanding his conviction. Lord
Bacon (the Attorney-General) developed this view of the
subject at length, and with characteristic grace, calmness
and power. The defendants excused themselves in a
polite manner, Sir John Hollis observing that ' Mr.

THE MURDER OF SIR THOMAS OVERBURY

Attorney had so well applied his charge against him that, though he carried the seal of a good conscience with him, he would almost make him believe he was guilty.' As for what he had said to Weston, he was there ' carried with a general desire which he had to be at the execution as he had done in many like cases before.' It was a common thing on such occasions to question the person about to be executed, and he had only followed his usual practice."

This is an excellent example of the difficulty of ensuring historical accuracy. Here we have two excellent sources of information (Howell's " State Trials " and Stephens' " History of Criminal Law ") drawing two totally different interpretations from the same facts. Who can tell at this distance of time which is correct?

I quote here a part of the speech made by Sir Francis Bacon in his prosecution of these two men to show, firstly, the style of eloquence of the Attorney-General, and, secondly, the slavish adulation of royalty characteristic of the times, even by such a man as Bacon :—

" The king, amongst many his princely virtues, is known to excel in that proper virtue of the imperial throne, which is justice. It is a royal virtue, which doth employ the other three cardinal virtues in her service. Wisdom to discover, and discern nocent and innocent : fortitude to prosecute and execute : temperance, so to carry justice as it be not passionate in the pursuit, nor confused in involving persons upon light suspicion nor precipitate in time. For this his majesty's virtue of justice, God hath of late raised an occasion, and erected as it were a stage or theatre much to his honour for him to shew it, and act it in the pursuit of the untimely death of Sir Thomas Overbury and therein cleansing the land from blood. For, my lords, if blood spilt pure doth cry to heaven in God's ears, much more blood defiled with poison. . . . First, it pleased my lord chief justice to let me know (that which I heard with great comfort) which was the charge which his majesty gave to himself first, and afterwards to the commissioners in this case worth certainly to be written in letters of gold, wherein his majesty did fore-rank and make it his prime direction that it should be carried without touch to any that was innocent; nay more, not only without impeachment, but without aspersion : which was a most noble and princely caution from his majesty; for men's reputations are tender things and ought to be like Christ's coat, without seam. And it was the more to be respected in this case, because it met with two great persons : a nobleman that his majesty had favoured and advanced, and his lady being of a great and honourable house : though I think it be true, that the writers say, that there is no pomegranite so fair or so sound, but may have a perished kernel. . . . Now I will come to the particular charge of these gentlemen, whose qualities and persons I respect and love : for they are all my particular friends : . . . That wretched man Weston, who was the actor or mechanical party in this impoisonment, at the first day being indicted by a very substantial jury of selected citizens, to the number of nineteen, who found *billa vera*, yet nevertheless at the first stood mute : but after some days intermission, it pleased God to cast out the dumb devil, and that he did put himself upon his trial : and was by a jury also of great value, upon his confession, and other testimonies, found guilty : so as thirty-one sufficient jurors have passed upon him. Whereupon judgement and execution was awarded against him. After this, being in preparation for another world, he sent for Sir Thomas Overbury's father, and falling down upon his knees, with great remorse and compunction, asked his forgiveness; . . . confessed that he was to die justly and that he was worthy of death. . . . For the offence of Sir John Wentworth and Sir John Hollis, . . . it was shortly this : At the time and place of the execution of Weston, . . . these gentlemen, with others, came mounted on horseback, and in a ruffling and facing manner, put themselves

THE MURDER OF SIR THOMAS OVERBURY 11

forward, to re-examine Weston upon questions: . . .
What was Sir John Wentworth's question: whether
Weston did poison Overbury or no ? . . . Weston . . .
turning to the sheriff, said, You promised me I should
not be troubled at this time. . . . For Sir John Hollis,
he was not so much a questionist : but wrought upon the
other's questions, and, like a kind of confessor, wished
him to discharge his conscience, and to satisfy the world.
What world ? I marvel ! It was sure the world at
Tyburn. For the world at Guildhall and the world at
London, was satisfied before : *teste* the bells that rung.
But men have got a fashion nowadays that two or three
busibodies will take upon them the name of the world,
and broach their own conceits, as if it were a general
opinion. . . . Of the offence of these two gentlemen in
general, your lordships must give me leave to say, that
it is an offence greater and more dangerous than is conceived. I know well, that as we have no Spanish inquisitions, nor justice in a corner : so we have no gagging of
men's mouths at their death, but that they may speak
freely at the last hour : but then it must come from
the free motion of the party, not by temptation of
questions. The questions that are to be asked, ought
to tend to further revealing of their own or others
guiltiness : but to use a question in the nature of a
false interrogatory, to falsify that which is *res judicata*
is intolerable. For that were to erect a court of commission of review at Tyburn, against the King's Bench
at Westminster."

The Earl and Countess of Somerset were also put on
trial for this murder. The Countess, who pleaded guilty,
was sentenced to death, but the sentence was not carried
out. She was imprisoned in the Tower for some five
years, and then released with the proviso that she should
remain at a country house, and not go beyond three miles
of this till the King gave further orders. In 1624 she was
pardoned, and died in 1632. The Earl was also found

guilty, but on him again the sentence was not carried out, the same treatment being meted out to him as to the Countess.

The juries concerned did their duty and found all alike, high and low, guilty. The Judge also showed no favour, sentencing all to death. The King alone failed in justice, hanging the four humble prisoners, but pardoning the two mighty and most guilty. Such was English justice under the Stuarts.

The torture of those who refused to plead, which has been referred to above, was not only threatened, as in Weston's case, but was on occasion actually carried out. Two prisoners, Spiggot and Phillips, were indicted for robbery on the King's highway in 1721. They declined to plead until some of their property which had been taken from them was returned. The Court refused, and as, in spite of every persuasion, they remained mute, the sentence was "that the prisoner shall be sent to the prison from whence he came, and put into a mean room, stopped from the light, and shall there be laid on the bare ground without any litter, straw, or other covering, and without any garment upon him, except something to hide his privy members. He shall lie upon his back, his head shall be covered, and his feet shall be bare. One of his arms shall be drawn with a cord to one side of the room, and the other arm to the other side, and his legs shall be served in like manner. There shall be laid upon his body as much iron or stone as he can bear, and more. And the first day after, he shall have three morsels of barley bread, without any drink: and the second day he shall be allowed to drink as much as he can, at three times, of the water that is next the prison door, except running water, without any bread: and this shall be his diet till he dies: and he against whom this judgement shall be given, forfeits his goods to the king." This sentence was read to the prisoners, but they still declined to plead, and were sent back to Newgate to be pressed to death. Phillips

THE MURDER OF SIR THOMAS OVERBURY

gave way, but Spiggot was put under the press, where he remained half an hour with 350 lb. weight on his body, but on the addition of another 50 lb. he also asked to be allowed to alter his mind. They were eventually both executed.

This barbarous law has, of course, long since been repealed by one of the many Acts passed in the reign of George III. for the more merciful treatment of crime.

Another instance is that of Burnworth, who was arraigned in 1726 at Kingston for murder. He " stood mute " and continued so, even after the usual warning. He was placed under the weight, and for nearly two hours bore a pressure of about 4 cwt., and then gave way and asked for mercy.

A most remarkable case of this dreadful punishment is that of Major Strangeways in 1685. He was accused of the murder of his brother-in-law. When before the coroner he was asked to take the dead body by the hand and touch the wound. It was at that time a popular superstition that a corpse would bleed when the murderer approached. Of course this did not happen, but negative evidence was no proof of innocence, and the Major was put to trial at the Old Bailey. He refused to plead, and this at that time meant he could not be convicted, and therefore his lands could not be forfeited, and would thus be preserved for his heirs. He was sent to endure the legal torture of *peine forte et dure*. A feeling, even at this time, had grown up that the punishment was too brutal, and so a merciful device had been invented of shortening the agony, and that was to place a sharp piece of wood under the prisoner's back, in order that death might be hastened ! In Major Strangeways' case this was not done, but instead a part of the mass of iron and stone was placed with a sharp edge over his heart. As this was not sufficient to kill him, the merciful attendants added the weights of their own bodies and crushed the life out of the victim, the whole operation lasting about ten minutes, after which the mangled body was exposed to the public gaze. This is an extreme example of the amount of pain which could be endured by a man who had almost certainly committed a callous murder, but who exhibited great brute courage in order to serve his heirs.

Medical jurisprudence was not recognised as of any importance in the detection of crime certainly till the sixteenth century, and the growth of the science was slow. Very little was known of the subject in this country till the Government instituted a Professorship of Medical Jurisprudence in Edinburgh University in 1803. Since then its strides have been rapid, and it is now a well-recognised branch of medicine. Practically no murder trial takes place at which medical evidence is not called.

The science of toxicology was of somewhat later development. The alchemists, the forerunners of the chemists, discovered many facts which have become part and parcel of the science of chemistry, and they invented and used various pieces of apparatus which are still employed in the laboratory. The evolution of chemistry from alchemy was a slow and gradual process, and the former science cannot be said to have attained any real position till the middle of the eighteenth century. Basil Valentine (which is a pseudonym framed to imply occult mastery over the metals), the author of a series of works on alchemy, who lived in the middle of the seventeenth century, was perhaps the man to whom the beginning of chemistry may be ascribed, for he made many discoveries which were the elementary facts from which arose the new branch of knowledge, though a 100 years were yet to pass before it can be claimed that this had attained the position of a real science.

It was only at the end of the eighteenth century that the chemical tests for the common mineral poisons could be said to be established on a scientific basis; toxicology made its modern start. To Orfila is due the credit of the foundation of the real science of poisons, his great work,

THE MURDER OF SIR THOMAS OVERBURY

"Traité de Toxicologie," being published in 1814. It says much for his marvellous ability that now, after 100 years, the majority of his processes, improved, of course, by modern technique, are used by the analysts. The alkaloids have been known for periods going back as much as 120 years, and the science of toxicology has kept abreast of the times. It has found tests for all the dangerous and powerful drugs of which any poisoner may make use. The scientific detective, the toxicologist, is more than a match for the criminal who indulges in murder by poison.

The first case of a trial for murder by poison in which medical witnesses were called to prove the cause of death, so far as I have been able to trace any record, is that of Mary Blandy, who was tried for murdering her father by means of white arsenic in 1752.

In this instance Dr. Anthony Addington and other medical practitioners gave evidence for the prosecution, but their testimony related to the clinical symptoms and the pathological findings, and no attempt was made to analyse the viscera, though many tests were known for the detection of arsenic, and were actually employed by the doctors to determine the nature of the powder administered to the deceased.

The subject of murder by poison has always had a peculiar fascination, and trials of poisoners always seem to attract an immense amount of public interest. There has been, and exists at the present time, a feeling that the power of poison is a very potent one and a very formidable help to the criminal. As a matter of fact, the knowledge of the chemist and the toxicologist has advanced at a more rapid rate than that of the poisoner, and probably very few instances of poisoning remain now undetected. In nearly all cases the circumstances are on more or less parallel lines. Sudden and extreme illness; symptoms consistent with and suggesting poison; detection of the poison in the body after death; possession of the poison traced to the suspected person ; motive, *e.g.*, the desire to get rid of a wife or a mistress, financial gain, etc.—all these elements together are almost equal to a certainty. In addition the murderer almost always makes some fatuous blunder (*e.g.*, Neil with his attempted blackmail of Dr. Broadbent, Crippen with his foolish lies to his dead wife's friends and his flight from justice, Lamson with his purchase of aconite, etc.) which helps to bring home his guilt. The Death Certification Act of 1836, although badly in need of amendment, did an enormous service in protecting the public from the risk of poisoning. This Act removed some of the easy facilities of disposing of dead bodies without any inquiry, and ensured a much closer watch by the authorities on the cause of death than had previously been the case. It is by no means an easy thing to obtain poison, to administer poison, and to escape detection. Probably at the present time with the Acts dealing with the sale of poisons, and the registration of death, and the advanced state of the science of toxicology, there are very few instances in which the poisoner is not brought to justice.

A QUEEN'S PHYSICIAN CHARGED WITH TREASON

IN order to understand adequately the meaning of the trial of Sir George Wakeman, physician to Queen Katherine, wife of Charles II., on a charge of high treason, some brief account both of the state of religious and political feeling in the reign of King Charles II. and of the life of Titus Oates (than whom probably no more unmitigated scoundrel adorns the pages of history) is necessary. Ever since the Gunpowder Plot, England had been ready to believe any tales, however wild and improbable, against the Roman Catholics. It was an undoubted fact that the King and his brother were at heart, if not in actuality, Catholics, and this together with the relaxation of the penal laws against the members of that religion, the victories of Catholic France, and the activities of the Jesuits, combined to rouse the suspicions and the fears of the nation. In 1678 the notorious Titus Oates came forward with his tale of a Catholic plot to murder the King and the Duke of York, and to establish the Roman Catholic religion in England. In spite of the absurd nature of the story, the ridiculous evidence in support of it, and the obvious falsity of the whole affair, so great was the prejudice against the Catholics that hundreds were arrested and some thirty-five executed on the perjured testimony of this wretched creature Oates. Sir George Wakeman owes his acquittal to the fact that Oates, who was a fool as well as a rogue, had implicated the Queen in this case, and therefore Charles had given instructions to the Judge who was to try the case. As a result, Justice Scroogs summed up in a very different way to that of the previous similar cases, and the prisoner obtained a fair trial.

The early life of Oates is not very clear. He was born about 1650, and after receiving his education at various schools, including one at Seddlescombe, in Sussex, he took Anglican orders and officiated in several parishes, including that of Hastings. Even at this early stage of his career his crooked mind showed itself. He brought malicious charges against various people, but his evidence was disbelieved, and he only just escaped prosecution for perjury. His next adventure was as a naval chaplain. He was soon dismissed for bad conduct. He then came in contact with Dr Tonge, rector of St. Michael's, Wood Street, one of the many fanatics then existing who lived on nothing but the belief in Jesuit plots, much as many people during the Great War did on the German spy mania. Oates offered to help Dr. Tonge to unearth these plots, and for this purpose joined the Roman Catholic Church, being admitted to the Jesuit college at Valladolid as Brother Ambrose. However, he was soon expelled, his conduct was so bad. Later he was admitted to St. Omer, but again his conduct was so disgraceful that he was a second time expelled. He then set himself to invent a popish plot, and by a skilful mixture of false and true and the production of forged documents he induced large numbers, who were only too ready to believe any nonsense as long as it told against the Catholics, to support him. After his failure in the case of Sir George Wakeman very little is heard of Oates in the reign of Charles II.; the pension granted by the Government of some £600 per annum allowed the professional perjurer to retire and live in quiet. A little before the death of the King, the Duke of York, his brother, brought a civil action against Oates, won his case, and was awarded £100,000 damages. Oates, needless to say, did not pay and was therefore arrested, and whilst in prison was indicted for perjury, in 1685. I cannot refrain from quoting some small part of Macaulay's description of this man : " On the day in which he was brought to the bar Westminster Hall was crowded with spectators, among whom were many Roman Catholics, eager to see the misery and humiliation of their persecutor. A few years earlier his short neck, his legs, uneven as those of a badger, his forehead, low as that of a baboon, his purple cheeks, and his monstrous length of chin, had been familiar to all who frequented the courts of law. He had been the idol of the nation. Wherever he had appeared men had uncovered their heads to him. The lives and estates of the magnates of the realm had been at his mercy. Times had now changed; and many, who had formerly regarded him as the deliverer of his country, shuddered at the sight of those hideous features on which villainy seemed to be written by the hand of God."

He was sentenced to be stripped of his clerical habit, to be pilloried in Palace Yard, to be led around Westminster Hall with an inscription declaring his infamy over his head, to be pilloried in front of the Royal Exchange, to be whipped from Aldgate to Newgate, and after two days from Newgate to Tyburn. If, against all probability, he should happen to survive this punishment, he was to be kept a close prisoner for his life, and five times a year to be exposed in different parts of London in the pillory. This rigorous but well-merited sentence was duly carried out. On the next day he was brought forth to undergo his first flogging. The hangman did his work thoroughly. Blood poured from his back, and though at first he showed a marvellous courage, at length his endurance gave way. His shrieks were terrible to hear. He fainted many times, but the flogging still went on. After two days, though unable to stand, he was brought out for his next whipping. He was dragged to Tyburn on a sledge, and had the incredible number of 1,700 stripes. He still retained his life, but his condition was appalling. He was kept in prison for three and a half years, and then, strange vicissitudes of treatment, was pardoned and granted a pension of £300 per annum.

Whatever punishment he endured he well deserved. He had been the means of bringing thirty-five innocent men to the gallows by his villainous perjury.

Sir George Wakeman, physician to the Queen, was charged at the Sessions House at the Old Bailey, together with others, in July, 1679, with high treason, the treason consisting of conspiring with others to overthrow the Government, murder the King, and establish the Roman Catholic religion as the religion of the country. Sir George pleaded not guilty.

Sir Robert Sawyer, who opened the case for the prosecution, stated that the prisoners at the bar stood indicted as principal actors and instruments in that late most bloody plot, discovered some time since. The design of the plot was against the King and Church. They well knew that so long as God should preserve the life of the King, and as long as the Church of England continued firm, neither the gates of hell nor Rome could prevail against it. On April 24th, 1678, there was a great meeting of Jesuits in London, and it was here that the foundation of the plot was laid. The prisoners at the bar were concerned in this meeting. It was resolved that the King must die. Some were for shooting him, others for stabbing, and there was a third party, which was for poisoning him. This was the party which included the prisoners, and he especially called the attention of the court to Sir George, who, on account of his experience and of his position as physician at Court, had exceptional opportunities of carrying out such a procedure. For this service he demanded a fee of £15,000. The prosecution further stated that they would prove that part of the bargain was that a portion of the fee should be paid in advance, and that an additional reward was to be given to Sir George, and that was the post of Physician-General to the new army which was to be raised.

Many witnesses were produced, but all they were asked was to testify generally as to the plot, until the notorious Dr. Oates appeared, when the first question he was asked was this :—

" Pray, sir, will you tell your whole knowledge of this matter, and apply yourself as near as you can to every one of the prisoners at the bar ? "

Oates.—My lord, in the month of July, Mr. Ashby came to town sick, and being sick and one of the society, the prisoner at the bar, Sir George Wakeman, was his physician, and being his physician, he did write him some instructions, how he should order himself before he went, and at the bath : that he should in the first place take a pint of milk in the morning, and a pint of milk at night and should drink no morning's draught but milk, and that he should have one hundred strokes at the bath, at the pump : I do not so well understand what that means but I suppose the court doth ; but these were the words of the instructions : in this letter Sir George Wakeman did write, that the queen should assist him to poison the king, and this letter was brought by a messenger to Mr. Ashby. Within a day or two after I saw Mr. Ashby and Sir George Wakeman, the prisoner at the bar, (he was so called but I had no acquaintance of him, but just the sight of him) I saw him sit in a writing posture, I saw him lay by his pen, rise up and go away and the same hand that he left behind him in a paper where the ink was not dry, was the same hand that writ the letter to Mr. Ashby. And, my lord, in that time of converse while he was writing this, Mr. Ashby did give him some instructions concerning the commission he had received of being physician to the army. Now, my lord, in some few days after there came a gentleman . . . with commands from the queen for the Fathers to wait upon her at Somerset House . . . and may it please your lordship we did attend at Somerset House and the Fathers went in to the queen, into a chamber where she was, and I waited in an ante-chamber,

and I did hear a woman's voice which did say she would
assist them in the propagation of the Catholic Religion
with her estate, and that she would not endure these
violations of her bed any longer, and that she would
assist Sir George Wakeman in the poisoning of the king.
Now, my lord, when they came out I desired that I might
see the queen, and so when I came in I had, as I believe,
a gracious smile. Now if it please your lordship, while
that I was within I heard the same voice speak thus to
Father Harcourt, and asked him, whether he had received
the last thousand pounds, and it was the same tongue, as I
can possibly guess, the same voice which I heard when I
was without: and I saw no other woman there but the
queen.

Oates then went on to state that Sir George refused
the sum of £10,000 as too little for the services he was
to render and demanded £15,000. He had seen the
handwriting of Sir George acknowledging the receipt
of the money in a book kept by the Jesuits at Wild
House. He had also seen the commission appointing
Dr. Wakeman physician to the army. When he was
asked by Sir George whether it were likely that he
would have been allowed to be at liberty if Oates
had told all this when examined before the King and
council on the matter, the witness replied that at
that time he was not well, that his intellect was not at
its best, and that the King had therefore excused him
from a prolonged examination. " My lord, Sir G. Wakeman had his liberty because I was so weak, by reason of
being up two nights together, one whereof was so very
wet, and being hot, wet, and cold, all in a few hours' time,
so that I thought it would have cost me my life: not being
used to such hard services, I did not charge Sir George so
fully."

Sir George Wakeman, who, as the law of treason then
stood, could not be represented by counsel, but had to

defend himself, made very pertinent comments on this evidence of Oates: " My lord, I have this to say, as I told you before, that I had my liberty for twenty-four days after my examination before the council. Mr. Oates called at the bar of the House of Commons, and there gave an account of this very letter he mentions now, . . . and thereupon the Commons sent an Address to the House of Lords with astonishment that I was not under confinement: and thereupon Mr. Oates was called to the House of Lords, and was commanded to give an account what it was he knew concerning me, that should create such an astonishment in the House of Commons: he told them of this letter and my Lord Chancellor said to him, Do you know it was Sir George Wakeman's hand? No, said he; How do you know it was his letter then? I know it only by this, said he, it was subscribed George Wakeman. If he had such proof as he says he hath now, if he had seen me writing and came into the room where the paper I writ was yet wet, whether he would not have mentioned it there when he was examined about the knowledge of my hand. . . . My lord Chancellor told me I was accused of the blackest of crimes: that I had undertaken to poison the King. I asked him who was my accuser, he pointed to Mr. Oates. . . . Says I, Mr. Oates, do you know me? Did you ever see me before? Mr. Oates said, No. Why then, said I, how came you to be my accuser? Said he, I will tell you: I was at St. Omers where there was a consult of the Jesuits at which Mr. Ashby, the rector of the College at St. Omers did preside: and in that consult it was debated who was the fittest person for that horrid undertaking of poisoning the King and unanimously it was agreed upon at that consult that you were. . . . Then, my lord, (said I to the Lord Chancellor) here is no proof, therefore I hope there is no need for any defence. . . . Then he pressed me to know what I could say for myself. Said I, my lord, I come of a loyal family, my father had suffered very much, to the value of £18,000 and more for the royal family. My brother raised a troop of horse for the King, and served from the beginning of the war to the end. He was major to the Marquis of Worcester, at Worcester fight, and lost his life by the wounds he received in the King's service. . . . I was suspected to be a favourer of the royal party and therefore was imprisoned and did not come out till I had given great security: and the second time I was committed, was, when I entered upon a plot, the only one I was guilty of, I conspired with Captain Lucy and several others to attempt something for his Majesty's restoration, when few durst appear for him. I was seized on in my bed: there were several arms found in my apothecary's cellar, and we were both committed to prison: and we should both have suffered death certainly if his Majesty's happy restoration had not prevented it."

The summing up of the Lord Chief Justice was very different from his performance in the cases of the previous victims of the villainy of Oates. He first pointed out to the jury that though several witnesses had given evidence in general of the plot without any mention of any connection of the prisoners with that plot, yet this was of importance, for it strengthened any evidence which might afterwards be given of the connection of the prisoners with the conspiracy. He told the jury that the assertion that the accused must be believed when they denied their guilt because they dared not die with a lie in their mouths must not be accepted, for " you are not going, according to your own doctrine, so immediately to Hell, I hope you suppose a purgatory where you may be purged from such peccadillos as this of dying with a lie in your mouths."

Dealing with the direct evidence which implicated Sir George Wakeman, he showed that Oates claimed to have seen a letter written to Mr. Ashby with this expression in it, " That the queen would assist him to kill the king." Oates was asked how he knew it was the handwriting of

Sir George. The reply was that, although he had never seen his writing before, he afterwards saw him either writing or in a writing posture, that he looked at the paper after Sir George had left, while it was wet, and the writing was to his thinking just like the writing of the letter he had seen with the treasonable sentiments in it. " Now I must observe this to you. First supposing it to be true, yet it is somewhat hard for a man that had never known a man's hand in his life, to see a hand to-day and sometime after to come and see his hand to a bill of physic, and to recollect the character so much backward, as to know, this is that, or that man's hand that I saw before. It is one thing to know a hand we are used to, but it is another thing if we see a hand we never saw before in our lives, and then by reflection at another time, and by comparison of hand to say this is the same, that is hard : but that is supposing it to be true. Sir George Wakeman as all people that are accused, does deny the fact, and says there was no such thing. Against him besides, he says he saw in a book that the Jesuit priests kept among them of their transactions and affairs, he saw in Harcourt's chamber, a book, wherin was written, this day . .¾ . Agreed with Sir G. W. for £15,000 to which he consented. And under was written, Received £5,000, part of £15,000. . . . George Wakeman. This he says he saw and he believes this to be the very same hand he saw before . . . he does not charge Sir George Wakeman to the best of my memory, with any positive things of his own knowledge, more than as I tell you of this matter."

Sir R. Sawyer. Yes, my lord, he says he saw his commission.

Lord Chief Justice. Indeed he does say, he saw a commission in his hands, to be physician general of the army that was to be raised. . . . The truth I leave with you gentlemen. . . . We would not, to prevent all their plots, (let them be as big as they can make them) shed one drop of innocent blood, therefore I would have you, in all these gentlemen's cases, consider seriously and weigh truly the circumstances and probability of things charged upon them.

The jury retired, and after about one hour returned to court, and gave their verdict of not guilty.

Immediately the Officer of the Court called to the prisoner, " Down on your knees ! " Sir George uttered the very laudable phrase " God bless the King and the honourable Bench." The prisoner was indeed lucky that he had escaped from the champion perjurer.

It is not often in criminal trials that the *rôles* of accuser and accused are reversed, but in the case of Sir George Wakeman and Dr. Oates this actually did in a way happen, for the former gave evidence against the latter in the trial in 1685 at the King's Bench, when Oates was indicted before the Lord Chief Justice, Sir George Jefferies, for perjury.

A copy of the record of the trial of Sir George Wakeman was produced, and then he gave the following evidence :—

Solicitor-General. Pray, Sir George Wakeman was Mr. Oates sworn against you at the trial ?

Sir George. Yes, Mr. Solicitor, he was.

Sol.-Gen. Do you remember what he swore against you at that trial ?

Sir George. Yes I do, Sir.

Sol.-Gen. Was that true, that he swore, by the oath you have taken ?

Oates. Is that a fair question ? I desire the opinion of the Court.

Lord Chief Justice. Ay, why not ?

Oates. He was legally accused : he cannot swear himself off.

L.C.J. But he was legally acquitted too : we have a record for that here.

Oates. Ay, my lord, he was acquitted : it is well known how.

PHYSICIAN CHARGED WITH TREASON

Sol.-Gen. Come sir, was that he swore against you at your trial true?

L.C.J. What do you say, sir?

Sir George. It was false, upon my oath my lord.

Sol.-Gen. What particulars did he swear against you?

Sir George. My lord, if your lordship please, I will give a little account what he swore against me before the King and Council.

Sol.-Gen. That will not do, Sir George; we do not ask you that.

L.C.J. No, it must be only the evidence that was given upon this acquittal, which is the record here produced before us: what did he swear against you then?

Sir George. He swore at that trial as near as I can remember, that I undertook for a certain sum of money, £15,000 as I think it was, to poison the King, and I was to do it by the means of the Queen. I was to provide this poison for her and she was to give it to the King. This he swore at my trial, which God forbid it should be true: nothing can be more false.

L.C.J. I ask you by the oath you have taken, you are now acquitted, and so in no danger: and being upon your oath, ought to speak the truth without malice or ill-will to him that did accuse you: was that he swore true or false?

Sir George. False, false, upon my oath: I speak it without any malice against the man in the world.

After the summing up of the Lord Chief Justice he turned to the jury and said, "Gentlemen, if any of you have a mind to drink at the bar before you go you shall have some got for you."

Jury. No, my lord, we do not care for drinking.

After a short time the jury returned with a verdict of guilty.

A few days later Oates was again tried on further counts for perjury and again convicted.

The judges consulted together a little while, and then

Mr. Justice Withins pronounced the sentence of the court :—

"Titus Oates, you are convicted upon two indictments for perjury, . . . one of the greatest offences that our law has cognizance of. . . . But your perjury has all the aggravations that can be thought of to heighten it. If a man kills another with the sword, and there be forethought malice in the case, he is to be hanged for it: but when a man shall draw innocent blood upon himself by a malicious, premeditated false oath, there is not only blood in the case, but like-wise perjury, corrupt malicious perjury. I know not how I can say, but the law is defective that such a one is not to be hanged. For, if we consider these dreadful effects which have followed upon your perjury, we must conclude our law defective: they are such, as no Christian heart can think of without bleeding for that innocent blood which was shed by your oath. . . . God be thanked, our eyes are now opened: and indeed we must have been incurably blind, if they had not been opened, first by the contradictions, improbabilities and impossibilities in your own testimony: but likewise by the positive, plain, direct and full proof of forty-seven witnesses to one point: against whom you had not one word to object, but they were papists and Roman Catholics, which is no objection at all: though at the same time it did appear that nine or ten of them were Protestants of the Church of England. That was all you had to say: you had not one word to justify yourself from that great and heinous perjury you were accused of. I hope I have not been thought a man of ill nature, and I confess, nothing has been so great a regret to me in my place and station as to give judgement and pronounce the sentence of law against my fellow creatures: but as to you, Mr. Oates, I cannot say my fellow Christian. Yet in this case, when I consider your offence, and the dismal effects that have followed upon it, I cannot say that I have any remorse in giving judge-

PHYSICIAN CHARGED WITH TREASON

ment upon you. And therefore having told you shortly my thoughts about your crime, and how readily I pronounce your sentence, I shall now declare the judgement of the Court upon you. And it is this: First the Court does order that for a fine, you pay one thousand marks upon each indictment.

"Secondly, that you be stript of all your Canonical Habits.

"Thirdly, the Court does award that you do stand upon the pillory and in the pillory, here before Westminster Hall gate, upon Monday next, for an hour's time, between the hours of ten and twelve, with a paper over your head (which you must first walk with round about to all the courts in Westminster Hall) declaring your crime. And that is upon the first indictment.

"Fourthly, on the second indictment, upon Tuesday, you shall stand upon and in the Pillory at the Royal Exchange in London, for the space of an hour, between the hours of twelve and two, with the same inscription.

"You shall upon the next Wednesday be whipped from Aldgate to Newgate. Upon Friday, you shall be whipped from Newgate to Tyburn, by the hand of the common hangman.

"But Mr. Oates, we cannot but remember there were several particular times you swore false about: and therefore as annual commemorations, that it may be known to all persons as long as you live, we have taken special care of you for an annual punishment. Upon the 24th of April every year, as long as you live, you are to stand upon the pillory and in the pillory, at Tyburn, just opposite to the gallows, for the space of an hour between the hours of ten and twelve. You are to stand upon and in the Pillory here at Westminster Hall gate, every 9th of August, in every year, so long as you live. And that it may be known what we mean by it, 'tis to remember what he swore about Mr. Ireland's being in town between the 8th and 12th of August. You are to stand upon and in the Pillory at Charing Cross on the 10th of August every year, during your life, between ten and twelve. The like over against the Temple Gate on the 11th. And upon the 2nd of Sept. (which is another notorious time which you cannot but be remembered of) you are to stand upon and in the Pillory for the space of one hour between twelve and two, at the Royal Exchange: and all this you are to do every year during your life and to be committed close prisoner as long as you live. This I pronounce to be the judgement of the Court upon you, for your offences. And I must tell you plainly, if it had been in my power to have carried it further, I should not have been unwilling to have given judgement of death upon you, for I am sure you deserve it."

In assisting in passing this well-deserved sentence, Lord Jefferies did about the only good deed of his life.

DR. CROSS, HIS WIFE, AND HIS GOVERNESS

THE trial in Ireland of Dr. Cross in 1887 for the murder of his wife is an example of a man well educated and belonging to a learned profession becoming, owing to his mad infatuation for a young girl, a criminal of the worst type, and ending his life on the scaffold. Dr. Philip Cross, after a long and successful career in the army as a surgeon, had, at the age of sixty-two, retired to Shandy Hall, in County Cork, with his wife and six children, to whom he appeared a devoted husband and father. He occupied himself by occasionally hunting and fishing, but as a rule he did not mix much with his neighbours and rather shunned female society. Had it not been for his wife, who was very popular, there would have been no entertaining or social life at the home. A time arrived when Mrs. Cross decided to engage a governess for the education of her children, and she selected for this post a Miss Skinner, a young lady who had held a similar position in the home of a friend. The governess, who was a beautiful and fascinating girl of twenty-one, became an inmate of the household and was at once exceedingly popular with Mrs. Cross and the children. For some short time the doctor appeared quite indifferent to the presence of Miss Skinner in the house; and it did not enter the head of Mrs. Cross that her husband, a man of sixty-two, who had shown a positive dislike to what he called " chattering females," could have an affair with the young governess, who was not of a flighty nature, and who was so devoted to the children and their mother. But where love is concerned there are no rules and regulations. The doctor, who when a young and handsome man, with every opportunity of mixing with and cultivating the society of the opposite sex, was indifferent to their charms, in middle age developed an overwhelming passion for the beautiful young governess who was an inmate of his house. He observed all her many favourable points. He recognised her beauty, her good nature, her capability in the management of the home and the children, her cheerfulness and good temper; all these completely overwhelmed him, and an ardent desire for possession took hold of him. His infatuation became noticeable to his wife, who spoke to him on the subject, but, needless to say, unavailingly. One day he startled the governess, who had never given him the slightest encouragement, by suddenly seizing her in his arms and passionately kissing her on the lips. She fled from him, despising his behaviour, and had it not been for her love for the children and Mrs. Cross, would have left the house for good. However, she said nothing to her mistress about the insult, and from this fact the doctor drew quite erroneous conclusions. He thought his passion was reciprocated, but, uncertain as to how far, he used every artifice and wile of which he was capable, to gain the love of the governess. It is quite certain that at first the girl was strictly honourable and straightforward to the wife who employed her; but Mrs. Cross could not fail to perceive the behaviour of her husband, and naturally was infuriated with both him and Miss Skinner. Mrs. Cross insisted that the object of the doctor's devotion should leave the house at once. He agreed and very plausibly convinced Miss Skinner that, owing to the ridiculous and unreasonable jealousy of his wife, a change would have to be made, Miss Skinner would have to go, and her life must suffer from the ungenerous and ungrateful conduct of Mrs. Cross. The governess believed him, and the idea that she had been very badly treated by her employer became firmly embedded in her mind. Her only friend was Dr. Cross. He was her protector and benefactor, and gradually she yielded to his persistent and ardent solicitations. At the suggestion of Dr. Cross, Miss Skinner went to live in Dublin, and they corresponded in assumed names. The doctor paid frequent visits to the capital, and it was not long before they were living as husband and wife during these visits. But this did not satisfy the doctor. He wanted Miss Skinner for his real wife. His dislike for his lawful partner grew intense, but he was very anxious to maintain his good name and position, and he determined to devise some means of getting rid of her without arousing any suspicion or scandal. The method he adopted was so silly and clumsy that it is difficult to imagine that an educated and clever man could have been so foolish. Detection was inevitable. Mrs. Cross when in perfect health was taken suddenly and seriously ill, complaining of a burning pain in her stomach and being frequently and continuously sick. Her husband attended her, calling in no other medical assistance, a most foolish action, to say the least. He expressed great anxiety about her condition, in which there was no improvement. She rapidly grew worse, and at last the doctor sent for his cousin, Dr. Godfrey, and asked his advice. The new doctor was told that the attack was enteric, and bowing to the opinion of his senior, he agreed with the diagnosis and treatment. Early on the morning of June 2nd, that is about a week later, Mrs. Cross died in agony. Her husband decided on a very early funeral. The coffin was at once ordered, and the interment took place at six in the morning of June 4th. The doctor had himself signed the death certificate of his wife, again a very unusual and unwise proceeding. Comments very unfavourable to the doctor were rife. He excused the haste with which the funeral was hurried on, on the ground that, as typhoid was the cause of death, he was desirous of avoiding any risk of infection of others.

The following is an interesting extract from the diary of the doctor : " Mary Laura Cross departed this life 2nd.

May she go to heaven, is my prayer. Buried 4th." These are words of regret. They were not supported by deeds, for fifteen days later the doctor married Miss Skinner at St. James's, Piccadilly. An attempt was made by him to keep the wedding secret, but the knowledge of it soon leaked out, and he then returned to Shandy Hall with his bride. Deep suspicions had been aroused. The infatuation of the doctor for the governess, the knowledge of the jealousy of his first wife, the sudden and mysterious illness during perfect health of Mrs. Cross, the fact that he alone had acted as her medical attendant until almost the last, and that he had signed the death certificate, the hasty burial and finally the marriage with the governess directly after his wife's death, caused the police to make the most stringent inquiries.

The body was exhumed, an inquest held, and an analysis of the organs made. Arsenic was found, and there was not the slightest evidence of typhoid fever. As a result of these discoveries, Dr. Cross was arrested. His trial took place at the Munster Assizes, and four days were occupied with the proceedings. Mr. Atkinson, afterwards Lord Atkinson, the famous Lord of Appeal, was counsel for Dr. Cross, and made a desperate and brilliant effort to save his client. How, he argued, was it possible to imagine that a doctor who had spent years in the East, and was familiar with all the subtleties of Eastern poisons, should employ arsenic, the most likely agent to arouse suspicion and the easiest to detect ? Could any sane man be so foolish ?

The prosecution was quite willing to acknowledge that as a doctor the prisoner might have been a very brilliant man, but they regarded him in his criminal capacity as a fool.

The purchase of arsenic was traced to the prisoner, the destruction of the medicine bottles used for his wife, the motive (his infatuation for Miss Skinner, and his adultery with her), all were clearly proved, and his culpability brought definitely home to him. The jury had no doubt as to his guilt, and Mr. Justice Murphy in passing sentence of death described his crime as one of the most cruel and bloodthirsty of the century.

The condemned man suffered agonies in the interval between the sentence and its execution. His hair turned white. His new wife, revolted by the terrible crime and the disgrace and misery brought upon her, refused to see him at all. He was hanged in January, 1888, suffering the last penalty of the law with great fortitude, and thus ended a life ruined by a mad passion for his wife's governess.

Arsenic is one of the oldest and commonest poisons made use of by murderers. Sir James Crichton-Brown, in his recent memoirs, declares that there is singular lack of originality among poisoners. Even doctors who have employed this method of homicide have seldom gone beyond Schedule A (the official poison catalogue).

"The same old implements are used again and again. There is an absence of anything like originality or ingenuity in the choice of ways and means. Wherever we turn in mediæval toxicology or that of the Renaissance, it is arsenic, arsenic, arsenic which was the mainstay, not merely of the murderous, fortune-telling hag, but also of the homicides of commanding intellect and power, like the Borgias and Catherine de Medici."

This is not quite correct, as cases described later in this book will show, *e.g.* Palmer used strychnine, Lamson and Pritchard, aconite, etc. But the fact does remain that arsenic is used more commonly than any other substance, probably because it is so much more easy to obtain.

TWO MEDICAL FORGERS

AT the end of the eighteenth century there lived in London two brothers named Perreau, twins, and so alike that it was difficult to tell them apart. They were both doctors: Daniel, a fashionable physician of Harley Street, and Robert (known to his friends as " Honest Perreau "), a general practitioner of Golden Square. They were popular and successful, but were bitten with the desire to make money more quickly than usually falls to the lot of medical men, and therefore started in the City as brokers. For this they needed capital, and Robert one day in March, 1775, presented himself at the well-known Drummond's Bank, in Charing Cross, and requested a loan of £5,000. For this he offered as security a bond signed by Mr. Adair, the army agent, but directly it was presented for inspection the signature was recognised as a forgery. Robert Perreau expressed astonishment, and willingly agreed to accompany the banker to the house of Mr. Adair in order to get the matter cleared up. This gentleman immediately disowned the signature, but Robert declared it must be correct for he had obtained the bond from his sister-in-law, Mrs. Daniel Perreau. She was fetched, and there entered the room a most beautiful woman, who at once acknowledged she had forged the bond ; but so fascinating was she, so experienced in the wiles of womanhood, so able to exercise her delightful charms, that the document was torn in two, and all agreed to let the matter drop.

A sensational *dénouement* followed. Robert at once charged his sister-in-law with forgery. This apparently insane procedure was really a measure of self-protection, for the Adair bond was not the only false one in circulation;

there were plenty of others. The brothers had already obtained £70,000 by means of such documents. The mean-spirited Robert, who had just been saved from arrest on a capital charge (forgery was in the eighteenth century punished by death), hoped to fasten all the other crimes on the unfortunate woman. This, of course, turned her into a bitter enemy of the Perreau brothers, and she determined to do all she could to destroy them and save herself. At the hearing before the magistrate Mrs. Daniel Perreau again exercised all her wonderful powers of fascination on those with whom she came in contact. She arrayed herself in a pink cloak trimmed with ermine, and a bewitching little bonnet. She was probably the most delightful apparition which had ever graced the dock of the Old Bailey. She told the story of the many forgeries, implicating the two doctors, who were arrested, whilst she herself was accepted as " King's Evidence " and was released.

Robert and Daniel had an immense circle of friends, and the usual crowd of fashionable nonentities appeared at the trial. The first sensation was provided when it was shown that the lady was not the wife of Daniel, but only his mistress. Her career had not been a very desirable one. She had married, when only seventeen, a drunken officer named Rudd, had left him to join Daniel Perreau, and had enriched him and herself by her friendships with many wealthy men. The sympathy of the people was with her, more especially as Lord Mansfield refused to allow her to appear as King's Evidence at the trial, although she had been accepted as such before the magistrates. After the witnesses for the prosecution had given their evidence a large number of people entered the box to testify as to the character of the prisoners, but, in spite of all these witnesses could say as to the very high esteem in which the brothers were held, the jury found them both guilty.

Mrs. Rudd, although she had not been called as King's

Evidence, endeavoured to obtain a decision that she should be released. Her lawyer produced an affidavit sworn to by Sir John Fielding, the blind magistrate and brother of the poet, that she had been admitted as a witness for the Crown against the Perreaus. Lord Mansfield, in delivering the opinion of the court on the different modes of accepting the evidence of accomplices in criminal charges, pointed out that Mrs. Rudd came within none of the various categories. In some cases, he said, there arose circumstances which rendered criminal witnesses, whose evidence for the Crown had been illegally admitted, fit objects for mercy; these circumstances were a decent behaviour and an absolute recital of the whole truth. In this instance he could see no reason for including Mrs. Rudd among those to whom mercy should be shown. In consequence of this judgment, she was tried at the Old Bailey directly after the two doctors had been found guilty. In her case the trial resulted in an acquittal.

Very determined efforts had been made to get the brothers pardoned, but all that their friends had been able to accomplish was to obtain a respite. Directly the acquittal of Mrs. Rudd had been announced this respite was at an end, and the brothers were ordered for execution early in the year. A petition signed by seventy-eight merchants and bankers of the City, and other appeals for mercy were ineffectual, and on Wednesday, January 17th, the execution took place. On this morning first Daniel came into the chapel, bowed to the company, went to the fire and warmed himself with great composure. Robert followed soon after, and turned to a table where the ropes with which they were to be bound lay. This sight upset him very much, and the surrounding spectators gave vent to their sympathy by uttering loud lamentations. Daniel helped to adjust the ropes round himself, but seemed very much unmanned when he saw them fixed on his brother. The doctors then took a last farewell of their friends and were taken to Tyburn in a mourning coach. In front of them were a man convicted of highway robbery and two Jews condemned for housebreaking, all in one cart. In addition there were two other felons, convicted for coining, who were dragged in a sledge. The procession left Newgate at nine, and took an hour and a half to reach Tyburn. The cart at once drove under the gallows, which was divided into two. The Jews were tied to one part of it, the highwayman and the two coiners to the other part. During this time, about a quarter of an hour, Robert and Daniel remained in the coach with a clergyman. Daniel first entered the cart, and was immediately followed by his brother. They were both in new suits of mourning, with dressed and powdered hair, but no hats. They were tied to the gallows like the other prisoners. All being made fast, the clergyman prayed with them, and asked them to acknowledge the justice of their sentences. They each handed him a paper. Then, after they had prayed a short time to themselves, the executioner put on their caps. The clergyman now took his leave, Robert and Daniel bowing to him as he departed. They then embraced each other most affectionately, and held hands. The caps were drawn over their faces, and the cart driven away. They behaved with the utmost firmness during this long-drawn-out ordeal, and died as brave men. There was, as usual, an enormous gathering of vulgar, morbid sight-seers. The bodies were driven away in a hearse and privately buried in the family vault.

The papers left with the clergyman were published soon after the execution. They contained the most solemn declaration of the innocence of the two victims.

A good deal of doubt still remains as to the parts played by and the relative guilt of the three charged with the crime.

COLLINS, THE ABORTIONIST

THE case of Dr. Collins, at one time surgeon to the Guards and fashionable West End practitioner, later professional abortionist and convict, presents many points of piquant interest. At the time of the trial it was followed with the greatest keenness, not only by the medical profession, but also by the lay public, and excited mingled feelings of satisfaction and regret, satisfaction because a rogue who was a disgrace to his profession had at last been tracked down, and regret that a man of such abilities and bright promise had been brought to shame and ruin.

W. Maunsell Collins, M.D., was born in Cork in 1844, and entered the army in 1866 as assistant surgeon on the staff, passing first of all the candidates of that year and gaining the same distinction at Netley. In 1870 he was appointed assistant surgeon to the Scots Guards, and surgeon in the Army Medical Department in 1873. In 1880 he became surgeon to the Royal Horse Guards, retiring with a gratuity in 1885. He subsequently practised in the West End of London, and ended his career with seven years' penal servitude. After his release his conduct was on a par with his previous behaviour. A lady living at Brighton, who had been attended by him in his palmy days, decided that she would like to end her life and wrote to Collins asking him to supply her with sufficient poison. He replied that it was a very dangerous thing for him to do, but if he were paid a fee of £300 he would take the risk. The amount must be paid in cash, and not by cheque. The patient sent her housekeeper to the bank, who changed a cheque for the requisite sum, which was handed to

Collins in exchange for a small packet. This the patient swallowed. It had no effect on her, for she had been given some harmless powder. The patient was helpless, as Collins well knew; she could take no action against him, for she was herself *particeps criminis*.

The crime for which Collins was tried was quite straightforward. Mrs. Uzielli, a lady who took a prominent part in so-called fashionable society, found herself pregnant. She did not desire any more children, and, on the recommendation of a friend, she went to Collins, who was well known in her circle as an expert abortionist. She paid him thirty guineas to perform the usual illegal operation. As the result of this the unfortunate woman died of septic peritonitis. As is usual in these cases, the septic infection took place because, with the secrecy essential to carry out these criminal proceedings, proper aseptic precautions were impossible and always will be impossible. Although his operations were quite well known, it was not till a death resulted that it was possible to bring home his guilt to the wretched criminal, and secure a conviction. This unfortunately is the case with nearly all those who are charged by the law with this crime.

The trial took place before Mr. Justice Grantham at the Central Criminal Court on June 27th, 1898, and subsequent days. The Attorney-General, Sir Richard Webster, Q.C., M.P., Mr. H. T. Sutton, Mr. Charles Matthews, and Mr. Bodkin appeared for the prosecution, and for the defence were Mr. C. F. Gill and Mr. A. E. Gill.

The Attorney-General in opening the case said that he had to put before the jury the facts which caused the death of Mrs. Uzielli on March 25th, 1898. Dr. Collins, the prisoner, practised as a medical man at 10, Cadogan Place, and had not been called to see Mrs. Uzielli till Monday, March 14th. She was then in good health. He attended her from March 14th to March 24th, and during this time, according to statements the doctor made to Mr. Uzielli, there was nothing in the condition of Mrs.

Uzielli to cause any alarm. He said up to the last moment of his attendance that there was not a single symptom to give rise to any anxiety. The jury had to consider whether or not her death was caused by anything done by Dr. Collins. Between March 14th and March 24th—a period of ten days—something happened. After Mrs. Uzielli's death there was a coroner's inquest and a post-mortem, and this disclosed the cause of death quite plainly. A wound, made by some blunt-pointed instrument, was found about one inch and a quarter on the inner side of the os internum of the womb. That this wound was the cause of death in Mrs. Uzielli was quite certain. Whether it was made by Dr. Collins was for the jury to determine. The prosecution contended that the wound was made on Tuesday, March 15th, and that all the symptoms which occurred after that date were consistent, to use no stronger expression, with the wound having been caused on that date. At the time of her first seeing the prisoner, on March 14th, she was, as the medical evidence would establish, seven or eight weeks pregnant. She was most anxious not to have a child, and had treated herself with various medicines with the object of restoring her monthly periods. When she came to London from the country she was undoubtedly a healthy woman about two months pregnant. A friend of hers, to whom she made a statement as to her condition, wrote to Dr. Collins asking him to see some one for her, not mentioning Mrs. Uzielli by name. The deceased went with her friend to the house of Dr. Collins on March 14th and saw him in his consulting room. Whether anything was done to her then he could not say. On the next day Mrs. Uzielli again went to see Dr. Collins, and this time paid a longer visit. The prosecution alleged that certainly on this day Dr. Collins had used an instrument on Mrs. Uzielli. He would deny it and say he had only made a digital examination, and possibly one with a speculum. Undoubtedly she went into the consulting room, and was there twenty minutes alone with the doctor. She went out, apparently well, on Wednesday and Thursday. On the latter day she sent Dr. Collins a cheque for thirty guineas. Dr. Collins suggested that he had told Mrs. Uzielli his fees were two guineas for the first visit at his own house and one guinea after, and two guineas at the house of Mrs. Uzielli. The cheque for thirty guineas was for payment for the visits already made and for future visits which he might make. On the Friday Mrs. Uzielli became ill, and Dr. Collins attended her three or four times a day. The next day her husband was very anxious about his wife and spoke to the doctor about this worry. Mr. Uzielli was not satisfied, dismissed Dr. Collins, and Dr. Stivens was called in. He at once saw that Mrs. Uzielli was suffering from a very dangerous illness, acute septic peritonitis. Sir John Williams saw her the next day and pronounced her case hopeless. She died the same day. It was for the jury to say what caused that state of things—was it something done by the prisoner, or was it not? The post-mortem disclosed the cause of the septic peritonitis. Whatever might have been the cause of the wound in the womb, it was undoubtedly this which set up the peritonitis from which Mrs. Uzielli died. At the request of Mr. Hall, a friend of Mr. Uzielli, Dr. Collins called on the morning after the death. He asked Mr. Uzielli if Dr. Stivens had refused to give a certificate and had suggested that he had done something illegal. It was for the jury to draw their own conclusions from these questions asked by the prisoner immediately after the death of Mrs. Uzielli. The coroner's jury had found Dr. Collins guilty of murder. The law was that in many cases, if in the course of an attempt to commit a felony or an unlawful act death was caused, it was or might be murder. But the jury would be told, no doubt, by his lordship, that if on the evidence they came to the conclusion that the act done, though unlawful in itself, was not such as of necessity to cause danger to life if not unskilfully performed, it was open to them to find the prisoner guilty of manslaughter and not of murder, assuming, of course, that they considered that death was occasioned by his act. It had also been laid down by great judges in the past that, as felonious intent was an implication of the law, the jury might disregard that intent if they did not think it established and find the prisoner guilty of manslaughter. The point for the jury to consider after hearing the evidence was, What was the cause of death, and was it caused by anything which the prisoner did?

Mr. Douglas Uzielli said he was a member of the London Stock Exchange, that his wife was about thirty years old, and that she had had two children. On the Friday before her death when he came home he found his wife had gone to bed. On the next day when he went home to dress, as he was dining out, he went in to see his wife and found Dr. Collins in the room. Up to that time he did not know that Dr. Collins was in attendance at the house. He asked the doctor how his wife was and was told she was quite all right. The doctor told him he was coming to see Mrs. Uzielli later on that night, and asked for the latch-key so that he might let himself in. He found his wife was gradually getting worse, so two days before her death he took a note to his own doctor, Dr. Lyne Stivens, of Park Street. On returning home he saw Dr. Collins coming downstairs. Witness asked how his wife was, and the doctor told him quite all right, and that there was no cause for anxiety. The doctor said he had noticed that Mrs. Uzielli's manner towards him had changed and that if witness wished he could call in another practitioner. Witness was not to consider prisoner's feelings. Witness told him he should obtain other advice. Dr. Collins called after the death and told witness how dreadfully sorry he was about it. He seemed very much upset and asked if there was any suggestion that he had done anything illegal. Witness told Dr. Collins he thought there was. The doctor asked if there was going to be an inquest, and he also asked if a certificate had been refused. He kept saying he had done nothing, and would not leave for a long time. Mrs. Uzielli had her own banking account, and on March 17th had drawn a cheque for thirty guineas for Dr. Collins.

Chief Inspector Moore, of the C.I.D., said he arrested Dr. Collins under a warrant for causing the death of Mrs. Uzielli by unlawfully using an instrument for the purpose of causing a miscarriage. Dr. Collins replied: " There is no truth whatever in the accusation. I never did anything to this lady except what was proper and legitimate." In the consulting room witness found a number of instruments, which he produced, one being a long black whalebone instrument, another a long yellow catheter.

Dr. Bertram Lyne Stivens, in the course of his evidence, said that when he first saw Mrs. Uzielli she was dangerously ill. She died shortly after from septic peritonitis. There had been a miscarriage. He had found at the post-mortem there was a place in the womb where the ovum had been attached. The wound in the uterus could not have come by itself; it must have been caused by something applied mechanically. Looking at the distance from the vagina to the entrance to the womb, he did not see how it could have been caused by a finger.

Mr. Thomas Bond said that, in consequence of an order from the coroner, he had made a post-mortem on the body of Mrs. Uzielli. On examining the uterus he found a recent wound about an inch and a quarter from the mouth of the womb. It was in a septic condition. He thought it must have been caused by a blunt-pointed instrument, like a sound. He did not think it had been caused by a curette.

What had been the cause of death?—Septic peritonitis.

Have you any doubt of that?—None.

Bearing in mind what you said about the wound, do you connect the wound with peritonitis at all?—I do.

Just tell us in your own way whether you think it is the consequence or cause, or what.—Septic peritonitis is caused by the introduction of germs into the blood through a wound. Here I found a septic wound, and my thirty years' experience would lead me to no other conclusion than that it was caused through the wound.

Sir John Williams said that, at the request of Dr. Stivens, he went to see Mrs. Uzielli. He found her in a dying condition suffering from septic peritonitis. He was not present at the post-mortem, but the parts taken away were shown him by Mr. Bond. The uterus had been pregnant about six weeks. About an inch and a half from the mouth of the womb was a wound, and he formed the opinion that it had been made by some blunt-pointed instrument. In his view it could not have been caused by a finger-nail. The miscarriage was the cause of the peritonitis, and this was due to the instrument used being septic. If curetting had been done so recently as five or six days before, there should have been visible evidence of it. There was none.

Mr. C. F. Gill then addressed the jury. He said that the prisoner was charged with constructive murder, but he was as much on his trial as if he had hated Mrs. Uzielli and had deliberately killed her. Dr. Collins had a patient named Mrs. Hope, and she had suggested to the deceased that she should consult the prisoner. One of the first points of difference between the case for the prosecution and that for the defence was the condition of health of Mrs. Uzielli in March. The prosecution alleged that she was a robust woman, and practically ignored her previous attack of peritonitis. That being the case, Mrs. Uzielli was in such a condition that peritonitis could be excited by a trivial cause. As to the medical evidence, he would remind the jury that if the case had been an action for damages against a railway company, they would have had one man of distinction going into the box and saying that the shock would be disastrous to the plaintiff, while the medical man for the railway company would say that the symptoms were trifling and would soon pass away. He (counsel) was not in a position to call medical evidence. Dr. Collins had not the means to place his case before the jury in that way, but he contended that he had proved in cross-examination that it was in his power to call medical experts who would controvert every point which had been put forward. The medical men who had been called were of such eminence that it would have been expected that they would have agreed, yet the jury had heard diametrically opposed opinions expressed by them. It had been proved that Mrs. Uzielli had previously suffered from pneumonia, a disease which left its effects for years, and that she had had influenza lately. So severe had been this attack that she had been in bed three weeks and had been attended daily by her doctor. When she was better she had gone to Eastbourne, and had there been so weak that she had had to remain in the house or go out in a bath chair. That was the condition of things till February, and it was not therefore remarkable that she should have missed her period. She was anxious to bring it on and had tried all sorts of things. She then returned to town, and it had been proved that she was being supplied with medicines from some unknown source. Was a quack doctor treating her? How was she getting these medicines? Was it going very much further to suppose that she either got some ignorant person to operate upon her or that she did herself some injury? Dr. Collins did not know whether Mrs. Uzielli were pregnant or not. Was it conceivable that any man would perform an operation under these circumstances? At least he would not commit a crime without some safeguard or without some motive. What was the motive if there had been any criminal intent? In March Mrs. Uzielli had drawn a cheque for self for £300, and there would have been no means of tracing the money if it had been paid to a man for an illegal act. If Dr. Collins had agreed to perform an illegal operation he would surely have insisted on being paid at the time and in cash, so that it could not be traced. But Mrs. Uzielli had sent him a cheque altered from being payable to bearer to order. This constituted a complete record of the transaction. Dr. Collins had told the nurse that Mrs. Uzielli had had an early miscarriage, and he had tried to remove some membrane with his finger-nail. The wound of the womb could have been caused at that time, and once the wound was made, there was abundant chance of sepsis. Dr. Collins had used a fine curette, as he failed to remove the membrane with his finger. No anæsthetic was given, and it was quite possible that Mrs. Uzielli had flinched and thus herself caused the wound. There ought to have been an independent man to perform the post-mortem, and Dr. Collins should have been given an opportunity of being present. What would have been the use even if he had called medical evidence? In the question at issue he could get sufficient material from the men who were called, but upon the question of the appearance of the body evidence would have been of no use unless he could call a man who had seen the post-mortem and who had had an opportunity of examining and forming an opinion. In conclusion Mr. Gill said that whatever was left to the prisoner in life was more important to others than to himself. His own career, after such a case, must necessarily be at an end. The only safe verdict was that the case had not been proved, and that therefore Dr. Collins was not guilty.

The Attorney-General then replied on behalf of the prosecution. He submitted that every fact in the case showed that Mrs. Uzielli was pregnant, that she knew that she was pregnant, and acted to bring about that which she wished, namely, miscarriage. He commented on the absence of medical men in the witness-box on behalf of the prisoner, and pointed out that in that great profession, which was generous and large-minded, there would have been no difficulty in procuring evidence in support of the views put forward on behalf of the prisoner if any one had held them. With reference to the suggestion made that Mrs. Uzielli was being treated only for suppressed menstruation, it was most important to observe that when she got back to the house after her visit to Dr. Collins she gave directions to the maid for something that was going to happen. Dealing with the post-mortem examination, the Attorney-General said there was evidence that there had recently been an ovum in the womb and that this ovum had been expelled. There was also evidence that four or five or six days before the death of the lady there had been a heavy discharge from the womb. It was perfectly clear that Mrs. Uzielli had died of septic peritonitis. This was not disputed. It was also known that a wound in the position in which the wound was found would be responsible for the mischief. It was known also that the ordinary course of septic peritonitis was that it developed from two or three days after the poisoning had taken place and was followed by rise of temperature, feverishness, and restlessness supervening about three or four days after the infection. It was practically established that the miscarriage had resulted from something done on the Tuesday, and that it was brought about by the puncturing of the membrane either by a metallic or other sound. The statement that the wound was the result of curetting must be discredited. If the curetting was done, it was a remarkable thing that there should have been no mark or sign of any kind of it. He protested against the suggestion of the defence that Dr. Collins had been treated in any unfair way, or that any improper attempt had been made to get up evidence against him. With regard to the law of the case, the Attorney-General pointed out that the prisoner was charged with constructive wilful murder, because, if he was committing an unlawful act, the law said that in one view death thereby occasioned was murder. But the law also said that if the act were not in itself of necessity dangerous, then the jury might find a verdict of manslaughter, and in that case it had been elicited by Mr. Gill from Dr. Stivens that the risk of procuring abortion from puncture of the membranes was practically *nil*. If the jury had any doubt whether the prisoner had caused the death of Mrs. Uzielli, he invited them to give the prisoner the benefit of that doubt. But if they had no reasonable doubt that her death was caused by the act of the prisoner, they were bound to do their duty and return such verdict as was in accordance with their conscience.

Mr. Justice Grantham, in summing up, said nothing could have been better than the defence made by Mr. Gill. With regard to the law, there was no doubt as to its meaning. A person who with intent procured the miscarriage of a woman by the unlawful use of an instrument was guilty of a felony, and assuming that the person did not die, was liable to penal servitude or any imprisonment that a judge might think fit to inflict. It could be well understood that there were cases where it was necessary, in order to save the life of a woman, that there should be a forcible miscarriage, and a properly qualified doctor had to say when that time had arrived. That was not unlawful. If in consequence of an unlawful operation the patient died, that was murder. But he could not ignore the fact that juries not unnaturally declined to find a verdict of murder when the person performing the operation did not do it against the will of the person operated on, when in fact he was bribed to do it. The operation was an illegal one, and any person who submitted to it was herself guilty of the same felony as the person who performed it. But unfortunately in most cases the woman had paid the penalty and had gone before another Judge. It had been suggested by Mr. Gill that prisoner had been unable to find medical witnesses owing to poverty, but there was very little foundation for that statement. It had also been suggested that Dr. Collins should have been represented at the post-mortem by an independent doctor, but Mr. Bond had been appointed by the coroner to be just such an independent witness. It would open the door to great difficulty if a person charged with an offence of that kind were allowed to be present while the post-mortem was going on. An accidental blow on the arm, an accidental fall of something, would obliterate the whole evidence that could be got. (In the Palmer case, of which doubtless his lordship was thinking, this very thing happened, except that the blow was not accidental.) His lordship then proceeded to review the evidence. There was no doubt that the case would not have been started but for the statement of Dr. Lyne Stivens, and his conduct had been commented upon ; yet in all the cases which he had ever tried he had never had one in which it was so clearly the duty of the doctor in attendance to do exactly that which Dr. Stivens had done on this occasion. The real questions for the jury were—(1) Was the woman pregnant, and (2) did she have a miscarriage ? Dr. Collins admitted that Mrs. Uzielli had had a miscarriage and stated that when he first saw her she had a retroverted womb, but the evidence of Dr. Stivens, Mr. Bond and Sir John Williams was that it was impossible that she could have had it because of the old adhesions. As regards the condition of Mrs. Uzielli on the day before her death, Dr. Stivens the moment he saw her knew what she was suffering from. That was only an hour or two after Dr. Collins had left, and it seemed incredible that he was ignorant of the true nature of the disease. It was difficult to understand why he should fear an inquest if he had been properly treating his patient. There was not a tittle of evidence to confirm the suggestion that the abortion was brought about by somebody else. His lordship then referred to the medical evidence. The uterus and other parts had been preserved, and they could have been examined, and other evidence could have been given to contradict what Mr. Bond, Dr. Stivens and Sir John Williams had said. The result of Sir John Williams' evidence was that death was due to septic peritonitis, and that this had been caused by the wound. How the wound was made was the question on which the whole case turned. If the evidence pointed out that it was brought about by artificial means, the question was : Who could have done it ? If the jury believed that Dr. Collins had given an untrue account of his position, then they would be justified in coming to the conclusion that the other evidence pointed strongly to the fact that his must be the hand that did it.

The jury, after deliberating for fifty minutes, found the prisoner guilty of manslaughter, and strongly recommended him to mercy. The foreman handed the Judge the following rider : " The jury wish to express their deep concern at and condemnation of the growing tendency on the part of certain classes of the community, as proved by the evidence in this case, to avail themselves of their marital rights and to try to evade the responsibility of their acts."

In reply to the question of why sentence should not be pronounced, the prisoner protested his innocence.

Mr. Justice Grantham sent Collins to penal servitude for seven years.

The professional abortionist will be with us as long as there are women determined to refuse maternity. The bribes offered in the shape of high fees seem to be such as a certain section of the profession are unable to refuse. They trust that all will go well, and, as a matter of fact, this is generally what does happen, and only when death results does discovery take place. The police often know these men and women well, but unfortunately are unable to secure sufficient evidence to procure conviction. The young medical man is sometimes tempted from feelings of real pity to help some unfortunate patient in this way. There is only one rule in these cases : to decline absolutely to allow any element of sympathy to enter into the matter and to refuse positively to perform an illegal operation under any circumstances whatever.

A MEDICAL FIREBRAND

The Trial of John Watson, Surgeon, for Treason in 1817

AFTER every great war, whether victory or defeat has resulted, there comes a period of industrial unrest. At the termination, by the battle of Waterloo, of the gigantic struggle of this country with Napoleon the depression in agriculture and commerce was great and unemployment was rife. The labouring classes were ready to seize any opportunity by which they might hope to better their condition. The opportunity of the irresponsible agitator was irresistible. Reformers were rampant. It was argued that the evil condition of the population was due to the fact that the labouring classes had no proper representation in Parliament, and until they had this representation there was no hope of improvement. Meetings were held all over the kingdom to promote this very legitimate desire, and, as is usual in agitations of this kind, the prime object was soon lost sight of, and other dangerous and objectionable doctrines were advocated. Crowds soon got out of hand and degenerated into mobs. Violent rioting ensued.

Among those who took a very prominent part in some of these meetings was Dr. Thomas Watson, a surgeon. He was one of the new party termed " Radicals," from their attempt to strike at what they considered to be the root of the industrial trouble—the inadequate representation of the labouring classes in Parliament.

The riots which led to the arrest of Dr. Watson started with a meeting held at Spafields, then a wild unenclosed space, in November, 1816.

A MEDICAL FIREBRAND

A flag bearing the words " Nature to Feed the Hungry —Truth to Protect the Oppressed—Justice to Punish Offenders," was produced and unfurled, violent speeches were made, and it was resolved to have a petition sent to the Prince Regent. It was decided to hold a further meeting on December 2nd, ostensibly to hear the result of the petition. The following is a copy of one of the placards advertising the second meeting :—

"ENGLAND EXPECTS EVERY MAN TO DO HIS DUTY

"The meeting in Spafields takes place at 12 o'clock on Monday, December 2nd, 1816.

"To receive the answer of the petition to the Prince Regent, determined upon at the last meeting held in the same place, and for other important considerations.

The present state of Great Britain.
Four millions in distress ! ! !
Four millions embarrassed ! ! !
One million-and-half fear distress ! ! !
Half-a-million live in splendid luxury ! ! !

" Our brothers in Ireland are in a worse state—The climax of misery is complete—it can go no further.

" Death would now be a relief to Millions—Arrogance, Folly, and Crimes have brought affairs to this dread crisis.

" Firmness and integrity can only save the country ! ! !

" After the last Meeting some disorderly People were guilty of attacking the Property of Individuals : they were ill informed of the object of the Meeting, it was not to plunder Persons suffering in these Calamitious times in common with others : the Day will soon arrive when the Distresses will be relieved.

"The Nation's wrongs must be redressed.

"JOHN DYALL, *Chairman*.
THOMAS PRESTON, *Secretary*.

"Scale and Bates, Printers, Tottenham Court Road."

At this meeting some 5,000 people assembled, and Dr. Watson, with a tricoloured cockade in his hat, made a most inflammatory speech. As a result the mob got out of hand, and led by Dr. Watson's son, attacked a gunsmith's establishment, shot and wounded the owner, who resisted, raided shops, and showed such violence that the military were called out to suppress them. Dr. Watson, his son, and Thistlewood (who was afterwards involved in the Cato Street conspiracy) escaped and made northwards for Northampton. On reaching Highgate they were seized by the patrol as footpads, suspicion being aroused by the sight of a pistol protruding from Dr. Watson's pocket. Thistlewood and Dr. Watson's son escaped, but the doctor was captured. He made an unsuccessful effort to get away, stabbing one of his captors with a cane sword. For this he was indicted at the Old Bailey in January, 1817, charged with cutting and maiming, but was acquitted. He was not, however, released, for a further and far more serious accusation was hanging over him.

The Government received information of a dangerous conspiracy against established authority, and among those involved in it were Thistlewood and the two Watsons. A charge of high treason was accordingly brought against them and they were committed to the Tower. The trial took place before the Court of King's Bench in June, 1817, before Lord Ellenborough and three other judges, the Crown being represented by the two chief law officers and four other counsel, whilst Dr.

Watson was defended by Mr. Wetherell and Mr. Serjeant Copley.

Numerous witnesses were called to prove the contention of the Crown that Dr. Watson was engaged in a dangerous conspiracy to overthrow the Government. A man named John Castles was the most important of those who testified against the doctor. His examination-in-chief was a very long one, occupying many hours. His evidence was to the effect that he had only recently become acquainted with Dr. Watson, and that he had attended with him a meeting of a society called the Spenceans, and had also met him at other similar meetings. After one of these Dr. Watson remarked that it was easy to upset a Government if a few good fellows would act together. He also said he had drawn up a plan that would debar the cavalry from acting, by means of a machine running on wheels, with sharp knives on each side and spikes in the middle. He had set up a committee which was devising the best means to carry out their schemes. Castles was asked to get as many men as he could to join; it should be made worth his while, and he should be made one of the generals.

Watson and Castles went to inspect the King Street barracks and the powder magazine in Hyde Park, to see how best they could set fire to the buildings. Among the various means employed to obtain recruits were the following. Unemployed and discontented labourers were approached, treated with beer, and offered a job. They replied that they were quite ready for a good row, and would rather be killed than remain as they were. They could at any time collect 500 or 600 men. Then some public-houses frequented by soldiers were visited and beer given freely. They were asked as to their feelings, and were encouraged in their grievances against their officers, their pay and their pensions. Next coal-heavers out of work were got at and arrangements made to recruit some fifty of them. A further meeting was held to perfect plans. London was divided into areas and the men told off for their various sections, the different barracks and other buildings which were to be attacked were arranged, and the officers who were to lead the attacks (all of which were to be made simultaneously) appointed. Thistlewood was proposed by Dr. Watson as the Commander-in-Chief. He with young Watson were to take the guns and two field pieces which were in the artillery ground in Gray's Inn Lane ; others were to attack the Tower, the barracks at Regent's Park and Portland Street Barracks. All these were to be assailed at a given hour and set fire to. Every one the rebels met was to be persuaded or made to join them. When the attacks had been carried out a volley was to be fired to announce success, and various points, such as Charing Cross and Westminster Bridges, Piccadilly Gate and Chancery Lane, were to be barricaded ; London Bridge and Whitechapel were to be guarded against the approach of troops, and the main body was to assemble at the Bank. When all had been successful a Committee of Common Safety was to be established and a new Parliament formed. A bounty of £100 was to be offered to every soldier who would join the new Government. Several meetings were held at beerhouses at Spitalfields, and at length it was determined to call a public meeting to get some idea of the number of adherents there were to the cause. The place decided on was Spafields, an uncultivated field, convenient in position to the Bank and the Tower. When this meeting was held it was arranged that Dr. Watson should address the crowd, and then, if he found them in the mood, they were to be led straight away to carry out the plans for attacking the Tower and other places. The Bank was to be surprised and assaulted, and men to be placed at the top of this building and neighbouring houses, armed with glass bottles and other weapons, to keep off the military. The books of the Bank were all to be destroyed, and thus the National Debt would be cancelled. A first public meeting was held at Spafields and adjourned for a fortnight.

Preparations were made for the second meeting. It was suggested that 200 young women dressed in white should head the procession in order to take off the attention of the soldiers. When the appointed day came, the mob, inflamed by the addresses delivered to them, started on their way. Dr. Watson led his contingent to attack the Tower. When he arrived he harangued the soldiers, who did not appear to take much notice of him. He went to try to obtain reinforcements, but, a band of thirty or forty soldiers appearing, the mob at once threw down their arms and fled. The leaders, including Dr. Watson, found that nothing more could be done, and they also disappeared with their followers.

Dr. Watson told Castles that after this he was going into the country. The people were not yet ripe enough to act.

At the close of Castles' evidence-in-chief, which had lasted many hours, the court was tired out, and the time of day was late. The Lord Chief Justice asked Mr. Wetherell if he would care to commence his cross-examination then.

Mr. Wetherell. " I am quite sure that your lordships will perceive my cross-examination must run into considerable lengths. As this witness is described in the list of witnesses to come out of custody, it may perhaps not be an unusual request that I might make that he should have no access till he is cross-examined to-morrow morning to any person whatever except his gaoler and his guard."

The Attorney-General gave an undertaking to do his best to see that the witness was not approached by any one during the period of the rising of the court.

The jury were also exhausted after listening for so many hours to the examination of Castles. They asked that they might be allowed to take a short airing round the place where they were, at six the next morning with their guard. One of the jurymen remarked that if they were confined in the court the time of the Judge would be taken up in a different way, for the jury would need doctors to attend them. Lord Ellenborough said he would give directions that, consistent with keeping them apart from all other persons, their wishes should be carried out.

The next day Mr. Wetherell commenced his cross-examination of Castles. Again many hours were occupied, and the brilliant forensic efforts of the doctor's counsel completely discredited the evidence of this man. He got Castles to admit he was a Government spy, and to acknowledge a most undesirable criminal career. A short extract from the cross-examination of this witness will show how Mr. Wetherell was able to demonstrate the unreliability of the evidence given and to undermine entirely the testimony of this man.

" Were you ever in commitment before this time ?—No.

" Never ?—No, never.

" Upon no charge whatever ?—Commitment, do you say ? Yes, I was.

" Were you ever at such a place as Guildford, in the county of Surrey ?—Yes.

" How many times have you been in commitment or custody before the present occasion ?—Twice.

" Where were you in commitment ?—Once at Abergavenny.

" Where was the other time ?—At Guildford.

" We will take the home circuit first, and then we will go to the Welsh circuit. What were you committed for for which you had occasion to go to Guildford ?—I daresay you perfectly well know.

" But I must take the liberty to ask you ; we had better have it from you than from me.—For putting off bad notes.

" Is not that what is commonly called forgery ?—No, I never understood it was.

" Or uttering forged notes ; is that the better way of putting it ?—Yes, uttering forged notes.

" You told me first you never were in commitment ; when you gave me that answer, did you not recollect you had been twice in commitment ?—I understood you different ; was I ever tried ?

" My question was, Were you in commitment ?—I misunderstood it.

" You made a distinction between commitment and tried ?—Yes, I did.

" You were not tried at Guildford ?—No, I was not.

" What happened that you were not tried ?—I was admitted as evidence.

" The same accident happened at Guildford as has happened upon this occasion ?—Yes, it did.

" Namely, that you were committed upon a charge and afterwards became a witness against the persons committed upon the same charge ; is that so ?—Be kind enough to repeat it ; I cannot understand you.

" Did the same accident happen at Guildford as has happened here, namely, that you became upon that occasion, as you are at present, a witness against persons committed upon the same charge as yourself ?—It did.

" What became of the man against whom you were witness at Guildford ?—What became of him ? He suffered the laws of his country.

" Did he die upon the scaffold as a victim ?—I was informed he did.

" Have you a doubt that he did ?—No, I have not."

Mr. Wetherell made a very eloquent and able speech for the defence. Commenting on the evidence for the chief witness for the Crown, Castles, he said, " I have no doubt, if this trial went on a little longer, I should have been able to prove that Mr. Castles had been guilty of crime under every letter of the alphabet. Under some letters there is a double alliteration of crime : for instance, under the letter B we have Bawdy-house keeping and Bigamy : . . . If we go on to the letter F we have more than double alliteration, we have forgery, felony and French Prisoners : he has allowed that he uttered forged notes, and he worked out the redemption of his life by sacrificing that of his companion : we have felony, for he has admitted stealing the chairs and tables of the room. . . . Mr. Castles was mixed up in one of the most infamous traffics in which a man could engage. I find him assisting the French Government in procuring the escape of French prisoners."

After a long and scathing condemnation of this witness, counsel appealed to the jury to say that at the most the offence committed was mere rioting and that it was ridiculous of the Government to attempt to make the wretched little affair into high treason.

The verdict of the jury was " Not guilty," and Dr. Watson was discharged. His companion Thistlewood was also released, but he was some few years later again put on trial for further offences in connection with what is known as the Cato Street conspiracy, found guilty, and hanged.

There can be no doubt that Dr. Watson was deeply implicated in whatever plot there was, but the brilliant efforts of Mr. Wetherell, his counsel, and the discredit he was able to throw on the evidence of the chief witness for the Crown, were sufficient to convince the jury that the case against the doctor had not been made out.

It is almost impossible to imagine that such a foolish and ridiculous plot as that described by Castles could have been hatched. No sensible men could have lent themselves to such nonsense. Whatever were the intentions of the leaders, the riot ended, as it was bound to do, in a ridiculous fiasco. Probably nothing more than the redress of political grievances was originally intended, but the mob, as usual, got out of hand and indulged in looting and violence. The Government, only too willing to be deceived, started this rather absurd prosecution mainly on the evidence of a notorious criminal, Castles, and such a prosecution supported by such evidence was as certain to fail as was the rioting which led to the criminal charge.

THE TRIAL OF DR. PRITCHARD

DR. PRITCHARD, a practitioner of Glasgow, who was hanged for poisoning his wife and mother-in-law in 1865, possessed a remarkable mentality. He posed as a friend of Garibaldi, whom he had never met, he lectured on places which he had never visited, and after poisoning his wife, he begged in broken accents that the lid of her coffin might be lifted so that he might kiss her dead lips.

The trial took place in Edinburgh, and the indictment charged him with the murders of his wife and of his mother-in-law, Mrs. Taylor, by means of opium, aconite and antimony. The prosecution was conducted by the Solicitor-General, and the defence by Mr. A. R. Clark, Mr. W. Watson and Mr. D. Brand.

The evidence of the servants and other inmates of the house was first taken. Mary Latimer, cook, said that Mrs. Pritchard was frequently sick during the month of February, and had severe cramp in the stomach. On one occasion she had said to her husband, "Don't cry, for if you do you are a hypocrite."

Mary M'Leod, a housemaid, sixteen years of age, whose evidence was of great importance—for the defence contended that she was the guilty party—was subjected to a very severe examination and cross-examination, lasting four hours. She said that during the greater part of Mrs. Pritchard's illness no doctor except her husband attended her. She was often sick after meals. On one occasion she was sick after taking some egg flip and complained of the bitter taste of the drink. Witness admitted that Mrs. Pritchard had seen the doctor kiss her in a bedroom. Witness offered to leave, but Mrs. Pritchard said no; she would speak to the doctor. He was a nasty, dirty man.

Witness also admitted that she had been made pregnant by Dr. Pritchard and had had a miscarriage. With considerable reluctance she admitted that Dr. Pritchard had said he would marry her if his wife died before he did. The prisoner had given her a ring, a brooch and a photograph of himself.

Mary Paterson said she entered the service of Dr. Pritchard as cook. She did not see Mrs. Pritchard till the night of Mrs. Taylor's death. She heard the voice of Mrs. Pritchard in the bedroom, exclaiming, "Mother, dear mother." Dr. Pritchard came out of the room and told witness that Mrs. Taylor was dead. He sent witness to prepare a fire in the spare room, and when it was ready he and his wife went down to that room. Witness and Mrs. Nabb prepared Mrs. Taylor's body for burial. She was dressed when she died. In stripping off the dress a bottle was found in the pocket. This bottle was half full of a brown liquid and labelled, "Two drops equal to three of laudanum." Dr. Paterson not having come when sent for, Mrs. Pritchard said to the prisoner, "Edward, can you do nothing yourself?" He replied, "What can I do for a dead woman? I cannot recall life." He added that Dr. Paterson had told him that Mrs. Taylor was paralysed on the left side. He asked what had been found in Mrs. Taylor's pocket, and witness gave him the bottle. He raised his hands and said, "Good heavens! Has she taken this much since Tuesday?" He also said, "Say nothing about it," as it would be bad for a man in his position to be spoken about. On the Monday before Mrs. Pritchard died witness tasted a piece of the cheese which Mary M'Leod told her her mistress had for supper the previous night. Witness took a piece the size of a pea. It tasted bitter and caused a burning sensation in the throat, and in twenty minutes witness was sick and felt a pain in the stomach. One night Mary M'Leod called witness to make a mustard poultice for Mrs. Pritchard. Witness took it up and saw the doctor and Mrs. Pritchard in bed. Mary M'Leod was in the room. Mrs. Pritchard was dead. Her body was cold. The doctor told witness to put on the poultice. She replied, " She is dead." He said, " Is she dead ? " Witness replied, " You should know better than I." He then said she must have only fainted. He told M'Leod to fetch hot water, but she said there was no use in hot water for a dead body. He then said, " Come back, come back, my darling ; don't leave your Edward."

Dr. Paterson said he was called on the night of February 24th to see both Mrs. Pritchard and Mrs. Taylor. Dr. Pritchard said they had been sick after taking bitter beer. Witness said Mrs. Taylor seemed to be suffering from the effects of some powerful narcotic, and Mrs. Pritchard seemed to be suffering from the effects of antimony. His impression was that she was being poisoned by this substance, and in cross-examination he said he formed this opinion simply by looking at her. (This appears to be a very remarkable statement, considering the very great difficulty there is in almost every case of making a diagnosis of poisoning, even after a very careful and thorough examination.) He refused a certificate of death to the registrar for Mrs. Taylor. He never mentioned poison to Mrs. Pritchard because the treatment he prescribed, provided she got nothing else, was quite sufficient to have brought her round. He did not say anything to the doctor, either. He thought it wiser not to. He wrote to the registrar that the death of Mrs. Taylor was extremely sudden, unexpected and mysterious.

Mr. Campbell, manager of the Glasgow Apothecaries' Company, said that the prisoner bought large quantities of strychnine, laudanum, tartar emetic, aconite, etc., from him. Within two or three months the witness sold the prisoner more tartrated antimony than he did all the rest of the Glasgow doctors together.

Four doctors who conducted the post-mortem on the bodies of the dead women deposed that Mrs. Pritchard had taken large quantities of tartar emetic, and that she had died as a result of this. They had found a considerable amount of aconite in the bottle of Battley's solution found in the pocket of Mrs. Taylor. (This preparation should not contain any aconite.) Mrs. Taylor had died as the result of aconite poisoning.

Mr. MacBrair deposed that Mrs. Taylor had made a will leaving £2,000 to Mrs. Pritchard, and in the event of her death to her husband, who was to get the interest till the children were twenty-one, and then he was to have the principal.

Various witnesses were produced for the defence, including two small children of the prisoner, who said their mother and father and their grandmother were all very good friends and seemed very fond of each other, and a Mr. Thompson, who said he was in the habit of buying Battley's solution for Mrs. Taylor in the name of Dr. Pritchard, but the evidence given by the witnesses for the prisoner had very little bearing on the facts which the prosecution had proved.

The Solicitor-General in his final address to the jury argued that the evidence had very clearly proved that there were only two people who could have committed the murders, and they were the prisoner and the girl Mary M'Leod. Was it possible that this gradual poisoning could have been carried out by a girl of sixteen? The hand of the doctor was very plainly indicated. He had had ample opportunities of administering the poison. Mrs. Taylor's death was due to aconite. This had been mixed with the Battley's solution, and the mixing had clearly been carried out by the doctor.

Counsel for the defence, Mr. Clark, maintained that the prosecution had not traced the poison to the prisoner. All that the Solicitor-General had contended was that there were only two possible poisoners: Mary M'Leod and Dr. Pritchard. They had not even asked M'Leod whether she had put any poison into any article of food, and yet the jury were told to believe that she was not guilty, and that therefore the prisoner must be. The whole evidence was nothing more than a probability and could not possibly justify a verdict against his client.

The Lord Justice Clerk went through all the points which had been given in evidence at considerable length. He pointed out that the contention of prisoner's counsel that Mary M'Leod might have committed the murder was very unlikely. The jury, however, must consider that possibility. Mary was a servant-maid only sixteen years of age. Was it possible that she could have conceived or executed such a crime? If she had got as far as to imagine such a thing, could she have carried it out, when she must have been subjected to the vigilance of the husband of the victim, himself a medical man? It would be very difficult to accept such a possibility. But, on the other hand, if the prisoner had been the designer of the crime, it was quite an easy matter to imagine that Mary M'Leod was the innocent instrument who carried it out. If the jury believed that the two ladies had been murdered, only those who had access to her could be guilty. Of all these it was clear that only the two mentioned need be considered. There was no suspicion of guilt against any of the others. The jury must decide between these two.

After considering the evidence for an hour, the jury were unanimously of the view that Dr. Pritchard was guilty of the murder of both the ladies. The Lord Justice Clerk said he quite agreed with the jury, for the evidence given could leave no reasonable doubt in the mind of any one. He sentenced Dr. Pritchard to be executed at Glasgow on July 28th.

Some days later the prisoner confessed to the murder of his wife, but still persisted that he had not poisoned Mrs. Taylor.

About a week before his execution he made the following further statement: "I, Edward William Pritchard, in the full possession of all my senses and understanding the awful position in which I am placed, do make free and open confession that the sentence pronounced upon me is just; that I am guilty of the death of my mother-in-law, Mrs. Taylor, and of my wife, Mary Jane Pritchard; and I can assign no motive for the conduct which actuated me, beyond a species of terrible madness and the use of ardent spirits. . . . I hereby confess that I alone, not Mary M'Leod, poisoned my wife in the way brought out in evidence at my trial. That Mrs. Taylor's death was caused according to the wording of the indictment I further state to be true, and the main facts brought out at my trial I hereby fully acknowledge, and now plead wholly and solely guilty thereto."

On July 28th, 1865, Dr. Pritchard suffered the penalty of the law. His execution was the last public one in Scotland, and was witnessed by enormous crowds, estimated at 100,000 people. The wretched criminal retired at about eleven the night before his execution, and slept till five the next morning, when he rose and dressed himself in the suit of mourning which he wore when arrested on returning from the funeral of his wife. At eight o'clock the executioner arrived and bound the convict. The procession then formed and made its way to the Court Hall, where Bailie Brown, the presiding magistrate, asked the prisoner if he had anything to say. Dr. Pritchard in a firm voice replied, " Simply to acknowledge the justice of my sentence." The procession once more set out on its way to the gallows. The doctor walked up the stairs to the scaffold, on to the drop, the bolt was withdrawn, and the execution was over. His body was left hanging for an hour.

A NINETEENTH CENTURY FASHIONABLE QUACK

THE career of John Long, a quack doctor practising in Harley Street, who was tried for manslaughter in 1830, reminds us that our forefathers of that period were at least just as credulous as are their descendants of the present day.

In August, 1830, Mrs. Cashin, a well-known lady of Dublin, became very worried about the health of one of her two daughters. Miss Cashin was suffering from consumption. Her mother having heard of the fame of Long, came to London, and took a house in Hampstead, where the quack doctor attended the patient. It was very soon clear to all that Miss Cashin was beyond cure, and that nothing more could be done for her. Mrs. Cashin then became alarmed about her other daughter and feared that she might develop the same complaint. She again consulted Long, asking him whether he could do anything to prevent the onset of the disease. At this time the elder Miss Cashin was twenty-four years old, and in the very best of health. But Long, no doubt seeing an excellent opportunity of putting a considerable sum into his pocket, told the mother that he advised treatment in order to protect her daughter from consumption. Long's pathology was delightfully simple. All internal diseases were due to something which should be let out of the body. He would make an outlet and carry off the cause through this. He duly made the promised outlet by means of an application which was of a secret nature, and which caused an external wound, but in a very short time this wound became much more serious than was anticipated. It increased rapidly in size, and the girl was taken so ill that the landlady sent for Long, telling him she feared very grave results from such a horrible sore unless something were done to stay its course. Long laughed at her fears, saying he would give a hundred guineas if he were able to produce such favourable wounds in other patients. It was pointed out to him that Miss Cashin was ill in herself, that she had constant vomiting, and that something must be done for that. Long announced himself as an enemy of medicine, but recommended mulled port wine. This, of course, did no good for the vomiting. The wound became worse and worse, but Long still was completely satisfied. At length even the credulous relatives could stand this no longer. They sent for Mr. Brodie, the celebrated surgeon of Saville Row. He did all he could, but the young girl died the next day. Mrs. Cashin had let Long know she had called in further assistance for her daughter. He said it was quite unnecessary, and he did not call again.

The death was investigated by a coroner's jury, and Mr. Brodie in his evidence said that when he was called to attend the deceased he found a wound in her back with considerable sloughing. He could not say how the wound was produced, but he had no doubt that it was the cause of her bad symptoms and of her death. He could not imagine how the production of such a wound could possibly have any effect either in curing or preventing consumption. A post-mortem examination of the body, at which eight doctors had been present, had demonstrated plainly that there was no disease except that occasioned by the wound in the back. (It was made clear afterwards that the method adopted by Long to produce the wound was the application of some very strong escharotic.) They agreed that the wound had been the cause of death.

It was shown in evidence that Mrs. Cashin, who had heard of Long through a book which he had published, was begged by her own doctors not to take the younger

Miss Cashin, who was in an advanced state of consumption, to London for treatment by Long, but she refused to listen to the advice given her. He had told the family that unless the sister put herself under his treatment she would be very soon seized with the same disease.

Long's advocate, speaking in his defence, said that, even if the treatment had caused the death of Miss Cashin, it was not manslaughter, for two judges had recently decided that if a man, whether ignorant or skilful, acted honestly and with intention to do good, he was not accountable for the result. Different practitioners adopted different modes of treatment.

Then, as generally happens in this class of case, there was produced the usual string of patients cured by Long's treatment, but, as the jury sagely remarked, this evidence had no bearing on the case under consideration, for, however many harmless acts Long might be responsible for, he would not be relieved from the consequences of one which was not harmless.

One is glad to notice that only one medical man came forward in support of Long. Sir Francis Burdett said he had sent patients to him, although he did not know the nature of the treatment they were to undergo. He had been to consult Long in reference to the Marquis of Anglesea, who suffered from facial neuralgia, as he understood Long had a cure for this disease.

The coroner in his summing up told the jury that if Mr. Long seemed to have the necessary skill and knowledge for carrying on medical practice, and had used due care and diligence in his treatment of Miss Cashin, they must come to the conclusion that he was not to blame for her death. It would be a lamentable thing if every medical man who committed an error of judgment were to be made responsible as if he had committed a criminal act. (The coroner appears to have omitted to pay due regard to the fact that Long was not a medical man.) In spite of the words of the coroner, practically asking the jury to whitewash Long, a verdict of manslaughter was returned. Great public interest was taken in the case. The room was crowded, and the verdict was received with mixed feelings, some of the audience applauding, others calling " Shame."

Long was tried at the Old Bailey, and again a verdict of manslaughter was pronounced. The punishment was the remarkable one of a fine of £250, which was at once paid.

Long was making far too good a thing out of his practice for this punishment (a very ridiculous and inadequate one for such an offence) to have any deterrent effect on him. Within a month he was again before the court on a charge of causing the death of another patient.

Public excitement and interest was aroused in the matter. On the one hand were those who supported the irregular practitioner with all their hearts, and on the other hand was the party who marvelled there could be people so credulous as to place their lives in the hands of a man who adopted such absurd treatment for the cure of real or imaginary disease.

The second charge against Long was investigated in a coroner's court at Knightsbridge, and was concerned with the death of Mrs. Colin Campbell Lloyd, aged forty-eight, wife of Captain Lloyd. Her death was alleged to have been caused by the treatment given to her by Long. This inquest roused even more attention than the previous one, the court being crowded to excess, and among the audience was a large number of members of the medical profession. The nature of the case will be best explained by the evidence given by the medical men who appeared for the prosecution. The chief witness was Mr. George Vance, of Sackville Street, Piccadilly, and he was supported by Mr. Brodie, of Savile Row, and Mr. Campbell, of Wilton Street, all well-known practitioners. Mr. Vance said he first saw Mrs. Lloyd on October 1st, ten days after the beginning of her illness. He was told that she had been attended by Long, that she had inhaled from a tube, and that she had been rubbed twice on the chest with a liniment. The first rubbing did not upset her, but the second caused a sensation of burning. Up to this time she was in very good health, and had been so for some years. When Mr. Vance saw her he found the tongue, mouth and throat eroded; on the chest where she had been rubbed was a sloughing sore, which extended from above the collar bones to below the nipples, right across the chest. The soft parts were gangrenous. Her general condition was bad, severe constitutional symptoms, such as fever, exhaustion and vomiting, being present. It was considered necessary to endeavour to remove the mortified parts, and Mr. Campbell assisted Dr. Vance to do this. They found that so deep had the sloughing gone that the breast bone was exposed, and the ribs and cartilages were reached. The patient gradually grew weaker and died in about a fortnight. The cause of death was gangrene, following the application of some corrosive to the skin of the chest. Mr. Vance added that the only complaint for which he had had to attend Mrs. Lloyd was *globus hystericus* (a manifestation of hysteria), otherwise she was a very healthy woman.

The husband gave evidence that the complaint for which his wife was attended by Long was this nervous affection of the throat. Nothing else was the matter with her.

The coroner put to the jury this question: Did the deceased come by her death from gross ignorance or inattention of her medical attendant (meaning Long), or did she die a natural death? The jury had no hesitation in returning a verdict of manslaughter.

They were asked by the coroner on what grounds they had reached that conclusion. " On the ground of gross ignorance and on other considerations," was their reply.

As the result of the finding of the coroner's court, Long was tried at the Old Bailey before Mr. Baron Bayley. Much the same evidence was adduced as at the former court, but in addition Mr. Campbell, the doctor who had been the first to attend Mrs. Lloyd when she had left Long, stated that he had found her with very extensive wounds, reaching from one armpit to the other, and from the throat to the bottom of the chest, the skin being off both breasts. In cross-examination an attempt was made to show that Dr. Campbell was responsible for the wound getting into such a state, and that if the patient was so bad he should have called in some eminent surgeon to assist him in the treatment, but this line of attack was of very little, if any, assistance to the prisoner.

After the prosecution had presented their case counsel for the prisoner contended he had nothing to answer, but Mr. Baron Bayley held that any man presuming to meddle with anything he did not understand, unacquainted with the principles of medicine, venturing to prescribe for the sick and thereby causing their death, incurred a heavy responsibility, and undoubtedly in some cases was guilty of manslaughter. It would be for the jury to decide whether Long's case came within this category.

The prisoner was then called upon to make his defence. He urged on the court that the death of Mrs. Lloyd was due, not to any fault of his, but to the inexperience and improper treatment of her medical attendant, Mr. Campbell. He said that the medical men who were only earning £3,000 or £4,000 a year were jealous of him, who was making £10,000 or £12,000. Although he was not a qualified doctor, he had spent large sums in attaining his present proficiency, and were he acquitted that day he had no doubt his former patients would flock back to him.

The usual string of dupes, which any quack is able to produce, came forward to give evidence in favour of the prisoner. His counsel wished his witnesses to testify to specific cures performed by Long, but the Attorney-General intervened, pointing out that were this done he should go into instances of his failure. The court held that all the witnesses could be asked was to give general evidence in favour of Long, but not evidence of any specific cure.

Baron Bayley in his summing up observed that the question the jury had to decide was whether the prisoner had been guilty of culpable ignorance. If the jury were of the opinion that the death of Mrs. Lloyd was due to the wound, they must find against Long, but if they entertained any doubt, the prisoner must have the benefit of that doubt. The jury, after considering the question for an hour, returned a verdict of not guilty. It was a most unfortunate decision. The fashionable crowd of ladies present in court heard the finding of the jury with evident pleasure.

Long had originally been a basket-maker, and nothing is known of his obtaining any training in medicine. He succeeded in his " profession " as many other quacks have done and will do in the future. He died, fortunately for the public on whom he preyed, a few years after his acquittal. This occurred just about 100 years ago, but how similar it is to present-day cases. We still have the same fashionable quack practising in a fashionable West End locality, the same large income, the same dupes to support him, even the titled surgeon to back him up. There always have been quacks and dupes ; there always will be quacks and dupes. Human nature does not change.

LEVI WEIL, THIEF AND MURDERER

LEVI WEIL, who in 1771 was accused of a very brutal murder, was a Jewish physician practising in London. His history is interesting, and causes one to wonder why he should have become the wretched criminal he did. He had a good education and studied medicine at the University of Leyden, where he obtained his degree. He came to England and started practice in the metropolis, making quite a success of his work. But some innate depravity caused him to pay less attention to his career of medicine in his desire to procure wealth and excitement. He deliberately set himself to organise a band of thieves who would help him to obtain both. He sent these men out by day to survey carefully premises which might be suitable for robbery, and then attacked the selected houses by night. As a medical practitioner he charged low fees, and soon made quite a big practice. In order to further his night adventures he himself sometimes investigated as far as was practicable the homes of his more wealthy patients, and was thus able at night to direct the attacks of his gang on these houses. Hundreds of burglaries and certainly three murders stand to the credit of Dr. Weil and his band.

The particular crime for which he was tried was an attack on the house of a Mrs. Hutchings in the King's Road, Chelsea, at that time quite a rural district, the building being known as the Farmhouse of Chelsea. Mrs. Hutchings was the widow of a well-to-do farmer, and had three children, two boys and a girl. On a Sunday evening Dr. Weil's gang of ruffians, many of whom had been imported from Holland, collected in Chelsea Fields, and at about ten o'clock approached the Farmhouse. Some of the family had gone to bed, but Mrs. Hutchings and two maids were still up. They were rather frightened by the noise made by the gang, and went together to the door to ask what was wanted. Directly this was opened members of the band burst in and threatened immediate death to any one who resisted them. Mrs. Hutchings bravely tackled them, but they soon overpowered her, fixing her skirts over her head to disable her and tying up the two maids back to back. Five of the men then commenced a search of the house, the remainder watching the three prisoners. They first visited the rooms of the children, and then came to one occupied by two labourers in the employ of Mrs. Hutchings. The men were sleeping so soundly that they knew nothing of what was going on. It was thought they might prove dangerous, so Weil, who was the most bloodthirsty of them all, aimed a blow at one of them, William Stone, meaning to kill him, but only stunning him. The other man, John Slow, sprang up and was at once shot by one of the band. He fell, calling out, " Lord have mercy on me ! I am murdered." They then plundered the house, collecting all the plate they could find, and were very disappointed to discover no cash. They threatened to murder Mrs. Hutchings unless she told them where her money was concealed. Their attitude was so threatening that she gave them her watch and £65, and they then made off. Mrs. Hutchings released her servants and attended to Slow, who was not dead. This victim of the gang lingered till the next day and then passed away.

For a long time no trace of the criminals was discovered, but at length a German Jew, named Isaacs, one of the band, betrayed them, and they were brought before the blind magistrate, Sir John Fielding, brother of the poet, who committed them to the Old Bailey. The trial took place in December, 1771, when Dr. Weil and five others were charged with felony and murder. Weil and three of the band were convicted and sentenced to death ; the other two were found not guilty, the evidence against them being insufficient.

It was usual, as far as possible, to try murder cases on Friday, the sentence being carried out on the following Monday, and this was the procedure adopted in the trial of Dr. Weil and his companions. Most unfairly, great public indignation was aroused against the whole Jewish community, as Weil and his ruffians were all of that faith. But the Jewish people of London showed how much they reprobated the crime by publicly condemning it in the synagogues, and one of the rabbis, who went to visit Weil and the others in Newgate, declined to attend them at the hanging or even to pray with them at his visit.

The execution at Tyburn was witnessed by immense crowds. The victims prayed together and sang a song in Hebrew; the sentence was then carried out and the bodies afterwards taken to Surgeons' Hall for dissection.

It is a remarkable fact that a gang of eight ruffians of this type should have had as their leader an educated man and a physician. He had imported the band from Holland, promising them a profitable livelihood by robbing and thieving, and under his leadership an immense number of successful burglaries was carried out. So well were these organised that no trace of the perpetrators was discovered, till fortunately, as so often happens when dealing with this type of criminal, one of the band betrayed his comrades, and the villainous career of the gang was ended.

THE TRIAL OF FLORENCE HENSEY, M.D., FOR HIGH TREASON AT WESTMINSTER HALL, JUNE, 1758

In 1756, in the reign of George II., owing to the unwarrantable proceedings of the French in the West Indies and North America since the conclusion of the Treaty of Aix-la-Chapelle in 1748, England joined with Prussia in the seven years' war against Austria, France, Saxony, and later Russia.

After the war had progressed for some considerable time suspicion was aroused that a certain Dr. Hensey was in treasonable correspondence with the enemy. The doctor, who had the unusual male christian name of Florence, was arrested, his house searched, and letters discovered which supported the suspicion. He was brought to trial in June, 1758.

Dr. Hensey was about forty-four years old, had studied medicine at Leyden, in Holland, where he qualified, and practised at Arundel Street, in the Strand. The accusation against him was that he was in the pay of France, acting as a spy for that country during war-time and giving information as to the distribution of the military and naval forces of King George. For this he received twenty-five guineas per quarter from the French Government. Among the items of information which he was especially accused of conveying to the enemy were the sailing of Admiral Boscowan to North America and the despatch of the secret expedition to Rochefort. He also advised the French to land in England, as, owing to the state of dissatisfaction of the populace and the bad financial condition of the country, the time was opportune.

Some of the letters were interlined with writing in

lemon juice, and this constituted the important part of the document, the ordinary writing in black ink being quite innocent.

This case was a trial at bar, *i.e.*, a trial which, owing to the importance of the legal questions raised, takes place before a full court of judges, a procedure very rarely adopted at the present time, the last occasion being the trial of the Jameson Raiders in 1896. A good deal of attention was attracted to this case. No other courts were sitting at the time, and great public interest was aroused. The proceedings opened at ten in the morning, and after the usual proclamation had been made the clerk proceeded to call over a list of the special jury who had been summoned to try this important case. About 130 freeholders from Middlesex were sworn, of whom eleven were challenged by the prisoner and two by the Crown. The only witnesses called by the prosecution were for the purpose of proving that the letters referred to in the charge were found in the possession of the prisoner and were in his handwriting. No evidence at all was called for the defence, which was based on legal objections to the various points raised by the prosecution. The counsel employed for the Crown were numerous and important: the Attorney-General, Pratt, afterwards Lord Chancellor Camden; the Solicitor-General, Charles Yorke, also later Lord Chancellor; Sir Richard Lloyd; Mr. Norton, afterwards Lord Grantley; Mr. Perrot, afterwards Baron of the Exchequer; Mr. Gould, later Baron of the Exchequer and Justice of the Common Pleas; and Mr. Serjeant Poole. Against this brilliant array of legal talent appeared Mr. Morton and Mr. Howard for the defence.

The lawyers engaged opened the case most fairly and humanely. The vast difference between a speech of this nature, outlining the facts with such excessive fairness, and the usual speeches by Crown lawyers in treason cases up to that period, impressed itself upon contemporary commentators. The procedure which our present-day

Crown prosecutors, always anxious to uphold the great traditions of the Bar and ensure the prisoner justice and a fair and impartial trial, take as a matter of course, was then regarded as something exceptional, opening up a new era in criminal justice, especially as applied to trials for treason.

Various witnesses proved the finding of letters in a bureau in the rooms of Dr. Hensey in Arundel Street, some of which letters were shown by the evidence of other witnesses to be in the handwriting of the prisoner. These documents contained the alleged treasonable utterances.

The evidence of James Newman, a postman, is very instructive, showing his remarkable powers of observation and deduction.

Do you know the prisoner at the bar, Dr. Hensey?—Yes, I know him very well. I have known him about eighteen months.

Tell the court and jury what you know relative to him.—I have often received from the prisoner at the bar letters of a post-night to carry to the office in Lombard Street, and have carried and delivered them to the office, as I used to do other letters, but at length I began to suspect them.

How came you to suspect the prisoner at the bar of carrying on a treasonable correspondence?—When I have got all my letters together I carry them home and sort them; in sorting of them I observed that the letters I received of Dr. Hensey were generally directed abroad and to foreigners, and, I knowing the doctor to be a Roman Catholic, and as I imagined in the interest of the Pretender, I advised the examining clerk at the office to inspect his letters, telling him that I had some suspicion that the writer of those letters was a spy.

Did you open any one of those letters yourself?—No, but I happened to challenge the letter about the secret expedition; and when it was opened at the post office and found to be what it is, after that I received

THE TRIAL OF FLORENCE HENSEY, M.D.

directions to bring every letter I received from the doctor's own hand, or from that house, directly to the office that it might be opened, and so I continued to do until the doctor was taken up.

Counsel for the prisoner cross-examined him.

How came you to know that Dr. Hensey was a Roman Catholic ? What had you to do with his religion ?—We letter-carriers or postmen have great opportunities to know the characters and dispositions of gentlemen in the several neighbourhoods of this part of the town from their servants, connections and correspondents ; but, to be plain, if I once learn that a person who lives a genteel life is a Roman Catholic, I immediately look on him as one who by education and principle is an inveterate enemy to my King, my country, and the Protestant religion. This led me to keep a watchful eye over Dr. Hensey and to suspect him of carrying on a correspondence with the King's enemies.

You say that you never opened one of the prisoner's letters. Why did you not ?—The first letter which I challenged, or suspected in my own mind, as I was one night sorting my letters, I held up to the candle, by which means I perceived that the body of the letter was wrote in French and that it began with the word " Monsieur." It being wrote in French increased my suspicion, and determined me to challenge the letter.

At the conclusion of the evidence counsel for the defence urged that it had not been proved that the letters found in the bureau were letters which were the property of the prisoner. Other people had access to the desk in which they were found, as had been admitted by witnesses in cross-examination, and these others might have placed them there. Was it likely that Dr. Hensey would have been so foolish as to leave treasonable papers in a desk to which so many people had access ? Then the two witnesses produced to testify that the letters were in the handwriting of the prisoner were very unsatisfactory.

One of them had seen the doctor write only once, and it was in the dark; the other merely said he recognised the letters as in the same handwriting as the doctor's. The similitude of writing was a species of evidence extremely uncertain. The comments of the defence on the evidence of Mendez da Costa, who had sworn as to the letters being in the handwriting of the prisoner, are interesting, and although Da Costa did not testify as a handwriting expert, but simply as one who was familiar with the handwriting of the doctor, these comments are very similar to those usually made by lawyers criticising the evidence of such experts.

"Again, gentlemen, to prove that the letters, writings and papers found in the said bureau, and some other letters said to be intercepted at the post-office, are the handwriting of Dr. Hensey, the prisoner at the bar, they have produced two witnesses that they are the handwriting of the prisoner; but how do they prove it? Why, one of these witnesses says himself that he never saw him write but once, and that was in the dark at night, in the evening at owl-light; and the other's evidence or testimony turns chiefly and principally upon the similitude of hands or of handwritings, and let me tell you that the doctrine of the similitude of hands and the similitude of writings is a species of evidence in itself extremely uncertain, vague and trifling. And as to the seeing of another write, what is there in that? All of you have seen me write to-day and write a good deal, but what avails that? Can any one of you from thence say, much less swear (swearing is a sacred thing), that you know my handwriting? That a person should know the handwriting of another so as to swear to the identity and sameness of it, it is certainly necessary that the person who takes it upon himself to swear to the similitude of hands should be well acquainted with that person's method and form of writing, with the very turn and make of the letters, and, in short, as every man almost has different genius, even with his style and manner of expression; but how is this possible to be done by any one of the evidence who now and then accidentally or occasionally sees the prisoner write I cannot conceive. In this case there is but one positive evidence to the prisoner's handwriting, and that is Mendez da Costa, who is very positive to the handwriting of the prisoner at the bar, and, indeed, he is so very positive that it almost destroys or brings into suspicion the credibility of his evidence. What has induced him to come into this court and here openly and positively swear, from the similitude of the writings, that the writings, letters and papers now before the court are the very handwriting of Dr. Florence Hensey, the prisoner at the bar, were wrote by him, and by him only—I say, what has induced the evidence to do this, must be left to himself and his own conscience, but charity forbids me to suggest that his motives for thus using his old acquaintance, and I suppose some time intimate and bosom friend, are any other than the affection and duty he owes to His Majesty, and the preservation of his long and precious life, and the love which he bears to this country and the inhabitants thereof; but these motives or any other which may or shall arise to you on considering this man's evidence are worthy of your serious consideration. If you believe him, it must go hard with the prisoner; but if you should not believe him, I shall have hopes of seeing the prisoner once more at large."

Finally, counsel argued that the letters, even if written by the prisoner, had never reached their destination, and therefore there was no overt act, and if there was no overt act, there could be no treason. After all, what was contained in the letters? Only a parcel of paragraphs taken from the newspapers, old and stale, which everybody knew, and which Dr. Hensey had written to his brother. There was not so much as one treasonable expression contained in the twenty-nine letters.

"Is the launching of a ship high treason? Is the embarking of the Duke of Cumberland at Stade, after crossing the Weser, treason ? Mr. Pitt and Mr. Legge are reinstated in the Ministry. The common people of England grumble at the great weight and number of taxes, at the scarcity and dearness of corn and, above all, at the loss of Minorca, and that the commanders of their fleets and squadrons do not do their duty and fight and destroy the French. Who can call these treasons ? Who can say that a bare and naked recitation of these matters of fact is high treason ? And this is all that has been done, so you will see, gentlemen, when you come to read and consider the subject of these letters and papers apart by yourselves, for you only are the proper judges whether the subject of the letters is treasonable or not."

Lord Mansfield in his summing up pointed out that the letters produced in court were undoubtedly letters belonging to and written by Dr. Hensey. The jury had to consider whether they were written by the prisoner at the bar in order to be delivered to the enemy and with intent to convey to them such intelligence as might serve and assist them in carrying on war against the Crown. Commenting on the point raised by the prisoner's counsel that no letters written by Dr. Hensey had reached the French Government, Lord Mansfield said, " That which constitutes an overt act in the eyes of the law is the accomplishment of the end proposed by the party acting to the best and utmost of his power. If a man endeavours to do an act of treason, and this act of treason fails through some intervening accident or occurrence, the party so endeavouring and acting to the best of his ability and power is deemed to be guilty of an overt act, as though he had done the thing he had proposed and intended. Thus, in cases of murder as well as treason, suppose a man firing off a gun or a pistol with a premeditated design to kill another, and by some accident or event the gun or pistol do not go off or the party shot at evades the blow, the party shooting is guilty of an overt

THE TRIAL OF FLORENCE HENSEY, M.D.

act, and is liable to be indicted as guilty of a capital offence." (This is not at the present time the law of England. The crime would be only attempted murder, and this is not punishable with death.) "It is the same here. The prisoner at the bar, as far as appears upon the evidence, . . . did intend to send the letters intercepted to the French king's agents."

The jury went out a little after eight, and soon after sent to know if they might have some candles. The officer who brought in the message said he was sworn not to let them have these unless it was so ordered. Lord Mansfield asked counsel on either side if they objected; and as they both agreed, candles were permitted. Obviously the treatment of juries at this time was more stringent than it is at the present day. In half an hour the jury returned and gave their verdict of guilty.

Dr. Hensey was then asked if he had anything to say why sentence should not be pronounced. The doctor more or less recapitulated the arguments of his counsel, and finally he prayed the court not to pass the death sentence or, if that could not be, to recommend him to mercy.

The death sentence was however pronounced, whereupon the counsel for the defence requested that a reasonable time should be allowed the prisoner before execution. The court agreed to a month, and Dr. Hensey was taken back to Newgate. He was, as a matter of fact, not executed, for, after repeated respites, he was finally set at liberty. The country had arrived at a time when even prisoners convicted of high treason were treated with a certain amount of consideration, and not with that brutal vindictiveness characteristic of the Stuart period.

DR. LAMSON

THE murder of Percy John, a lad of eighteen, by his brother-in-law, is an example of a carefully planned and long-thought-out murder with a very trifling motive. Lamson chose aconitine as the poison with which to get rid of his victim. This is a very unusual substance to employ. Mr. Montagu Williams in his defence claimed that so little was known about this poison that all the evidence in connection with it was pure speculation. There had been only one previous case of murder by aconite. He was wrong in this. There were at least three other instances. There was the case *Reg.* v. *McConkey*, and also the two described in this work: that of Dr. Warder and that of Dr. Pritchard. The murder by Dr. Lamson was quite a *cause célèbre*, and excited a great deal of attention at the time.

The trial took place at the Central Criminal Court in March, 1882, before Mr. Justice Hawkins. Great interest was taken in the trial, the court being crowded both by members of the Bar and of the general public. The Director of Public Prosecutions was represented by the Solicitor-General, Sir Farrer Herschell, Mr. Poland and Mr. A. L. Smith. The prisoner was defended by Mr. Montagu Williams, Mr. Charles Mathews, Mr. E. Gladstone and Mr. W. H. Robson. Dr. Lamson pleaded " Not guilty."

The Solicitor-General in opening the case said that the prisoner stood charged with the most serious crime known to the law, that of wilful murder, and if he were guilty, the murder was of the very worst type, because the victim of the crime was the prisoner's brother-in-law, Percy John, a boy of eighteen. He had been for some time at a school kept by Mr. Bedbrook at Wimbledon, and was there at the time of his death. During the three years he was at Blenheim House School the boy enjoyed good health, with the exception of a crippling defect, and required no medical attendance. On Saturday, December 3rd, the prisoner called at about seven o'clock in the evening. Percy John was brought up to see him. The prisoner was offered some sherry by Mr. Bedbrook and accepted a glass. He asked for some sugar to neutralise the effect of the brandy which he said the wine contained. He put some sugar in his wine and then produced from his bag a Dundee cake and some sweets. He cut some of the cake with his penknife, and both Mr. Bedbrook and the boy had some. The prisoner also partook of the cake. After talking for some little time on general matters, the prisoner said, " Oh, by the way, Mr. Bedbrook, when I was in America I thought of you and your boys. I thought what excellent things these capsules would be for your boys to take nauseous medicines in." He then produced two boxes containing capsules from his bag, and asked Mr. Bedbrook to try one to see how easy it was to swallow. Mr. Bedbrook did so and found it quite simple. The prisoner then filled one with sugar and handed it to the deceased, saying, " Here, Percy, you are a swell pill-taker. Take this and show Mr. Bedbrook how easily it is done." The deceased took it and swallowed it quite easily. The prisoner then said he must be going. He told Mr. Bedbrook he did not think the boy would live long. Lamson left behind him the boxes of empty capsules. A little later Mr. Bedbrook saw Percy, who complained of heartburn. Soon after he said, " I feel as I felt after my brother-in-law had given me a quinine pill at Shanklin." When seen again by his schoolmaster, the deceased was in great pain and was violently sick. Two doctors, who happened to be in the house as guests, attended Percy. He died at about eleven that night. Mr. Bedbrook informed the police, who took possession of the capsules and also various other medicines found in the boxes of the deceased, some of which had been sent him by the prisoner. A post-mortem was made by Dr. Bond, of Westminster Hospital. There was no evidence of death from natural causes. The stomach showed that some vegetable poison had been introduced into it and had acted on the nervous system, and so caused death. Portions of the viscera and vomit were submitted to two eminent chemists, Drs. Stevenson and Dupré, and in the viscera, the vomit and the urine was found evidence of some vegetable alkaloid. With regard to these vegetable alkaloids, there were not the means of chemical analysis applicable to the discovery of many poisons. The presence of a mineral poison and its actual nature could be ascertained beyond question by chemical tests that were perfectly sufficient and absolutely sure. But that was not the case with vegetable alkaloids. The presence of an alkaloid was, indeed, placed beyond doubt by the investigations of the medical men, but then arose the question of the nature of the particular alkaloid present. While there was no certain chemical test by which the presence of aconitine could be distinguished, there was a test which would afford to a competent investigator a sure and reliable result, and that was taste, and that test was applied. The taste was an extremely characteristic one, of course not easy to describe in words, but perfectly easy to recognise by any one who had tried it. There was produced on tasting the substance found in the vomit a sort of biting and at the same time a sort of numbing effect on the tongue, which continued even to a painful degree for several hours afterwards. The effect was exactly similar to that of some aconitine purchased for the purpose of comparison. The medical men further tried injecting under the skin of a mouse a small quantity of aconitine. In a few minutes there were symptoms of poisoning, and in about a quarter of an hour the animal died. Using some of the alkaloid found in the viscera and vomit submitted to them in the same way on another mouse, precisely similar effects followed as when aconitine was used. Enough of the poison was found in the vomit to have caused death, showing that a large dose must have been administered to the unfortunate boy. Supposing from the symptoms that the deceased had died from the effect of aconitine, the natural question was, who administered the aconitine? There could be no doubt that the last person from whom Percy John received any food or anything he swallowed was the prisoner at the bar, and within about a quarter of an hour from the time he received the capsule from the prisoner he began to complain of feeling ill. He had taken nothing else since he had had his tea. The next fact of importance to notice was that the prisoner had become possessed of aconitine a very few days before these transactions took place, and that before this he had tried to obtain some from another chemist, but had been refused. On November 24th the prisoner went to Messrs. Allen and Hanbury's in Plough Court, Lombard Street, asked for two grains of aconitine, and being requested to give his name, wrote it down on a piece of paper: "George H. Lamson, Doctor, Bournemouth." As the name was in the Medical Directory, the prisoner was supplied. In the boy's box were found some powders, most of which were quinine, but in some of them there was also aconitine. These powders had been made up by a chemist at Ventnor for the prisoner, and were pure quinine. He had no aconitine in his shop. There was also found at the bottom of one of Percy's boxes a pill-box containing pills, and this was labelled "George Henry Lamson, M.D., care of Messrs. Gilling and Co., 499, Strand." Upon analysis these pills were found to contain aconitine. The jury would learn that aconitine was a very powerful poison, and was not generally used by medical men internally. It was, of course, immaterial to prove any motive, but there was actually a reason, though a slight one only, for Lamson getting rid of his brother-in-law. By the death of Percy John, prisoner would benefit to the extent of £1,500. Lamson was at the time of the death in very embarrassed circumstances and in urgent need of money.

The evidence of the witnesses bore out the opening statement of the Solicitor-General. Mr. Thomas Bond, M.B., F.R.C.S., Lecturer on Forensic Medicine at Westminster Hospital, said he had had a large experience in making post-mortem examinations ; in about a dozen of the cases the patients had died of poison. In his judgment there was nothing to account for death from natural causes. He believed death was due to a vegetable alkaloid. He had never seen a death from aconitine except this one.

Asked if the fact that the aconitine was contained in a gelatine capsule would delay the onset of symptoms, he replied this was so, as the gelatine would have to dissolve before the poison could take effect.

William Dodd, an assistant at Messrs. Allen and Hanbury's, Plough Court, said that about November 24th the prisoner came into the shop and asked for two grains of aconitine. He wrote the order " Aconitia, two grains.—G. H. Lamson, M.D., Bournemouth, Hants." Witness referred to the Medical Directory, and found the name Lamson there, so supplied the drug ordered.

No entry was made in the register when poison was sold to medical men. If an ordinary member of the public wanted to buy poison, they required the purchaser to be introduced by some one known to them. If they were satisfied that the buyer was a doctor, they need not by the Act enter the sale. They just referred to the Directory to see if there were such a medical man.

Mr. Justice Hawkins. Supposing I went in, and having got hold of the Medical Directory and taken a name—say Mr. Brown—would you serve me with two grains of aconitia ?—That would not be sufficient.

What would be ?—You would have to write your name in a formal manner.

What then ?—If I were satisfied that you were a medical man I would let you have it.

Then do I understand that any one of respectable appearance and well dressed might apply, and that without any means of satisfying yourself that he is not an impostor and not telling you what is untrue you would supply him ?—The only test would be the style of writing which is characteristic of medical men.

Mr. Justice Hawkins. That hardly seems satisfactory. It strikes me that any one could go and represent himself as a medical man and be supplied without difficulty. Though the matter is not before us in this case, it may be that the law requires amendment in this particular.

John Stirling, of Messrs. Bell and Co., Oxford Street, said the prisoner came to buy aconitine. He said it was for internal use. Witness declined to serve him and recommended him to go to some place where he was known.

Dr. Thomas Stevenson, M.D., F.R.C.P., Lecturer on Medical Jurisprudence and Chemistry at Guy's Hospital and Examiner in Forensic Medicine at the University of London, said he had had large experience in chemistry, especially in toxicology. He had frequently been employed by the Home Office during the last ten years. He had, in conjunction with Dr. Dupré, examined all the various articles in connection with this case, including the viscera. The methods of examination were arranged between Dr. Dupré and himself at every step. From the fluid in the stomach was obtained, by Stas's process, an alkaloidal extract, which was tasted and produced a sensation of aconitine. He had never found that sensation with any other alkaloid, and he had tasted a great many. He had made experiments on mice both with extracts from the viscera and with preparations of aconite, and the effects had been identical. He had only known of one fatal case of aconitine poisoning in a human being, and the dose then had been between $\frac{1}{13}$ and $\frac{1}{21}$ of a grain. His opinion of the cause of death had been founded on what he had heard of the symptoms—the taste test, the experiments on mice, his knowledge of the poison aconite, and what he had read of in a case of aconitine poisoning. He agreed that too much reliance must not be attached to experiments on animals. Asked whether cadaveric alkaloids were not to be found in the body after death independently of poison, he said the matter was still *sub judice*, and there was no certain knowledge on this subject. Questioned as to whether the cadaveric alkaloids would produce the same effects as vegetable alkaloids, he said they had been described as doing this, but he had no knowledge of any of them producing the same symptoms as aconitine. Asked whether, supposing the cadaveric alkaloids to have existed, there was any means of distinguishing them from vegetable alkaloids, he replied: " There is said to be a test which distinguishes them from all natural alkaloids except morphia and veratrine, certainly from aconitine."

Mr. Montagu Williams called no witnesses. In his address to the jury he said he proposed to place before the jury two propositions. The first was, Did this unfortunate lad die from aconitine poisoning ? Was it proved beyond any doubt ? If there was any reasonable doubt, the prisoner was entitled to be acquitted. The second question was, If you are of opinion beyond any reasonable doubt that the deceased died from aconitine poisoning, are you satisfied that the aconitine was wilfully administered by the prisoner ? He proposed to comment on the two propositions in the order in which he had placed them, not taking the evidence of witness after witness as they had been called before the jury, but dealing with the medical evidence first. He could not help thinking that to rely upon it when human life was at stake would be most improper. Who knew anything about aconitine ? What was it ? It was the root monkshood. Aconitine was the active principle. Up to the present moment, with the exception of one reported case, there was not a single authority of any kind upon the subject. What was the evidence of the medical men called before them? It amounted, with one exception, to a confession of ignorance. He did not blame them, nor was he for one moment attempting to cast a slur upon the honourable profession of which they were members. It was admitted, in effect, that they knew nothing at all about it. The first medical witness was Dr. Berry. He had not suspected poison till after the boy's death, and he admitted he knew nothing about vegetable alkaloids. Dr. Little, the other doctor who attended the deceased in his fatal illness, admitted much the same. Then came Dr. Bond. He said he came to the conclusion after making the post-mortem that death was due to some vegetable alkaloid, but admitted he had never had a similar case. They were therefore asked to come to the definite conclusion that death was due to aconitine poisoning on the evidence of two doctors who had seen the boy during life and knew nothing as to the cause of death, and of another doctor who had not seen the boy alive and also knew nothing as to the cause.

They then came to the evidence of Dr. Stevenson. He was a man of very great scientific attainments. His was the first knowledge or supposed knowledge of the mysterious vegetable alkaloids. What were the tests by which he had arrived at the conclusion which he had placed before them? He said there were no individual tests which would prove the presence of aconitine. The tests on which Dr. Stevenson founded his opinion were on the symptoms detailed to him, upon the taste and upon the experiments on mice, and by his reading. Most of the symptoms were consistent with other causes. What were the tests applied in this case by Drs. Stevenson and Dupré? They had had submitted to them the viscera, and they obtained from these what they believed to be certain vegetable alkaloids, and having obtained them, they tried them on the lower animals, and also by the sense of taste. They experimented on some mice, for whose sufferings they had but little care, and they came to the conclusion that the alkaloid was aconitine. He had thought of reading to them from an article on vivisection, in which it was pointed out that too much reliance must not be placed on experiments on animals. The operations on the mice were effected by pricking them in the back, and they had it in evidence that so delicate were the little creatures that one of them died because the needle was stuck into it a quarter of an inch too far. Mice would even die of pure fright or from the injection of simple water. Yet they were asked to say that this poor boy had died from aconitine poisoning from experiments like this. Then what was the next test ? The taste. Was that to be relied on ? Because a certain substance was bitter and gave a sensation on the tongue something like aconitine, was it to be presumed that it was this alkaloid ? He had asked Dr. Stevenson questions as to the possibility of the bitter taste being caused by cadaveric alkaloids formed in the body after death, but the answer given was that this subject was still *sub judice*. But, at any rate, it was clear that the question of cadaveric alkaloids was being discussed among experts. There had only been one previous case of poisoning by aconitine, and they were asked by the prosecution to say that the tests made on this almost unknown substance were sufficient to convict a man of murder. He did not think it would be justifiable to sacrifice the life of even one of the mice on the evidence given. He might be asked why he had not called medical evidence to refute the evidence given by the doctors for the prosecution, but this was impossible, for the whole matter was so purely theoretical that all his witnesses could have said would have been in the region of speculation, and therefore of no value.

Mr. Montagu Williams complained bitterly of the refusal of the authorities to allow a medical man to be present at the analysis on behalf of the prisoner. He had been told it was contrary to all practice. If this was so, the sooner this practice was abolished the better. It had taken away the only chance the prisoner had of calling medical evidence of any value. He now came to the question whether, if aconitine had been administered, had it been by the prisoner? Supposing he wished to commit this terrible crime for the paltry sum of £1,500, would he not have waited three weeks, till the holidays commenced, and when he would have had the boy at his own home in Chichester, and where he would have been under his own care, and where there would have been no one to have any suspicion, and where he would have even signed the death certificate himself? This was, in counsel's opinion, unanswerable.

The Solicitor-General, in his reply for the Crown, remarked that his learned friend had said that the jury would have to traverse a region of science which was at present unexplored, and that they would have to pronounce a decision upon a drug but little known. All they had heard about it was mere speculation and theory, and ought not to guide them to any judgment. If this argument were pressed too far it would come to this, that any one desirous of taking the life of a fellow-creature by poison had only to select one seldom used and little known, and then to ask the jury to declare him innocent. No doubt from time to time fresh material was discovered for the commission of crime, but science was full of resource and was able to track down these fresh materials. He agreed with his learned friend that the jury had two propositions to consider: firstly, Was the death of the boy caused by aconitine? secondly, Was this substance administered by the prisoner? The evidence of the doctors was quite clear that the boy did not die a natural death. His learned friend had said that it was impossible for him to call medical evidence on this matter because it was all mere speculation, but surely, if he had thought he could dispute any point made by the prosecution, he would have done so. It was satisfactory to know that the prisoner's counsel had had the assistance of gentlemen of the highest skill and experience, who had been able to suggest questions and advise him as to how he should cross-examine the witnesses for the prosecution. If there had been, to their knowledge, any natural cause of death consistent with the symptoms, it must surely have been suggested. Had such a cause existed, it would have been possible to have put medical men in the box to state what that cause was. This would not have been a matter of speculation. These facts and these symptoms, then, had been studied by medical men of great experience, anxious, of course, in the interest of the prisoner, to detect some explanation consistent with natural death, and they had failed to do so. Considering all this, would the jury doubt that death was due to poison? The next question was, Whose was the hand that gave the poison? His learned friend had complained that the application of the solicitor for the prisoner that some one should be present on his behalf during the analysis was not granted. It was said that to reply that it was contrary to practice was not sufficient reason for the refusal. Of itself it would not be satisfactory, but the question was whether that practice was not, on the whole, a right and satisfactory one. The scientific gentlemen appointed by the Home Office to conduct the analysis were independent experts, of the highest experience and skill, and they were nominated as men of science calmly to investigate the facts and say what had happened. They were not appointed to bolster up a theory. To have some one nominated over whose appointment they had no voice, who might at a critical moment of the very delicate analysis interfere either by word or action, would be a very serious matter. But, happily, the results could be tested, for those arrived at by Dr. Stevenson and Dr. Dupré depended upon certain facts. If the jury could trust them as to actual facts, they could trust them as to their analysis, and the presence of any number of persons would not have made that analysis more reliable. Dr. Stevenson had detailed all the minutiæ of his analysis, recounting step by step everything he had done, and there were listening to that record critical ears, gentlemen of great experience who had had the opportunity of reading and studying—for most of the evidence was given in the police court—the statements of Dr. Stevenson. If there had been any weak link in that chain, these gentlemen were present to detect it and point it out; if there had been an error in the process used, that error could have been exposed; if anything was done which might have led to mistake, the jury surely would have heard of it. Men of science could have been called to show that the process Dr. Stevenson used could not have led to any certain result, that it was open to this or that danger; but no such evidence had been produced. It would have been evidence all-important; it might have been evidence fatal to the case presented on behalf of the Crown; and therefore he relied upon the fact that no such evidence had been produced.

The jury might then depend upon it that the process used by Dr. Stevenson was the right one to enable him to obtain the ultimate result, an alkaloid, and that he had used the proper tests to prove that this alkaloid was of vegetable origin. When he came to the test of applying it to his tongue, he used the best test known, for if there had been any better one they would have had evidence to that effect from the defence. Therefore they were asked to rely on what was not mainly theory or speculation, but matter of hard, bare fact. Could they have any doubt that the vegetable alkaloid found was aconitine? Dr. Stevenson did not rely only on the taste test. There were the experiments on the mice, in which the injection of aconitine and the injection of the substance obtained from the body of Percy John produced identical effects. In reference to the cadaveric alkaloids which it had been suggested might have been present, Dr. Stevenson had pointed out that these were only to be found when there was decomposition of the body. In this case Dr. Bond had said that when he placed the specimens in spirit for analysis there was no decomposition. Dr. Stevenson had also said he had tasted the cadaveric alkaloids, and they did not produce the effect that aconitine did, and, moreover, they did not when injected into mice produce death or illness, in fact appeared to have no effect at all. Here again the effect of these alkaloids was not a question of theory, but of proved fact. So these facts were definite, that there was no natural cause of death and there was clear evidence of poisoning.

The Solicitor-General then dealt with the suggestion that the boy had taken the poison himself. No suggestion had been made by the defence as to any means by which the boy could have done this, and there was absolutely no evidence to support such a supposition. It had been remarked that if the prisoner had intended to commit murder, he had acted more like a lunatic than a sane being. Unhappily, experience showed that when men, even men of education and intelligence, did commit crimes of this nature, they rarely failed to blunder. It was surprising, but the truth was that men who committed crimes of this nature did not place before themselves that those crimes were likely to be discovered. If they did, the offences would never be committed. As to motive, the prisoner was so pressed for money that he had committed an indictable offence in drawing cheques on a bank where he had no account. He was just in the position where temptation to get money at any cost would prevail with him.

Mr. Justice Hawkins then commenced his summing up of the case to the jury. He reviewed the whole of the evidence in a most impartial manner. He pointed out that the testimony of Drs. Stevenson and Dupré had not in any way been contradicted, and that they had obviously conducted the analysis in a most careful manner.

He went into the details of the last meeting of the prisoner and his brother-in-law. When they were in the room together, the prisoner seated himself at one side of the table, and a yard from him was the poor deceased boy, and five or six feet to his right was Mr. Bedbrook. The prisoner produced a Dundee cake and some sweets. They were all asked to partake of the sweets and cake, which the prisoner distributed. He then told Mr. Bedbrook that he had not forgotten, when he was in America, either him or his boys. He had seen there some capsules which would do very nicely for them to take their medicines in. He produced two boxes of these capsules from his bag, and one of them he pushed over to Mr. Bedbrook. The latter took one and swallowed it without the slightest ill effect. The prisoner then took a little spoon and filled one of the capsules with sugar. This capsule was taken from the other box. Handing it to Percy, he said, "Now let Mr. Bedbrook see what a swell pill-taker you are." The boy took the capsule and swallowed it, and within five minutes the prisoner left the house. The boy was soon after this taken seriously ill, and died in a few hours' time. The suggestion of the prosecution was that in this capsule was some aconitine, that this had been put in by the prisoner in order to kill his brother-in-law, and that his motive was to obtain the sum of about £1,500 which would come to him on the decease of Percy John. It was for the jury to determine whether these suggestions had been proved to their satisfaction by the evidence produced before them.

The jury retired, and after about half an hour returned to court with a verdict of "Guilty."

Mr. Justice Hawkins sentenced the prisoner to death. He had no doubt that the verdict of the jury was correct. Lamson was taken to Wandsworth Gaol to await execution.

The jury added a rider to their verdict, expressing their opinion of the necessity of strengthening the law in the direction of making it much more difficult to obtain deadly poisons. The judge said he fully concurred with this expression of opinion.

It is difficult to understand how any sympathy could have been felt for such a cold-blooded murderer, but Mr. Williamson, head of the Detective Department at Scotland Yard, relates how he was pestered by women who wanted to see Lamson, and that baskets of hot-house flowers and costly grapes were sent by these hysterical creatures to show their sympathy with this brutal criminal. Many American " experts " sent to the Home Secretary documents expressing their view that Lamson was insane. Whatever value these papers might conceivably have had was negatived by the fact that they had never seen the man they were prepared to certify as a lunatic.

On the representation of President Arthur through the American Ambassador, the convict was respited on the ground that documents were on their way from New York which would throw a new light on the case, but investigation showed that these were of no importance, and Lamson was hanged at Wandsworth Gaol on April 28th, 1882.

Mr. Justice Hawkins in his reminiscences relates the most remarkable view he took of the method which he believed Lamson adopted to give Percy John the poison. He did not believe that it was administered in the capsule, but that it was put in one of the raisins in the cake and given that way. Why the learned Judge should have gone out of his way to imagine such a fantastic theory it is difficult to understand. The evidence makes it quite clear that the poison was put in the capsule and handed to the boy. If it had been put in a raisin in the cake it is very difficult to imagine how Lamson could reasonably have expected that he would be able to manipulate that particular piece of cake so that it should go to his brother-in-law, or even how he could possibly know in what particular raisin in an uncut cake the poison was contained. There is no necessity to advance such a far-fetched supposition, especially when the real method is so strikingly plain.

Lamson had reckoned that he had been so careful in his preparations that his crime would remain undetected. He had chosen as his agent a rare alkaloid, about which very little was known, and his victim was a boy far from robust. He believed that even if any suspicion of poisoning should arise, it would be impossible to detect the presence of a fraction of a grain of a very uncommon vegetable alkaloid. But these beliefs were, unfortunately for him, ill founded; chemical science was too much for him, and his well-merited punishment followed.

Mr. Montagu Williams looked upon this as one of the most difficult cases he had had to deal with, because it required so much medical knowledge. He spent days before the trial in study, being assisted in technical matters by Professor Tidy, the celebrated analyst. Mr. Williams had no doubt as to Lamson's guilt; in fact, he said that he believed Lamson had murdered Percy's brother Herbert, by whose death he came into a considerable sum of money, and also that the convict confessed to both crimes before his execution.

DR. HUNTER AND THE "PALL MALL GAZETTE"

THE libel action brought by Dr. Hunter against the *Pall Mall Gazette* in 1866 had many interesting aspects, the most important from the point of view of the medical profession being the able charge of the learned Judge, Lord Chief Justice Cockburn, to the jury. This charge puts the considered opinion of an intelligent layman on the subject of quacks and their evils with extreme lucidity, and is so well worth following that it is quoted at some length. The jury, whilst finding for the plaintiff, marked their estimate of the value of his reputation by giving one farthing damages.

The action was brought in the Queen's Bench, and Mr. Coleridge appeared for Dr. Hunter. Counsel said that Dr. Hunter was the son of a medical man, an English physician, who had brought up his three sons to the same profession. Plaintiff was educated at a medical school in Canada and afterwards took his M.D. degree at New York. He practised in that town, and made diseases of the lungs a speciality. He developed such a large connection that he engaged four doctors, each holding an English qualification, to assist him. In 1858 he came to England, where he published a book setting forth his abilities, and he also advertised in the newspapers. In 1855 a patient, Mrs. Merrick, accused him of committing rape on her, and whilst that charge was under investigation the libel complained of was published. It was headed " Impostors and Dupes," and it said, " One of the evils which are a curse to English society is the advertising practices of a certain class of medical impostors," and referred to plaintiff as one of these. The article also said, " The Merrick-Hunter story is a fresh illustration of the state of the law in the matter of these abominable advertisements."

Dr. Hunter was able to procure several doctors to appear as witnesses for his system of quackery, and he also produced several of his dupes.

A large number of eminent medical men, including Dr. C. J. Williams, consulting physician to the Brompton Hospital, Dr. Richard Quain, and Dr. Hodgkins, were called, by the defence. They all agreed that not only was the theory of the cause of consumption put forth by Hunter absolutely ridiculous, but also his suggested remedies could not possibly do what he claimed.

Lord Chief Justice Cockburn summed up at very considerable length, reviewing carefully the whole of the evidence. He said it was an important case to the plaintiff, because upon the verdict of the jury would depend his professional position and his personal character. It was also important because incidentally they might have to consider how far the character and dignity of an honourable profession might be sullied and tarnished by recourse being had to a system of puffing by advertising, to which the plaintiff had thought fit to resort. The article undoubtedly was libellous, unless it could be justified on the score of its truth or excused as privileged. To say that a man was an impostor, that he first frightened people into becoming his patients and then treated them by pretended remedies, and that he did all this for the sordid purpose of putting money into his pocket, was unquestionably a matter of a very serious and libellous character. The defence was raised upon two grounds. In the first place, the defendant said, " What I have written and published is true ; and as by the law of England truth is not libellous, I am justified in writing the article complained of." In the second place, he said, " Even if I should fail in making out to the necessary extent the plea of justification, nevertheless I say that, looking at all the circumstances of the case, I, having exercised all needful caution in the matter, having exercised my judgment to the best of my ability in discussing a subject concerning the public, was justified in writing the article in question."

First came the question whether the defendant had established his plea of justification, in other words, whether they were satisfied that the facts set forth, however damaging to the character of the plaintiff, were true. The charge was that the plaintiff in dealing with one of the most fearful diseases to which the human frame is subject, with the intention of gaining profit for himself, began by exciting unnecessarily the fears of those who might read his publication, and then proceeded to hold himself out as the only person who could cure them effectually, that he induced them to trust in the remedies which he prescribed, which he knew to be delusive, and that thus he tampered with their health and trifled with their hopes for the sordid purpose of putting money into his pocket. If the charges were true, hardly anything could be worse than the conduct of the plaintiff. If it were true that the plaintiff had intentionally, fraudulently, and dishonestly put forward such statements, no language could be too strong in which to describe his conduct, for he would be not only an impostor, but an impostor and swindler of the worst possible character. The jury must consider that part of the alleged libel on which the defendant had offered no evidence; that was the charge relating to the proceedings in the police court in Mrs. Merrick's case. Did they believe that in writing those passages the author intended to convey that Dr. Hunter was guilty of the offence with which Mrs. Merrick charged him, or did they believe that the charge at the police court had only been made use of as the occasion, and was not the substance, of the article against the plaintiff? These points, however, although they might enable the plaintiff to obtain a verdict, were not the real matters of contest between the parties. The plaintiff had been acquitted of the charge brought against him by Mrs. Merrick, and therefore the article in question could not injure him in that respect, although it was doubtless published at a most inopportune moment, namely, when the charge was hanging over his head. The main question between the parties was this: Was the system which Dr. Hunter had propounded one which an honest medical writer and practitioner would have put forward? Was it put forward for the mere purpose of enlightening the profession and the public as to his system of cure, or was it a system of quackery which he promulgated for the purpose of monetary gain? The plaintiff came forward professing to understand, as others had not understood, the true cure of consumption; he came forward professing that whereas the whole medical faculty had abandoned the hope of curing this terrible disease, he had discovered means whereby in its incipient stage certain cure could be effected, while even in its more advanced stages the patient who submitted to his system might be restored to health. The method of curing the disease was by the administration of oxygen by inhalation in his special way. They were told on the highest medical authority that the whole of the supposed discovery was purely delusive, and that the views of Dr. Hunter were quite untenable. However, it was not because a man put forward erroneous views of science that he was to be held up to universal scorn. It was not, therefore, because they might be satisfied that the views held by Dr. Hunter were erroneous, that he was to be branded as an impostor, a swindler, and a scoundrel. They must ascertain the motives of the plaintiff in publishing his views. His book warned patients who had colds, elongated uvula, bronchitis, etc., that if they resorted to their usual medical attendants for advice, although they might apparently improve in health, they were the certain victims of consumption. There were two or three passages in the book which might enable them to arrive at an accurate judgment as to the honesty or dishonesty of the plaintiff. In one part of the work he stated that a common cold in the head, if not checked, would tend to the loss of the bones of the nose. Then he said that a sore throat must lead to consumption unless immediately cured, adding that a patient having such a complaint would soon find how short a step led from a sore throat to consumption if he remained under the hands of his usual medical adviser. It was also startling to hear that the tickling of the throat from a long uvula might be the precursor of a speedy decline. It was for the jury to say whether they believed the medical men who had given evidence in the box or the plaintiff. Were his statements put forward honestly to warn people, or were they for the purpose of making money? Undoubtedly the tenor of the book was to show that it was useless to go to the ordinary practitioner for advice as to the treatment for consumption. It mattered not what confidence might be placed in the medical man; if there was anything the matter with the respiratory organs, he was unfit to remedy the evils, and the patient must necessarily turn to the advertiser. They knew, as a matter of history, that from the earliest ages men sought to impose upon the credulous by acting upon their fears and by pretending to be possessed of the power of healing all the diseases to which humanity was subject, men who trifled with the misery of their fellow-creatures for the purpose of their own sordid interests. The denouncement of such pretenders was, perhaps, one of the most meritorious actions in which a public writer could exercise his power. The jury must not confine their attention to the book alone. They must look at the method of advertising adopted by the plaintiff. The object of a scientific medical man in publishing a work was to enlighten the members of his profession and to enable them to treat patients according to his method, whereas the object of the quack was to conceal his method and thus keep his system of cure secret for the purpose of making money for himself. In this respect the book was silent, and no medical man by reading the work could apply the system of the plaintiff to his patients. But this book was said to have passed through edition after edition with unexampled rapidity, and he could not see the necessity for publishing the advertisement of it in *The Times*, since it had passed through fifty-six editions in a month. Could it be supposed that these were ordinary editions ? Again, there were prefaces to the work purporting to be written by two physicians, who turned out to be merely assistants to the plaintiff. Would it not have been as well if the plaintiff had made that fact public instead of inducing people to believe that two gentlemen high in the profession had stamped the work with their unqualified approval ? The plaintiff, however, was not satisfied with the repeated editions of his work. He had resorted to the extraordinary expedient of taking his book to pieces and of publishing it by instalments in the daily papers. Even the learned counsel who appeared for plaintiff did not approve of this, and endeavoured to excuse it on the ground that the plaintiff came from America, where advertising to any extent was legitimate. But they were not in America, they were in England, and whatever might be the practice in the former country, he was happy to say that such a practice had not extended to this country. The rule here was that quacks advertised, but professional men did not. What would be thought if a member of the Bar adopted such practices ? Such an individual would be scouted from the profession which he had disgraced.

The jury found a verdict for the plaintiff, and assessed the damages to Hunter's reputation at a farthing, probably a good deal more than it was worth.

DR. SPREULL AND THE TORTURE

IN 1681 John Spreull, apothecary, of Glasgow, was indicted at Edinburgh for treason and rebellion. The indictment was, " that where notwithstanding be the common lawe, lawe of nations, lawes and acts of parliament, and constant practique of this kingdom, the ryseing of his majesties subjects, or any number of them, the joyning and assembleing together in arms, without and contrarie to his majesties command, warrand and authoritie, and the assisting, abaiting, recepting, intercommuning, or keeping company, or correspondence with such rebells, either with or without armes, and supplieing of them with levies of men, horse, money, armes, and furnishing them with meat, drink, powder, ball, or other munition bellicall, most detestable, horrid, hynous, and abominable crymes of rebellion, treason, and lese majestie, and are punishable with forfeiture and escheat of lyff, land and goods."

The particular act of rebellion which was laid to the charge of Spreull was that he had joined the band of fanatics who after assassinating Sharp, Archbishop of St. Andrews, the head of the Episcopal Church, combined with the Covenanters to rise against the King. They were eventually defeated at Bothwell Brigg by the royal forces, and the frantic desire of the Government for revenge is well illustrated by the vindictive pursuit of Spreull.

Mr. Walter Pringle, one of the counsel for the defence, opened the trial by claiming that his client, having been subjected to torture by order of the Scottish Privy Council and having maintained his innocence whilst under torture, was by law entitled to release. Sir George

M'Kenzie, the King's Advocate, argued that it would be a miscarriage of justice to release a man simply because he was obstinate under torture. The most he could claim in law was that he should not be tried on the questions for which he was tortured, that Spreull was indicted for other points than those for which he had been subjected to this punishment. His denial during the torture could not acquit him, because those who maltreated him had not been authorised by the Scottish Privy Council to ask these particular questions. (It seems absurd that the King's Advocate should seriously have suggested that the poor racked victim should have argued with his persecutors the particular questions they were entitled to put to him.) In this case there could not be any doubt of the legality of the trial, because the prisoner had confessed his guilt previous to the application of the torture.

Long legal arguments took place on this and other points, and eventually the judges ordered the trial to proceed.

It is a curious fact that of the small number of witnesses produced in this case there were four doctors : John Layne, chirurgeon, of Hamilton ; Charles Mowatt, apothecary, of Glasgow ; James Mortown, apothecary, of Hamilton ; and Thomas Alstoun, doctor of medicine. The witness who was most instrumental in securing the acquittal of John Spreull was another man of exactly the same name, also of Glasgow, who came to court having taken the benefit of the indemnity offered, and stated that he was at Bonny Brigg. This witness answered the description given of the wanted man (*e.g.*, colour of eyes, dress, colour of his horse, etc.) much more accurately than did the prisoner.

The verdict of the jury was as follows : " The Assyse, having considered the Depositions of the whole witneysses led and adduced against John Spreull, *una voce* finds nothing proven of the crymes contained in the Lybell which may make him guilty."

Unfortunately for Spreull, the Government were so vindictive against him that the Lords of the Privy Council, notwithstanding the verdict of not guilty, ordered him to be detained in prison in order that they might have him tried on other counts. He was brought before the Privy Council in 1681 and fined 9,000 marks for refusing to make any statement about his attendance at conventicles, and he was ordered to be sent to the Isle of Bass till he paid it. Here he remained in prison for six years, when he was released by order of the Privy Council after the receipt of a letter from the King, who for some reason, which we may be certain was for his own advantage, decided to be a little less brutal to those who did not belong to the established religion.

The whole question of the legality of torture bristles with difficulties. It is the boast of the common law of England that it has never recognised this practice as legal. In spite of this, it was in exceptional instances practised, but generally by some tribunal of extraordinary authority, such as the Star Chamber, which did not profess to be bound by the rules operating in common law. In Scotland things were different. Torture was long a recognised part of criminal procedure and was acknowledged as such by many Acts of Parliament and warrants of the Crown and Privy Council. In 1689, in the Claim of Right, the use of torture without evidence or in ordinary cases was declared illegal. It will be noticed that it took no objection to torture as a whole. It merely limited it to cases where there was evidence which had already been produced, or where the crime was of great gravity, thus admitting the dangerous principle laid down by Roman law, that the seriousness of a crime justifies a departure from the ordinary principles of justice. The various instruments employed demonstrate the fiendish ingenuity of the inventors. The methods of use of some of them, such as the iron boot and the thumbscrew, are known, but of many, such as the pilniewinkis, the caschie-

DR. SPREULL AND THE TORTURE

laws and the lang irnis, not much but the name is known. Crookshank's History quotes the following from the records of the Council: "Whereas the boots were the ordinary way to expiscate matters relating to the government, and that there is now a new invention called the thumbkins, which will be very effectual to the purpose and intent aforesaid, the lords of his majesty's privy council do therefore ordain that when any person shall, by their order, be put to the torture, the said boots and thumbkins both be applied to them, as it shall be found fit and convenient."

But although not recognised by the common law of England, torture was undoubtedly carried out all too frequently in the Middle Ages. The rack, with all its horrors of forcibly wrenched joints, and the scavenger's daughter (which, by means of iron bands drawn very tightly, crushed the doubled-up limbs into the body) are two well-known instances; and there were plenty of others in addition.

In one form, torture could be ordered by a judge, not to obtain evidence, but to compel a prisoner who "stood mute" to plead or to punish him if he did not do so. Before the infliction of the *peine forte et dure* (a matter which has been referred to more fully in another chapter) the prisoner was warned three times and the dreadful penalty explained to him. He was then given a few hours to think the matter over. If the accused were still obdurate, whether man or woman, the judgment of penance was pronounced and carried out. The sentence was not left to any discretion of the judge, for he was by law compelled to pass it in cases where an accused person refused to plead. The wording of the terrible judgment was as follows: "That you be taken back to the prison whence you came, to a low dungeon into which no light can enter; that you be laid on your back on the bare floor, with a cloth round your loins, but elsewhere naked; that there be set upon your body a weight of iron as great as you can bear and greater; that you have no sustenance save on the first day three morsels of the coarsest bread, on the second day three draughts of stagnant water from the pool nearest to the prison door, on the third day again three morsels of bread as before, and such bread and such water alternately from day to day till you die."

Mr. Maclaurin in his "Introduction to Criminal Trials" makes the following observations on torture in Scotland : " On the 24th of June, 1596, John Stewart, Master of Orkney, was indicted for consulting with Alison Balfour, a witch, for the destruction of Patrick, Earl of Orkney, his brother, by poison. The confession of Alison Balfour was libelled upon." (In Scots law a libel means a document containing the plaintiff's allegation.) "He gave in a written declaration by way of defence, bearing, *inter alia*, as to the confession, ' No regard can be had to it, in respect the said confession was extorted by force of torment, she having been kept 48 hours in the caspie-laws.'" (This was an old Scotch instrument of torture said to have been invented by the Master of Orkney in 1596. Its action appears to have been forcibly to draw together the body and limbs of the victim and hold him in this cramped position, much the same as in the instrument referred to above as the scavenger's daughter.) "Her old husband, a man of about ninety years of age, was put in heavy irons ; her son put in the buits, where he suffered 57 strokes ; and her little daughter, about seven years old, put in the pilniewinks," (a board with holes into which the fingers were thrust and pressed upon with pegs), " all in the poor woman's presence to make her confess."

Lord Royston observes : " The instruments in use amongst us in later times were the boots and a screw for squeezing the thumbs, thence called thummikins. The boot was put upon the leg, and wedges driven in, by which the leg was squeezed sometimes so severely that the patient was not able to walk for a long time after ; and even the thummikins did not only squeeze the thumbs, but frequently the whole arm was swelled up by them. Sometimes they kept them from sleep for many days, as was done to one Spence, A.D. 1685. And frequently poor women accused of witchcraft were so used. Anciently I find other torturing instruments were used, as pinniewinks or pilliewinks, and caspitaws or caspicaws, in the Master of Orkney's case, June 24, 1596, and tosots, Augu. 1632. But what these instruments were I know not, unless they were other names for the boots and thummikins."

The boots and thummikins were, it is said, imported into this country from Russia by a Scotchman, who had long been an officer in the service of the former country.

"No inferior judge could torture. It was employed by the Privy Council and justiciary only, by the last never during trial before the jury, but by way of precognition. What the person who underwent it confessed was proved at his trial."

Among the other methods employed to torture the prisoner Spence, referred to above, was the use of a hair shirt and pricking, by means of which he was kept five nights from sleep, till he was half demented.

In the case of Felton, tried for the murder of the Duke of Buckingham in the reign of Charles I., the question of the legality of the torture was again raised. The King had it put before the judges of the land. First, the Justices of Serjeants' Inn, in Chancery Lane, met and agreed that the King could not in this case put the prisoner to the rack. Afterwards all the justices assembled, and agreed unanimously that by law he could not be put to the rack, for no such punishment is known to or allowed by our law.

Baron Weston, the judge who tried Elizabeth Cellier in 1680, in the reign of Charles II., made the following observations on the question of torture: "But you must first know the laws of the land do not admit a torture, and since Queen Elizabeth's time there hath been nothing of that kind ever done. The truth is, indeed, on the 20th year of her reign, Campion was just stretched upon the rack, but yet not so but that he could walk: but when she was told it was against the law of the land to have any of her subjects racked (though that was an extraordinary case, a world of seminaries being sent over to contrive her death, and she lived in continued danger), yet it was never done after to any one, neither in her reign, who reigned 25 years after, nor in king James's reign, who reigned 22 years after, nor in king Charles the first's reign, who reigned 24 years after; and God in heaven knows there has been no such thing offered in this king's reign."

Lord Coke, in the case of the Countess of Shrewsbury in the reign of James I., appears, by implication, to express the opinion that torture was allowed by English law. Hargrave, commenting on this, says: "It is surprising that doctrine so reflecting on the law of England should escape from one of Lord Coke's character. His language, as Attorney-General, at the trials of the Earls of Essex and Southampton implies the same obnoxious tenet. But in his third Institute he gives it as his opinion most decisively that all tortures of accused persons are contrary to our law. (This latter view was freely quoted in the trial of Mr. Picton, referred to later.) As to the instances of torture collected by a most respectable writer of the present time, they only prove an irregularity of practice. The use of torture appears to have been continued in Scotland until the Revolution. It was abolished by an Act of Parliament of Queen Anne.

The following is a brief account of a very brutal punishment of a criminal in France: "There was in this country an instrument called the brodequin, which corresponded to the boots in Scotland. The instrument is a strong wooden box made in the form of a boot, just big enough

DR. SPREULL AND THE TORTURE

to contain both legs of the criminal. The legs are inserted, and a wooden wedge is then driven with a mallet between the knees and forced right through. A second larger wedge is then inserted and the same procedure repeated. The prisoner in this particular instance was a man named Ravillac, who was accused of parricide and convicted. His sentence was not only death, but torture to precede it. He was first ordered to be put to the torture of the brodequin. The first, the second, and then the third wedges were driven in, when he fainted away. Wine was forced into his mouth, but he could not swallow it. He was released from the brodequin and laid upon a mattress till he recovered his senses. Three hours later he was put into the tumbril and drawn to the scaffold. When he ascended the platform, his right hand, holding the knife with which he had committed the murder, was burnt, while his breast was torn with red-hot pincers, and afterwards melted lead and scalded oil were poured upon his wounds. Next he was attached to four horses, which dragged upon him for half an hour at intervals, the populace lending a hand at pulling on the ropes. A man passing, seeing the horses were tired with their efforts, lent the fresh animal he was riding, in order to assist in the torture. At length, when the horses had drawn for some considerable time on his limbs without pulling them out, the crowd with knives, sticks, and other weapons threw themselves upon him, tore his limbs from his body, dragged them through the street, and burnt them in different parts of the city."

This appalling brutality was not the work of an uneducated mob, lost to all feelings of humanity. It was the deliberate sentence of a properly constituted court of justice. The wording of the sentence pronounced was as follows : " . . . From thence he shall be carried to the Greve and, on a scaffold to be there erected, the flesh shall be torn with red-hot pincers from his breasts, his arms and thighs, and the calves of his legs ; his right hand, holding the knife wherewith he committed the aforesaid parricide, shall be scorched and burned with flaming brimstone, and on the places where the flesh has been torn with pincers melted lead, boiling oil, scalding pitch, with wax and brimstone melted together, shall be poured. After all this he shall be torn in pieces by four horses, his limbs and body burnt to ashes, and dispersed in the air. His goods and chattels are also declared to be forfeited and confiscated to the King. And it is further ordained that the house in which he was born shall be pulled down to the ground (the owner thereof being previously indemnified) and that no other building shall ever hereafter be erected on the foundation thereof, and that within fifteen days after the publication of this present sentence his father and mother shall, by sound of trumpet and public proclamation in the city of Angoulême, be banished out of the kingdom, and forbid ever to return, under the penalty of being hanged and strangled without any further form or process at law. The court has also forbidden, and doth forbid, his brothers, sisters, uncles, and others from henceforth to bear the said name of Ravillac. . . . And before the execution thereof the court doth order that the said Ravillac shall again undergo the torture. . . ."

Were the record of this ghastly sentence not obtained from a source beyond doubt accurate (Register of Parliament), it would be difficult to believe, even in France in 1610, that such savage brutality could have been devised by civilised beings.

At the trial of Mr. Thomas Picton, late Governor of Trinidad, for causing torture to be inflicted on Luisa Calderon, a free Mulata in the Island of Trinidad, early in the nineteenth century, the question of the legality of torture in England, and therefore in an island under English government, arose and was in fact the whole essence of the case. Some of the remarks of Mr. Nolan in his argument before the court are of very great interest in their bearing on this matter: "Now, my lords, it becomes necessary, in the first place, to see upon what grounds and principles it is that torture cannot be applied in this country. If such a practice is expressly forbidden by Magna Charta; if it is repugnant to the fundamental principles of the British Constitution; if it is as absurd as it is cruel and unjust, inasmuch as it attempts by a very ineffectual mode to procure that which by our law cannot be extorted, namely, a confession of the party against himself, and by means which our law prohibits, namely, by punishing him previously to the time when he is arraigned and tried, I shall then contend that exemption from torture is one of the indefeasible birthrights of the British subject, which he carries with him into whatever country he may go which is under allegiance to the Crown of England. . . . I know my learned friends agree with me that torture cannot be inflicted by the law of England; but they differ with me upon a point which is the very essence and vital principle of this argument, namely, whether the rule which prohibits the infliction of torture in this country is a mere matter of positive regulation, or whether it is one of those rights which are formed upon Magna Charta and the principles of the British Constitution; upon this point, as it appears to me, will mainly depend the question whether it has ceased, or whether it remains in an island under the British dominion by conquest. . . .

"The next authority I was going to cite to show that torture is contrary to the principles of the British Constitution is Mr. Justice Blackstone. Your lordship will find it in the first book and the first chapter of his commentaries. At present I shall only observe that whenever the *constitution* of a state vests in any man, or body of men, a power of destroying at pleasure, without the direction of laws, the lives or members of the subject, such constitution is in the highest degree tyrannical, and that whenever any *laws* direct such destruction for light and trivial causes, such laws are likewise tyrannical, though in an inferior degree, because here the subject is aware of the danger he is exposed to, and may by prudent caution provide against it. The statute law of England does therefore very seldom, and the common law does never, inflict any punishment extending to life or limb unless upon the highest necessity; and the Constitution is an utter stranger to any arbitrary power of killing or maiming the subject without the express warrant of law. 'Nullus liber homo,' says the Great Charter, 'aliquo modo destruatur, nisi per legale judicium parum suorum aut per legem terræ,' which words 'aliquo modo destruatur, according to Sir Edward Coke, include a prohibition, not only of *killing* and *maiming* but also of *torturing* (to which our laws are strangers) and every oppression by colour or an illegal authority. Therefore, according to the opinion of this most learned judge, it appears that the practice of torture is not only forbidden by the *law* of this country, but by the *Constitution* of this country. . . .

"It has also been contended that torture has not been prohibited as being contrary to the law of God or to the constitution, but merely as contrary to the custom of of the realm and the peculiar local positive institutions of the country. But Lord Coke considered it as contrary of the fundamental principles of the Constitution, and declares torture to be contrary to the laws of God, in a quaint manner certainly, but not with less force on that account. It is further relied that torture is not repugnant to the principles of the British Constitution because the law of England permitted the *peine forte et dure*. Now, unless I very much mistake all the authorities upon the subject, no cases are more dissimilar than the infliction of the *peine forte et dure* and that of torture. . . . Instead of being a punishment to compel a person to accuse himself, it was a positive judgment. It was not inflicted to extort a confession of the truth by the rack under torment, but a judgment the effect of which was that the party was to be kept under the punishment until he died."

It is clear from the instances cited and the opinions expressed by the celebrated lawyers quoted that the practice of administering the torture in England was illegal, and when carried out, the law was broken by the high-handed action of the executive.

THE FIRST CASE OF MURDER BY MORPHIA

An interesting case, the scene of which is laid in Paris, is that of Dr. Edme Castaing, a young physician, accused of murder in 1823. It is one of the earliest, if not the earliest, example of poisoning by the newly discovered drug morphia. The trial took place in November at the Paris Assize Court. The prisoner, who was only twenty-seven years of age, was accused of poisoning Hippolyte Ballet by morphia, of having destroyed the last will and testament of the deceased, and, lastly, of having poisoned Hippolyte's brother, Auguste Ballet, also by morphia. The motive alleged for the murders was a pecuniary one. Castaing was a profligate and extravagant young man with very small means and, therefore, without the opportunities of indulging his tastes.

He was medical adviser to Hippolyte, and some fortnight before the death of the patient a large quantity of morphia had been bought by him (Castaing). He had previously been engaged in experiments with different poisons, and had made inquiries as to those most likely to escape detection. When a post-mortem was made on the body of Hippolyte the conditions found were said to be those which might be found in any one dying either from inflammation of the lungs or from poison. Castaing, who previous to Hippolyte's death had been very pressed for money, suddenly became affluent, and, according to the theory of the prosecution, this was due to the fact that he had destroyed the real will, and forged another by means of which a large sum was secured by Hippolyte's brother, Auguste. The prisoner had obtained 100,000 francs from him for this service. But this did not satisfy Castaing. He must have more money, and in order to obtain this, so it was alleged, he poisoned the brother Auguste with the same narcotic after persuading him to make a will leaving all his money to himself (Castaing). He had inquired of a lawyer whether a will made in favour of a physician was valid. A few days after this inquiry Castaing, though he was supposed to be in active practice in Paris, went on a visit to St. Germaine and St. Cloud with Auguste. On the morning of May 29th they set out for St. Germaine-en-Laye in a small carriage and without servants, although Auguste had plenty of horses and a carriage of his own, and his servants were doing nothing. At St. Cloud they went to the Blackamoor's Head, and Castaing asked for some warm wine for his friend. He said it was not necessary to put any sugar in, as he himself had bought some in the town. He had also bought lemons, and these, it is suggested, were for the purpose of disguising the bitter taste of the morphia which he put in the wine in place of sugar. Auguste was so disgusted with the bitterness of the taste that he took very little of the wine, but even this quantity made him feel very ill. He could not get up the following day. At four o'clock the next morning the prisoner roused the people of the inn to open the doors, ostensibly that he might go for a walk in the park, but actually in order that he might go to Paris and secure some more morphia. On his return he called for a glass of milk, and gave it to Auguste to drink. He was at once seized with a violent attack of vomiting and diarrhœa. He asked that a physician from Paris might be sent for, but instead Castaing secured the services of a medical man in the neighbourhood. This doctor, M. Pigache, ordered a soothing draught for the patient. Castaing gave him a dose of it, and within a few minutes Auguste had a fit, became unconscious, and died. The physicians made a post-mortem and found all the signs which they would have expected in morphia poisoning.

The witnesses in this case were very numerous, sixty-five for the Crown and twenty-six for the defence.

The medical evidence was somewhat unusual, but it must be remembered that acetate of morphia was a new discovery, that the chemical tests were also new, and that there was no similar previous case to guide the experts. M. Lherminier and M. Segalas, both doctors, agreed that two years previously Hippolyte was suffering from pulmonary tuberculosis; their opinion was that he might have lingered for some considerable time with this complaint. At the post-mortem they found inflammation of the chest; the same appearances would have been present if Hippolyte had died from any vegetable poison. They agreed that certain vegetable poisons, even when administered in sufficient quantities to cause death, might not leave any traces behind them either in the stomach or in any other part. M. Segalas had been a member of the commission to investigate the new drug. This commission had unanimously declared that eight grains of the acetate of morphia would produce death, though no trial of it had been made on human beings. M. Segalas added that, after experiments which he had since made, 14 grains of this substance when given to animals had not caused death. (At the present time a dose of one grain is considered fatal to a human being, much larger quantities being necessary to cause death in such an animal as a dog.)

M. Laennec said that the prisoner was one of his students, but had been very unsuccessful in his medical studies. He attributed the death of Hippolyte to apoplexy, but whether this was produced by violent or natural causes he could not say. All poisons produced apoplexy: nearly all of them left no trace behind, even when given in quantities sufficient to produce death. The president of the court then asked him what he thought Hippolyte had died from. He replied that as a physician he did not know, but that as a man he suspected poison. The President turned to Castaing and asked him what he had to say. " I am not guilty of the crime which is imputed to me. I can look you in the face " (turning to the image of Christ which was in the court). " I can throw myself at your feet and say I have not committed it."

Dr. Michel, the usual medical attendant of Hippolyte, said he had been called in in April and found him suffering from pulmonary tuberculosis. The complaint was making such slow progress that he thought that Hippolyte would live many years. He was greatly surprised to hear four months later that death had taken place. He was asked to read the result of the autopsy, and to give his opinion from this as to the cause of the death of Hippolyte. He read this document and then said that the congestion of the brain might have arisen from natural causes, but that some of the signs found might have resulted from morphia poisoning.

M. Billoin, a druggist, said that the prisoner had in January, 1823, bought considerable quantities of acetate of morphia from him. He was told that it was wanted for experiments on animals.

M. Orfila, Professor of Toxicology in the Faculty of Medicine, said that from inspection of the *procès verbal* of the post-mortem on Auguste he could not say whether the death had been produced by natural causes, or by poison. An important point in the evidence was missing, for none of the vomit had been analysed. If the vomit and the liquid contents of the stomach had been submitted to him, he could have answered much more satisfactorily. " My course of legal medicine leads to the establishment of a great point of public interest, that of revealing crime by showing the existence of poison. By means of exact analysis I could easily discover in a pint of liquid a single half-grain of acetate of morphia." The witness then proceeded to give the methods of his analysis : " Two or three years ago it was a common error to suppose that certain vegetable poisons left no trace ; . . . that was even an axiom of legal medicine. At present chemistry has made great progress, and it is almost as easy to discover the vestiges of vegetable as of mineral poisons." (The contents of the stomach had been analysed, but no poison was found.)

M. Pigache said he had been called in on the day before Auguste's death. He asked to see the matter which had been vomited, but was told that it had been thrown away. The next day being more and more astonished at the singular nature of the illness, and seing M. Auguste at the point of death, he went to the Mayor of St. Cloud to tell him the circumstances. The Procureur du Roi was accordingly sent for, and on his arrival with the Gens-d'armes witness at once proceeded to make an autopsy.

Did you think that the cause of death was natural?— It might be natural, or it might be the result of poison. It was the uncertainty I felt that led me to go to the Mayor and demand that the body should be opened.

Did the patient mention to you his having felt any disturbance, on the second night, from the noise of cats and dogs?—He did not mention any such thing to me; he only said he had passed a very unquiet night.

The President: Prisoner, how was it that the deceased spoke to nobody but you of this pretended noise of the cats and dogs?—He attached less importance to it than I supposed.

The President: He attached so much importance to it that, by his desire, you went to Paris to procure poison to rid him of these disagreeable animals.

The next witness was Dr. Pellatan, a professor in the School of Medicine. He said that on Monday, June 1st, he went from Paris to St. Cloud, in great haste, in consequence of a letter which was brought to him from M. Pigache by a black servant. On his arrival at the Blackamoor's Head, he was introduced to Dr. Castaing, and the sick man, M. Auguste Ballet. He did what he could, but it was too late. Seeing the condition of M. Ballet growing worse and worse, he wrote an account of what he had observed for the information of the legal authorities. The patient had stertorous breathing and very contracted pupils. M. Pigache and witness then went out, and during their absence the patient died. He saw Dr. Castaing shedding tears, and overwhelmed with grief. The witness told prisoner that he was in a dangerous position. Circumstances were against him. He had come with his friend to pass two or three days. He was a physician, and he was legatee for a large amount, and his patient had died whilst under his care. Castaing asked witness whether he thought suspicion would fall on him (Castaing). Witness said, Certainly, and the least that could be done was to take every step in their power to definitely ascertain the cause of death. He should request that there should be a post-mortem. Later witness saw prisoner in custody. He was very anxious to learn the result of the examination. He was told no poison had been found. He then asked whether the authorities would release him. Witness said he did not know.

M. Malassis, a lawyer, said that Castaing had called to see him to ask whether a will made by a patient in favour of his physician would be valid. "I told him that it was in certain circumstances. He came back some time afterwards and told me that one of his friends, who was ill in the country, had made a will, and had left him 10,000 francs a year. That friend was attacked by an incurable disease and had only one sister, to whom he did not intend to leave a farthing on account of a bitter quarrel with her. He asked what were the formalities required for a will that was written throughout in the testator's own handwriting. His friend wanted his will deposited with a third person. I suggested his employer, but Castaing said he preferred me as a depositary. Prisoner later left the will produced on my desk."

Dr. Laennec was recalled by the President and asked to give his opinion on the following. A healthy man of twenty-five years of age takes in the evening warm wine in which has been put some lemon and a quantity of acetate of morphia sufficient to cause death or to produce considerable illness. He has this draught at nine in the evening. The next day at nine in the morning he takes some cold milk, to which again there has been added morphia. At six in the evening he is given a draught which contains the same poison. What would be the probable result of the last draught? Dr. Laennec replied that acetate of morphia was a new drug and had only been used very recently indeed. Very few physicians had as yet employed it. Physiologists had made many experiments on animals with it, but it was not possible to conclude from these experiments what would be the effect on human beings. It would vary, but if any substance extracted from opium caused sickness, the result would not be the same as if no vomiting had been caused. The results would depend on the individual. One might take 100 grains with impunity; another might die from a dose of ten. (The usual dose of morphia is a small fraction of a grain, about one sixth to one quarter.)

Castaing then produced his witnesses, of whom the first was Dr. Chaussieur, a physician, aged eighty, who said he had known several instances of death in circumstances as extraordinary as those of M. Auguste Ballet, in which there was not the slightest ground for suspecting that the deceased had been poisoned, although in these cases autopsies had been made. If the red spots observed in the stomach of M. Auguste had been due to poison, he would have expected they would have been spread over the organ generally, instead of being merely local. The President asked him if they might not have been due to poison. Dr. Chaussieur replied: "Let us not lose ourselves in the vagueness of possibility; you know as well as I that *ex posse ad actum non valet consequentia.*"

The President: You are not wanted here to teach the President his duty, but simply to answer such questions

FIRST CASE OF MURDER BY MORPHIA 129

as may be put to you. May the poison have been the cause of Auguste's death ?—Dr. Chaussieur: Death may be caused by a thousand circumstances.

M. Roussel, counsel for the prisoner, then asked the doctor whether after the death of M. Auguste his pupils were contracted, and whether that was the natural effect of narcotic poison. The doctor replied: "No; on the contrary, those poisons dilate the pupils." (One of the most marked effects of morphia on the body is the contraction, to a very small size, of the pupils.)

Several witnesses of the poorer classes spoke in strong terms of gratitude of the careful attention which they and their families had received from the accused. He attended them when ill, and would take no fees.

This brought forth the remark from the President that although this showed the goodness of his character, it also pointed to the fact that his practice was not among the wealthy classes. How then could he have saved the money he claimed he had? Castaing said he had only called patients who had special cause to be grateful to him. He had not asked any of his patients who had paid him fees to attend the court.

The jury acquitted the prisoner of the murder of Hippolyte, but found him guilty of the destruction of the will and of the murder of Auguste. This verdict was the opinion of seven of the jurors, five of them dissenting. The Court announced that it agreed with the majority, and sentenced him to death, and to pay 100,000 francs towards the costs of the prosecution. Castaing was afterwards executed, protesting his innocence to the last.

The medical evidence, looked at after one hundred years, appears curious. Morphia, which is a drug administered in fractions of a grain, and of which a grain is usually regarded as fatal, is here spoken of in amounts of ten and even 100 grains. M. Orfila was proud to say he could detect half a grain by analysis. The science of toxicology was then in its infancy and its methods crude.

The present-day chemist can recognise without difficulty $\frac{1}{5000}$ of a grain. The doctors spoke of signs at the post-mortem which might be due to morphia poisoning. As a matter of fact, there is nothing characteristic found in the body after death from morphia, except the presence of the drug itself. This case was decided mainly on other grounds than medical, but there is no doubt that Castaing was properly convicted.

THE MURDER OF DOCTOR BY DOCTOR

THIS case is a very remarkable one, and fortunately very unusual, for, unlike so many other examples contained in this work, the criminal doctor was not one of the scum of the profession, but a learned and respected professor at a university.

Dr. Webster, the accused man, was Professor of Chemistry at Harvard University, and a member of many learned societies in his own and other countries. He unfortunately had extravagant tastes, and was unable to meet the expenses thereby incurred, from his earnings. He resorted to borrowing money; and among those from whom he obtained loans, and to whom he mortgaged property, was a Boston practitioner named Parkman. Dr. Webster was not honest in his dealings, but he was so successful in concealing his monetary embarrassments from his friends that he was able to lead the double life of brilliant college professor and dishonest financier for a long time without discovery. But there came a time when his creditor insisted on the repayment of his loans, threatening exposure unless he received his dues. Dr. Parkman most unaccountably disappeared on November 23rd, 1849, after a visit to Dr. Webster at the college. Suspicion was very soon aroused, the general feeling being that there had been foul play. The authorities offered a reward of 1,000 dollars for the discovery of the body of Dr. Parkman. For some reason or other Dr. Webster was from the outset suspected. His rooms were searched, but nothing whatever was found to inculpate him. But there still remained the feeling that Dr. Parkman had never left the building after his interview with Dr. Webster. There was a part of the college which the police had not searched, and that was the vault underneath the Professor's laboratory. This laboratory rested on piles, the tide ebbing and flowing through them. After a very thorough search of the vault, portions of a human body were discovered, and Dr. Webster was at once arrested. The pieces of the body were shown to Dr. Webster. They consisted of the pelvis with the right thigh and leg. At the same time a jaw-bone, some artificial teeth, and some buttons, which were found in a furnace used in the laboratory, were exhibited. Later the police found a tea-chest in Dr. Webster's room, which contained further portions of the body. An inquest was held, and the jury found that the remains were those of Dr. Parkman, and that he had met his death at the hands of his colleague, Dr. Webster.

At the subsequent trial the evidence proved very clearly the guilt of the Professor.

The dentist who had looked after Dr. Parkman gave evidence to prove that the mouth of the deceased was so deformed that his case had impressed itself on the memory of witness. He produced his model of the mouth, which corresponded in the most minute detail with the plate found in the furnace of Dr. Webster.

The securities for the debt to Dr. Parkman were found in the possession of the prisoner, and he was totally unable to say how he could have redeemed them. It was proved that he had sent letters and messages which were ingeniously contrived to put the relatives of the missing man off the real scent when they commenced to search for him.

The jury had not the slightest hesitation in returning a verdict of guilty, a verdict which overwhelmed the accused and left him prostrate.

A very long period elapsed between the sentence and the execution. This period of five months gave the prisoner the impression that he would be pardoned, but when he found that the hope was not to be realised, he made a confession. It was a very long document, and the main gist of it was that the crime was not premeditated. According to this, Dr. Parkman on his visit to Dr. Webster made bitter speeches and used threatening gestures. Dr. Parkman produced an old letter which went to show that he had been the means of getting Dr. Webster appointed to his post. " You see, I got you into your office, and now I'll get you out of it." He pushed his fist into Dr. Webster's face, and taunted him beyond endurance ; self-control was lost by Dr. Webster. He seized a heavy piece of wood and struck Dr. Parkman a violent blow on the the back of his head, killing him on the spot. There was nothing left to do but to endeavour to conceal the crime. The dismembering of the body and the attempt to burn it were prompted by the fear of discovery. All the details brought out at the trial were woven into the confession, and made to fit in with this version, but after the Executive Council of State had caused a very careful examination of this confession to be made they came to the conclusion that the statement was not consistent with the evidence which had been given at the trial.

Dr. Webster was executed on August 30th, 1850, and the spectacle appears to have aroused the same morbid curiosity as similar sights in this country. From the roofs of neighbouring houses a view of the scaffold could be obtained, and seats were sold at a high price. There were present 125 persons in the prison yard with passes from the sheriff. At half-past nine the presiding officer addressed those whom he had admitted, and told them they were assembled, by invitation from him, as lawful witnesses of the execution of John White Webster, convicted of the crime of murder. He expressed the hope that they would observe silence during the proceedings. The sheriff, the reporters, and the spectators went to the condemned cell, where religious offices were at once performed. The procession then started for the scaffold. The prisoner walked firmly, but with profound dejection.

The rope was adjusted, and the condemned man shook hands with the gaoler and others, and thanked them for their kind treatment of him. The sheriff said, " In the name of the commonwealth of Massachusetts and in accordance with the warrant of the Chief Executive, I now, before these witnesses, proceed to execute the sentence of the law upon John White Webster, convicted at the March term of the Supreme Judicial Court of the murder of Dr. George Parkman." He then placed his foot on the spring which released the drop. The body, after hanging some thirty minutes, was placed in a coffin and delivered to the family of the dead man.

Two days after the committal of the murder Dr. Webster attended Divine service and heard the brother of his victim preach the sermon!

THE CASE OF DR. EDWARD SHERIDAN

THE PROCEEDINGS BEFORE THE COURT OF KING'S BENCH IN IRELAND IN THE CASE OF DR. EDWARD SHERIDAN FOR MISDEMEANOURS IN VIOLATION OF THE IRISH CONVENTION ACT, NOVEMBER, 1811

In order to understand the action of the English Government against Dr. Sheridan, it is necessary to appreciate the state of Irish feeling at the end of the eighteenth and the beginning of the nineteenth centuries. Of all the many grievances which Ireland cherished against the mother-country the religious was the most reasonable. As far back as 1691, the date of the Treaty of Limerick, religious freedom had been promised to the Irish, but, instead of keeping faith with them, the Test Act was imposed on Ireland for the first time. From 1795 to 1815 ensued a period of penal legislation the like of which fortunately has never been paralleled in our history. Under the new Acts no Catholic could set up a school, nor could any Catholic be sent abroad for education. The lands of a Catholic must be split up at his death between all his sons, unless one of them had become a Protestant, when all went to him. This had the effect of dividing and subdividing all the great Catholic properties. No Catholic might buy land from a Protestant, or keep weapons for his defence, or own a horse of more than the value of five pounds. A Catholic who tried to convert a Protestant committed a punishable offence. No Catholic priest might come to Ireland from abroad.

So atrocious were these penal Acts that the law officers were extremely loth as a rule to prosecute under them, and juries were equally unwilling to convict. But still the Acts were there. The Test Acts prevented a large number of Catholics from entering the public service. The Irish were not prepared to sit still tamely under these galling conditions.

In the middle of the eighteenth century signs were evident that there was a national opposition arising, and about 1760 the secret societies began to make themselves felt. They were not at first definitely political, but later they taught the peasants the power of concerted resistance to authority. The Catholic Committee was formed to obtain the repeal of the disabling laws. The difficulties of the American war and the fear of a French invasion compelled the Government to weaken. They allowed the enrolment of an Irish volunteer corps, and this corps had the Government at its mercy, for no English troops could be spared for Ireland. Various measures were passed by the Government not from conviction of right, but from fear; however, these concessions by no means satisfied Ireland. The United Irishmen, led by Wolfe Tone, Emmet and others, a society originally formed for the purpose of obtaining Catholic emancipation and parliamentary reform, gradually became a company of rebels, and turned for help to the French people. Pitt decided to prepare the way for the removal of all Irish disabilities by uniting the Parliaments of the two nations, and the Act of Union was passed. What a disastrous failure this was history has shown. The promise of Catholic Emancipation remained a dead letter, largely owing to the opposition of George III., the Sovereign at that time unfortunately taking a personal and active part in party politics.

Early in the nineteenth century efforts were again made by the Irish Catholics to obtain redress from the religious disabilities under which they laboured. The English Government, in order that they might have the power to suppress legally the various societies which had been formed in Ireland with the object of assisting Catholic freedom, passed the Irish Convention Act.

This Act was one " to prevent the election or appoint-

THE CASE OF DR. EDWARD SHERIDAN

ment of unlawful assemblies under pretence of preparing or presenting public petitions or other addresses to His Majesty or the Parliament." One of the clauses said: "Provided also that nothing herein contained shall be construed in any manner to prevent or impede the undoubted right of His Majesty's subjects of this realm to petition His Majesty, or both Houses or either House of Parliament, for redress of any public or private grievance."

Under this statute Edward Sheridan, M.D., was charged with a misdemeanour before the Irish Court of King's Bench in November, 1811.

Great importance was attached to the case by both the prosecution and the defence. It was the first under the Act and therefore a test case. The large array of eminent counsel engaged on both sides, the long and able arguments on important points of law, the great eloquence of the speeches both for the prosecution and the defence, the important historical and legal references in these speeches, all combine to make the trial a memorable one. In addition to the Attorney-General and the Solicitor-General, the Crown retained eight counsel, and the defence employed no less than eighteen barristers. Dr. Sheridan's counsel ably argued every point which could be of possible assistance to their client. They complained that no copy of the information had been furnished to the prisoner, and that therefore they were unable to prepare the defence; they claimed the right to challenge members of the Grand Jury, which they asserted had been packed by the Crown; they objected to any reply by the Attorney-General, on the ground that the defence had produced no witnesses; in short, they left no point unargued which could by any possibility be of use to their client. They were overruled on all these questions, although they did their utmost to convince the judges of the legality of their contentions, especially on the question of challenging the Grand Jury. Counsel regarded this as most important, as they believed the jury to have been unfairly selected by the Crown. Many days were occupied by these legal arguments on both sides before the actual trial commenced.

The charge against Dr. Sheridan was that being a person professing the Roman Catholic religion, together with divers other ill-disposed persons professing the same religion, they, on the 31st day of July, 1811, at Liffey Street, Dublin, met and assembled themselves together for the purpose of appointing five persons to act as representatives of all the inhabitants professing the Roman Catholic religion of the parish of St. Mary in a committee of persons to be thereafter held, and to exercise a right to represent the Roman Catholics of Ireland under pretence of preparing petitions to Parliament for the repeal of all laws remaining in force in Ireland whereby any Roman Catholic was subject to any disability by reason of his religious tenets.

The Attorney-General in his comprehensive opening statement said that he was in full expectation that the result of proceedings against Dr. Sheridan and the others would be to frustrate the designs of treason and to give an effectual check to those extremes to which folly had proceeded. "The project against which the present prosecution is levelled is one which you will find detailed in certain resolutions entered into by an assembly, assuming to itself the denomination of 'A General Aggregate Meeting of the Catholics of Ireland,' held on the 9th of July last. This aggregate meeting sprang out of the resolution of a committee, which is well known, I am sure, to every gentleman who hears me, which for the last eighteen months has been acting a very distinguished part indeed in the country under the name 'A General Committee of the Roman Catholics of Ireland.'

"When I talk of treasonable motives as connected with this measure let me not be misunderstood. I am fully persuaded that the great portion of the educated Roman Catholics of Ireland are loyal to their king, and

THE CASE OF DR. EDWARD SHERIDAN

have no intention of conducting themselves otherwise than agreeably to the laws of their country; nay, that many of them look with as much disgust as any of us upon the lawless and seditious proceedings which have been carried on for a considerable time past falsely under the name and authority of the Roman Catholics of Ireland. . . . Many of them are young men of ardent minds, whose passions have been inflamed by engaging in a political pursuit, who are not actuated by any more criminal motive than the vanity of raising themselves into notice."

The Attorney-General then recited the resolutions of this treasonable assembly:—

(1) "That, being impressed with the unalterable conviction of the undoubted right of every man to worship his Creator according to the dictates of his own conscience, we deem it our duty thus publicly and solemnly to declare our decision that no Government can inflict any pain, penalty, or privation for obeying that form of Christian faith which in his conscience he believes to be right."

(2) "Resolved, that we again petition the Legislature for a repeal of the laws affecting the Catholics of Ireland."

(3) "That in exercising our undoubted right to petition we will adhere to the ancient forms of the Constitution."

(4) "That a committee be appointed to inquire into the penal laws and make a report within one month of the ensuing session of Parliament."

(5) "That the committee to be appointed to prepare petitions to Parliament do consist, first, of Catholic peers and eldest sons of peers and Catholic baronets; second, Catholic prelates; third, ten persons chosen from each county, and the survivors of the delegates of 1793, to form an integral part of that number; fourth, five persons from each of the parishes of Dublin."

(It is difficult to imagine in our day how such very harmless and desirable resolutions could by the most distorted or prejudiced mind have been construed into anything approaching treason.)

The Attorney-General followed with an interesting dissertation on the disabilities under which the Catholics of Ireland had laboured, the Acts of Parliament which had been passed to remove many of these disabilities, and the list of disadvantages which still remained to the Catholics on account of their religion. In his opinion, they were so slight that the presentation of the petition could not be the real object of the calling of the National Convention. He suggested there was another reason for the existence of this convention. "If we can suppose that there exists a rebel party in this country, a remnant of the United Irishmen, who are labouring to effect by artifice that which they could not accomplish by force, who are labouring to undermine that constitution which in 1798 and in 1803 they attempted to carry by assault, I can well conceive that they may have an object in having such an assembly established within the metropolis. . . . I am sure I offer no disparagement to the Roman Catholics of Ireland when I say that in point of rank, fortune, education, and character the Roman Catholics of England are at least equal to those of Ireland. They are not only subject to all the incapacities to which the Roman Catholics of Ireland are subject, but also to several from which those of Ireland are exempted. They, no doubt, are as desirous as the Roman Catholics of Ireland to be delivered from the operation of the Test Act, but they would hold no aggregate meeting; they countenance no seditious speeches or proceedings; they issue no mandates for convening a provincial election; they claim not to hold a National Convention. Now see whether the conduct which they observe or that which the Roman Catholics of Ireland are pursuing be most conducive to the success of their petition."

Various witnesses testified as to the presence of Dr. Sheridan at the meeting and his active participation in the proceedings. The evidence of one of the witnesses, which is typical of all, is quoted to illustrate the flimsy nature of the charge.

James Sheppard was called by the prosecution.

In what situation or employment are you ?—I am a peace officer.

Were you directed to attend any meeting at Liffey Street Chapel ?—I was.

Do you know Dr. Sheridan ?—I saw him there and saw him in court this day.

Was there an assembly in Liffey Street Chapel upon that day ?—There was, and what I considered a very large one.

Did you see any person in the chair presiding at that assembly ?—I did. I saw Dr. Sheridan in the chair.

Did you hear any person address Dr. Sheridan in the chair ?—I did.

Who was that person ?—Mr. Kirwan, for one.

Do you recollect what was the nature and substance of his first address to Dr. Sheridan ?—The first motion was for a petition to the Prince Regent and both Houses of Parliament for a repeal of the penal laws existing against the Roman Catholics of Ireland, or to that purpose.

Was there a question put upon that motion ?—There was.

Who put it ?—Dr. Sheridan.

Was the motion carried ?—It was, unanimously.

Do you recollect any other motion made by Mr. Kirwan at that meeting to Dr. Sheridan ?—There was a motion made for appointing a committee of five.

For what purpose ?—For the purpose of representing that parish on the general committee of the Catholics. The words may not be exactly so.

You are not certain as to the exact words ; do you say that is the substance ?—That was the substance.

Prisoner's Counsel : Gentlemen of the jury, I beg you will attend to that. He does not recollect the *exact words*, and yet they are very important.

Witness : My lord, I omitted to state that to " prepare

a petition " was part of the motion, and to " conduct the business of the Catholic inhabitants of that parish."

Court: Do you mean to say that was part of the motion?—Yes, my lord.

Was the motion for appointing a committee of five persons put?—It was.

Who put it?—Dr. Sheridan.

Was it carried?—It was.

Was any proceeding adopted in consequence of that resolution?—There was.

What was it?—There was some difference of opinion as to the mode of election. It was at last proposed that seven persons not candidates for the committee should be chosen, and that those seven should retire and select five out of a list which was given to them.

Was that proposal of appointing seven persons carried?—It was.

Did those persons who retired, as you say, return to the meeting?—I saw but two of them afterwards. The situation I was in was such that I could not see all the people: I was in the gallery.

Did any of the persons who returned hand in anything to any other?—They did.

To whom?—Dr. Sheridan.

What was it?—A slip of paper.

Was it read?—It was.

Were there any names read from it?—There were.

Pray, sir, after these names were read, did Dr. Sheridan continue in the chair?—No, sir; he was removed from the chair.

Who took it?—Dr. Burke.

What was then done?—He put the question upon Dr. Sheridan's election as one of the committee; it was carried unanimously.

After this election did you hear any persons address the chair?—I did.

What was the subject of their address?—Expressing their thanks for the honour which was done them.

THE CASE OF DR. EDWARD SHERIDAN

As soon as thanks were returned was there any other motion made to Dr. Sheridan? Did he continue in the chair?—It was moved that he should leave the chair, and Mr. Taafe took it.

Was any motion made to him?—There was a motion returning the thanks of the assembly to Dr. Sheridan for his proper conduct in the chair.

Was there any other business done at the meeting except what you have stated?—Nothing else that I observed.

On this evidence of one of the chief, if not the most important, of the witnesses, it appears impossible for any reasonable-minded person to see anything approaching treason or rebellion, and one is at a loss to imagine how any Government could have been so ridiculously absurd as to institute a prosecution, launch it with so much formality, and make every effort to secure a conviction.

There is not a village in the country at the present time where meetings are not being held freely and frequently at which reforms much more violent are advocated, at which language infinitely more " treasonable " is used, and at which sentiments far more revolutionary are expressed. It is taken as an absolute matter of course that no interference by the Government or any other body will take place, the public having a perfect right to express their views on political matters when, how and where they like, provided they are not a nuisance to their fellows.

The cross-examination of this Crown witness adds additional proof to the harmless character of the alleged treasonable meeting.

Of what religion are you?—Of the Established Church.

Then you did not go to the chapel in Liffey Street as one of the meeting?—No, sir.

The meeting was open to any person of any religion?—It was.

No concealment whatever?—None.

No abuse of any individual or of the Government ?—Not a word.

Or anything seditious ?—No. From the respectability of the meeting I would not expect any such a thing.

Do you not believe that they really did intend to present a petition to Parliament ?—I do.

Upon your oath did you not say (you may now unsay it if you choose) that the object of the meeting was to prepare a petition and nothing else ?—That was the object of the meeting.

Upon your oath, if anything was said about the appointment of persons, do you not believe that it was an appointment of persons to prepare the petition ?—I believe the object of the meeting was to petition.

A good many other questions were asked, but the tendency of them will be seen from the above.

The speech for the defence by Mr. Burrowes was a magnificent oration, bristling with adroit legal points and eloquently appealing to the jury to recognise that the Roman Catholic population of Ireland was strictly within its legal rights in endeavouring to obtain Catholic emancipation.

Mr. Burrowes first bitterly complained of the way the jury had been packed with Protestants, and every Roman Catholic excluded. Twenty-two Protestants were actually challenged because they were thought to be too liberal-minded. He argued that it was absurd to say the meeting was a revolutionary or treasonable one; the kind of meeting the Act under which the prosecution was undertaken was intended to suppress was quite different to this. " What was the evil which in 1793 induced the Attorney-General and the Government of the day to introduce this Bill ? In stating it, I am vindicating the memory of that Attorney-General and of that Government from the misconstruction and the misapplication of the Act by their successors of the present day. There existed, shortly previous to the enactment of that law, a body representing the whole province of Ulster in the illegal and dangerous sense which I have ascribed to the term. They sat at Dungannon; they acted and resolved in their own names, as general *representatives* of that province. They abstained from no subject, legislative or executive. . . . Their avowed purpose was to destroy or new-model all or most of the ancient and venerable departments of the State and Constitution. They would annihilate the boroughs, purge the House of Lords of ecclesiastical intermixture, extend the elective franchise to the whole rabble, interfere with the executive in the prerogative of making peace and war and in short control and dictate upon every subject. In the name of God, can any man say there is any resemblance between an assembly such as I have described and a Catholic Committee (such as I acknowledge is now in existence) for the sole *bonâ fide* purpose of preparing a petition for the subsequent ratification and adoption of individuals of their body?"

The summing up of Lord Chief Justice Downes is not of any very particular interest. He recapitulated the facts proved in evidence, and pointed out the law as laid down in the Irish Convention Act: " Upon the whole of this case, we are of opinion that the statute provides, and means to provide, against all representative and delegated assemblies meeting for the purpose of procuring, either by petition or otherwise, an alteration of matters established by law in Church or State; and we are of opinion, even although it should appear that there was in reality an intention to petition, that the cloak of a petition cannot protect an assembly of that description from the penalties of the Act. If Dr. Sheridan had acted in a manner that would bring him within the interpretation of the Act as laid down above he must be adjudged guilty, otherwise the jury must acquit him."

The jury returned a verdict of not guilty.

Dr. Sheridan's colleague, Mr. Kirwan, was tried and found guilty. The Judge in his address to the prisoner, on sentencing him, said, " The Court entertains the most sanguine hope that this Act of Parliament, which has never before been awakened into action, will be allowed to assume its long slumber in the Statute Book, and in that hope has resolved to inflict upon you a nominal punishment. . . . The sentence of the Court is that you, Thomas Kirwan, be fined one mark and discharged."

The mark was equal to 13s. 4d.

DR. NEIL CREAM, WHOLESALE POISONER

THE series of callous, cold-blooded murders committed by Dr. Thomas Neil Cream are as remarkable and unique as any recorded. The great probability is that he would never have been detected had it not been for his own amazingly foolish conduct. The first of these apparently purposeless murders was that of a girl named Matilda Clover, a prostitute, whom he got to know when he was living in rooms near Waterloo Station. He prescribed for her, whether at her own or his request is not clear, and he gave her two pills which contained a large quantity of strychnine. She died in a few hours. Her death certificate was signed by her regular medical attendant, who, however, had not seen her for about twelve days, and the cause of death was given as alcoholism. This poor girl would never have had any inquiries made about her had not a letter with the signature " Malone " been received by Dr. (afterwards Sir) William Broadbent accusing him of poisoning the girl Clover, and offering to destroy the evidence which the writer declared he had in his possession if Dr. Broadbent would give him the sum of £2,500. Dr. Broadbent naturally looked upon this as the work of a lunatic and sent it on to Scotland Yard.

Soon after the death of Matilda Clover a girl named Donworth was taken to St. Thomas' Hospital in a moribund state. Before she died she asserted that a strange man had given her some pills which she had taken. A post-mortem was held and strychnine and arsenic found in the body. There was no clue whatever as to the person who had given her the pills, and there did not appear any likelihood of one being found, but a letter signed " W. Bayne " was received by Mr. F. Smith, one of the well-known firm of booksellers, accusing him of being concerned in the death of the girl Donworth, and offering to help him escape the consequences if he would engage the writer. A notice was to be put in the shop window in the Strand if Mr. Smith agreed. This was done, and detectives watched, but without result.

The next two victims were two young women named Alice Marsh and Emma Shrivell, with whom Neil had had relations, and to whom he gave some of his pills. Both died as a result of taking these pills.

The mentality of Cream was abnormal. Reckless, foolish and careless as he had been, he feared discovery. He tried to plant the crime on others and repeated his former tactics. A young medical student named Harper lived in the same house with him, and he wrote to the father of this student, a doctor in Barnstaple, accusing his son of being guilty of these murders and offering to destroy the evidence if the doctor would pay £1,500, signing the letter "W. H. Murray." But this did not satisfy Cream. He met a friend, an engineer, to whom he said that he knew the murderer of the two girls, and also of another woman named Lou Harvey. It was, he alleged, a medical student. He took his friend to the house where Lou Harvey was supposed to live, and named the music hall where the medical student and Harvey had met. In fact, he entered into a wealth of imaginary details, and finished by telling the engineer that the father of the student, Dr. Harper, of Barnstaple, was doing all he could to save his son from the consequences of his acts. Cream's friend naturally asked him why he did not communicate with Scotland Yard. The reply was that it was undesirable to get mixed up with such cases. However, the engineer to whom Cream had given this information was not happy about things and determined himself to go to Scotland Yard. There he saw Detective-Sergeant M'Intyre, but no mention was made of Cream's name, in accordance with a promise given. There was no record at Scotland

Yard of any one named Lou Harvey having died under suspicious circumstances, but M'Intyre promised that the matter should be fully inquired into. This was done, and for two months investigations were made, but without any satisfactory result.

Dr. Harper sent the letter he had received to his son. He naturally thought it was the work of an insane person. Young Harper forwarded the letter to Scotland Yard, and by good fortune it came before M'Intyre. He already had had another communication, signed "Murray," addressed to the coroner conducting the inquest on the two dead girls Marsh and Shrivell. The police had not the slightest clue as to the authorship of the two letters. They had no knowledge whatever of Cream. But Cream, with the incredible foolishness which he had shown all along, played into the hands of the authorities. He called at the Yard to complain that he was being followed morning, noon and night by people who worried him. M'Intyre promised he would look into the matter. Cream gave him the name of Thomas Neil Cream, and said he was a commercial traveller. This sort of complaint was, of course, very common at Scotland Yard, but something roused the suspicion of the detective staff, and they looked into this rather more thoroughly than usual. It was found that the constable who was on the beat in the neighbourhood where the two girls had been murdered had seen a man leave the house early on the day of the murder, and the description of this man would tally quite well with that of Cream. M'Intyre therefore himself visited Cream, and talked to him in a most friendly way to put him off his guard. He asked him if he were still followed about, and was told that all that had ceased. The two then went into a public-house, where, by arrangement, there were present the constable on the beat mentioned and an inspector.

They got Cream talking, and he contradicted himself so often that from that moment he was very carefully shadowed

The handwriting of the letter addressed to Dr. Harper was quite different to that of the one sent to Dr. Broadbent. M'Intyre determined to set to work to trace the notepaper of the communications, and eventually, having received a hint that the paper was Canadian, cabled to the police at Quebec, who sent him word back that it was the manufacture of a Canadian mill, that none of it was exported, and that therefore probably the letters had been written by some one who had recently been in Canada. M'Intyre by guile got Cream to write him a note, and found that the paper was identical with that of one of the letters. By this time Cream had become suspicious, and made this curious remark to the detective: " I'm going for a few days' holiday. Do you think I will be arrested before I go?" When asked why he should think of arrest, he replied that he had the idea that he was still being followed, and that it was all very worrying. M'Intyre suggested that Cream should come to Scotland Yard with him, and he would then make inquiries to see if there were anything known there about the matter. Cream agreed that this was sensible advice and started to go with the detective, but as they got near he suddenly refused to accompany M'Intyre any further. The two then parted, but care was taken that Cream was followed, and a watch kept on his movements.

The authorities had by now got a good grip on the affair. The bodies of Clover and Donworth were exhumed and examined, strychnine found, and no doubt was entertained that Cream, who it had been discovered was a doctor, and therefore more easily able to obtain poisons than the ordinary individual, was the murderer. Cream decided to fly to America, but just as he was about to depart he was arrested on a charge of sending a blackmailing letter to Dr. Harper. When he appeared before the magistrate the further charge of murdering four women was preferred.

The trial took place at the Old Bailey in October, 1892,

DR. NEIL CREAM, WHOLESALE POISONER

before Mr. Justice Hawkins. There appeared for the Crown the Attorney-General, Sir Charles Russell, Q.C., M.P., Mr. C. F. Gill, Mr. Sutton and the Hon. Bernard Coleridge, Q.C., M.P. Counsel for Neil Cream were Mr. Geoghegan, Mr. Warburton, Mr. C. Luxmore Drew and Mr. Scrutton.

The prisoner was charged under the name of Thomas Neil, which was the name by which he was usually known, though rightly his full name was Thomas Neil Cream. He was about forty years of age. He was accused of the murder of four women, but the count on which he was actually tried was that of poisoning a girl named Matilda Clover. The Attorney-General in outlining the case stated that Cream's father was a Scotchman, who emigrated to Canada when his son was a boy. The family settled in Quebec, and young Cream received his medical education in America, where he took the degree of M.D. He claimed that he had studied at St. Thomas' Hospital and at Dublin and Edinburgh, but this is doubtful.

He practised in Chicago, but later, in 1891, he came to London, and put up at Anderton's Hotel in Fleet Street. He had not long been there when he met in the streets a young woman named Elizabeth Masters, a prostitute, and having struck up an acquaintance with her, he went with her to her rooms. He afterwards took her to Gatti's Music Hall, where they met another girl of the same class, named Elizabeth May. Prisoner said he would write to Masters in a few days, and he did so on October 9th, arranging to call and see her on that afternoon between three and five. When Masters and her friend May were looking out of the window for him they saw him pass, evidently following a girl whom they knew—Matilda Clover, the deceased. Their curiosity was aroused, and the two girls watched Dr. Cream and Clover till they saw them enter the house where she lived. They waited half an hour, but did not see him come out. On October 21st

Clover was murdered at 27, Lambeth Road, where she occupied two rooms. On the morning of the 20th a servant at the house found a letter, which she read, and this letter contained a request that Clover would meet the writer outside the Canterbury Music Hall at 7.30 that evening, and it also asked that she should bring the letter and the envelope with her, evidently so that the writer might make sure that both were destroyed. Between eight and nine that evening Clover returned, accompanied by a man the description of whom would apply to Cream. Clover went out, apparently to buy some beer. Later she was heard to see her visitor out and say good-bye to him. At three o'clock the next morning the house was aroused by shrieks of agony. The mistress and the servant went to the room from which the sounds proceeded, and found Clover very ill indeed and in great pain. As she was well known to be addicted to alcohol, they attributed her illness to this cause. They sent for a doctor, but he was out or, at any rate, did not come, but they obtained the help of Mr. Coppin, the assistant of another doctor. He was told the circumstances, and he also thought the trouble was due to alcoholism, and prescribed certain remedies, but these had no effect. The poor creature died in agonising convulsions at 8.45 that morning. Next day a Dr. Graham, with almost criminal culpability, signed a death certificate that he had attended the deceased in her last illness and that she had died from delirium tremens and syncope. The certificate stated that she had died on October 21st, and that he had last seen her alive on that day. These statements were in fact all untrue. Clover was buried the next day at Tooting by the parish. Her wretched and obscure life was closed; she was lying in a pauper's grave, thought of and remembered by few.

In this month of October a very curious thing occurred. Prisoner spoke to a young woman, a Miss Sleeper, and told her he thought that a girl in Lambeth Road had been

DR. NEIL CREAM, WHOLESALE POISONER 153

poisoned, and he asked Miss Sleeper to go and find out if she were dead. No one so far had had the least suspicion of poison in this case. About a month later Dr. W. H. Broadbent, a very celebrated London physician, afterwards Sir William Broadbent, received a letter, signed " M. Malone," saying that a girl had died at Lambeth Road from strychnine poisoning, and that among her effects evidence was found which showed not only that Dr. Broadbent had given the girl the medicine which had poisoned her, but also that he had been hired to commit the murder. For £2,500 the writer agreed to suppress the evidence. If Dr. Broadbent agreed, he was to put a notice in the personal columns of the *Daily Chronicle*. The alternatives were offered him of paying £2,500 or of ruin, shame and disgrace. " I am not humbugging you. I have evidence enough to ruin you for ever."

Dr. Broadbent, who looked upon this as emanating from a lunatic, at once did the perfectly correct thing and handed the letter over to the police.

In the Life of Sir William Broadbent, edited by his daughter, there occurs a letter written by Sir William in connection with this trial. " I hear that people in the neighbourhood are excited about this dreadful poisoning case, in connection with which my name has again appeared in the papers, and you will no doubt be interested to hear the facts direct from me. I suppose I was selected as one of the victims because I was attending Prince George. This was at the end of November. I at once put the matter into the hands of the police, and a trap was laid for the writer. An advertisement was put in the *Chronicle*, as he directed, and he was told to come to the house, where we had two detectives in ambush for two or three days. However, he never turned up, nor made any further sign, and I thought no more about it till the new case of blackmailing came out, and the man was caught, when, of course, I recognised the work of the same scoundrel. But I should not have taken the trouble to proceed against him, and should not have appeared in the case, had it not been that the girl he accused me of poisoning was not known to have been poisoned at all. When the police observed this, they began to make inquiries and soon found that the certificate of death had been given by a medical man who had not seen the girl, and that the symptoms had been like those of strychnine poisoning, upon which an order to exhume the body was obtained, and it was ascertained that she had actually died from the effects of strychnine. It was, of course, at once clear that this man, who was the only person who knew that the wretched girl had been poisoned, was the man who had poisoned her. The letter to me was thus of cardinal importance: it pointed out the criminal, and once having the right clue, other evidence has rapidly accumulated, and a perfect network of proof appears to have been thrown around him. When the police inspector explained this to me, I had no choice but to give evidence first at the police court on Monday, then at the inquest on Thursday, and I shall have to attend again when the final trial comes on at the Old Bailey. It has cost me a good deal of time, and caused me great inconvenience, so that the scoundrel has blackmailed me after all, though not exactly to his own advantage. He little thought that in writing to me he was putting his neck into the noose."

The letter sent by "Malone" was in the handwriting of the prisoner, and, as at this time no one but the actual murderer could have known that the girl Clover died from strychnine poisoning, Cream had by writing this letter, as Dr. Broadbent says, "put his neck in the noose."

Prisoner had visited America in 1892, and there met a man named M'Culloch, who would be called as a witness. Cream had told this man of the wretched life he led with women in London, and said he used strychnine in connection with the prevention of childbirth. (This was literally true, for he killed the poor creatures whom he had defiled, though it was not in this sense that Cream meant his friend to understand him.)

Sir Charles Russell said it would be necessary to refer to the deaths of some of the other victims in order to prove that Clover's death was not an accident, and that it was deliberate, for the other victims had died from similar poison, and after these deaths Cream had, as in the case of Clover, written blackmailing letters, demanding money to suppress the evidence he alleged he had in his possession which would incriminate those to whom he wrote.

In the case of Donworth, he wrote to Mr. F. Smith—the son of the well-known politician Mr. W. H. Smith—saying he had found two letters connecting the former with the murder, and offering to save him from disgrace and ruin if he would employ the writer of the letter to assist him. He also wrote to Mr. G. P. Wyatt, Deputy Coroner for East Surrey, saying he could produce evidence to convict the murderer of Donworth if the Government would guarantee to pay him £300,000.

On the evidence presented to them the jury must come to the conclusion that the woman Clover had died from strychnine poisoning. Who gave it? The prisoner had access to strychnine; he had in his possession many pills containing strychnine. These facts, together with the other evidence of the association of the prisoner with Clover, the letter he had written, and all his actions in connection with the case, were sufficient to point to him as the guilty party.

Witnesses were called to prove the visits of Cream to the house of Clover in Lambeth Road, and his connection with her.

Mr. Francis Coppin, assistant to Dr. M'Carthy, said he was sent for to see the deceased at about 7 a.m. on October 21st. He was told of her alcoholic habits, and after examining her he came to the conclusion that she was suffering from alcoholism with an epileptic attack. He did not think of strychnine poisoning. He had never seen a case of poisoning by that substance.

Mr. Robert Graham, medical practitioner, said he had attended Clover for drink. He saw her about twelve days before her death. He gave the death certificate from symptoms described by Mr. Coppin.

The Attorney-General : I suppose you are aware that you were guilty of a grave dereliction of duty in doing so ? —I am not aware of it.

Dr. Thomas Stevenson, Lecturer on Medical Jurisprudence at Guy's Hospital and analyst to the Home Office, said he had examined the exhumed body of Clover with Mr. L. A. Dunn, Senior Demonstrator of Anatomy at the hospital, and that they had found no signs of any disease. He had found strychnine in the organs. The symptoms described by the witnesses were those caused by strychnine. Less than half a grain had proved fatal, and one grain was regarded as a lethal dose. He had found strychnine in the pills sent him for analysis. The spasms caused by strychnine came on about three-quarters of an hour after the administration of the poison, but they might be delayed by various conditions, *e.g.*, sleep. The symptoms, the result of his analysis by the colour test, the result of his physiological experiment on a frog with some of the material extracted from the viscera, and the fact that his examination proved that there was an alkaloid in the body were the grounds on which he arrived at the conclusion that death was due to poisoning by strychnine.

Louisa Harris, who said she was known by the name of Lou Harvey, said she was at the Alhambra one evening in October when the prisoner spoke to her. He asked her to go to a hotel in Berwick Street, and she passed the night there with him. In the morning he said he noticed she had some spots on her forehead, and that he would give her some pills for them. He brought her the pills

DR. NEIL CREAM, WHOLESALE POISONER 157

that evening. She pretended to swallow them, but actually did not. She threw them away.

Mr. Geoghegan intimated that he would call no evidence. He pointed out to the jury that, as this prosecution had been conducted by the Attorney-General in person, the law left him with the right of final reply, in spite of the fact that the defence had called no witnesses. He considered this was a distinct disadvantage to the prisoner, because it allowed the prosecution to hear all the points raised for the defence and afterwards to reply to them. There were three propositions which the prosecution had to prove affirmatively. The first was that Clover died from strychnine poisoning ; the second, that the brain and hand concerned in such an infernal murder as that they were inquiring into were those of the prisoner ; the third was that the strychnine was administered feloniously. Clover went out on the night of her death and came back accompanied by a man. The description of that man would apply to 30,000 or 40,000 in London. The man stayed in the house about one and a half hours and then left. Clover went out again and returned, and at three in the morning screams were heard, and she was found in a state of agony. If death were due to strychnine, the body should be rigid. The Attorney-General explained the absence of rigidity when the body was examined as due to the length of time which had elapsed since the burial. If this woman had been poisoned by strychnine, how was it that she, who was under treatment for incipient delirium tremens, and therefore had her nerves very much unstrung, should have lived so long after she was supposed to have taken the deadly drug ? Cases in which the onset of symptoms was delayed had been cited, but here they were dealing with healthy subjects for whom medical attention had been procured. He contended that on the very threshold of the case doubt arose whether it was possible in any known circumstances that a woman of the constitution of Clover could have lived so long after the administration of the poison.

Mr. Geoghegan dealt with the four tests used by the prosecution to prove the presence of strychnine. There was first the colour test, then there was the shape of the crystals, next the bitter taste, and finally the experiment on the frog. In Matilda Clover's case the amount of crystals found was so small that nothing ought to be inferred from it. The bitter taste was by no means characteristic of strychnine. Substances due to decomposition in the body might account for that. Strychnine was a vegetable poison and much more difficult to analyse than mineral poisons. The physiological test on the frog was one from which no analogy could be drawn. All the tests were untrustworthy, and they could not make a sound rope by mixing together four strands which were in themselves rotten. Dr. Graham and Mr. Coppin, the latter of whom especially had had very great experience of drink cases, both said that death was due to drink, and nothing given in evidence had shaken those opinions. Counsel made the very most of every point which could by any possibility tell in favour of the prisoner, and concluded with the following eloquent peroration: "I remember the first time I ever heard sentence of death pronounced in this court. It was a long time ago, and it was before my lord the Judge. I remember hearing four men who were rightly convicted of murder sentenced to death. I was a much younger man than I am now, and I remember going away and trying to picture to myself what those men must have felt as they lay under that sentence. I have endeavoured not to let my natural nervousness prevent me from doing the duty which my client has a right to demand of me; but I cannot help thinking that, if you come to appreciate what sentence of death means, you will feel, as I do, that my task is enough to strain the energies and faculties of the greatest advocate of his time. That sentence means separation from one's fellow-men ; it means being immured in a prison cell ; it means that the condemned is about to stand on the threshold of the most awful of all mysteries, and that, when that mystery is solved, his name shall be a hissing, a byword, and an abomination, even to his nearest and dearest. But there is one illusion which I have had from that day when I first heard sentence of death pronounced. It is an illusion of which I cannot get rid, although, God knows, the scenes and tragedies which we who practise in these courts see take place under our eyes are enough to conquer any illusions we may have had. I say, between you and the prisoner at the bar, between the bench and the prisoner, there stands a figure, and that figure is the genius of the law of England. It is the best protector a man can have in his hour of need. It demands that the guilt of the accused shall be brought home to him as clear and as bright as the light of heaven streaming into this court now ; it is to the protection of that figure that I leave my client, Thomas Neil."

The Attorney-General in his final address to the jury traversed the various points raised by counsel for the defence, urging that they were untenable and sometimes contradictory. His final words were just as eloquent and impressive as those of Mr. Geoghegan, and are a striking tribute to the unfailing spirit of justice which is exhibited by counsel for the Crown : " You have been told in words of warning, eloquent and solemn, that you have a grave duty to perform. That duty you ought to perform in accordance with the spirit of law as it prevails and is administered in this land. I join my learned friend in his appeal to you. The law of England deems every man to be innocent until the constituted tribunal of fact—the jury—has pronounced otherwise. That jury is composed of a number large enough to prevent the views of one prevailing over the good sense of all, although to each member of the jury is the individual sense of responsibility to be preserved ; large enough, therefore, for the good sense of all to operate on the minds of all; small enough, therefore, to preserve to each man amongst you a sense of individual responsibility for the verdict as if it were his alone. If, after you have heard my lord, there remains in your mind a doubt—not a doubt to be conjured up, but a real doubt—such as would operate on your minds in any important affair of daily life, by all means let the prisoner have the benefit of that doubt. But if the course of this evidence has driven into your minds and left resting there a solemn conviction that this man is guilty, why, then you will discharge your duty conscientiously; you will discharge your duty with fortitude."

Mr. Justice Hawkins then summed up. He said he could not commence his observations to the jury before he expressed sincerely to the learned counsel on both sides his great obligation for the assistance they had given to him and to the jury. On the one hand, no case was ever put before a jury with more temperate comment than the present case had been put before them by the Attorney-General. Every word of his had been in a spirit of fairness. On the other hand, a very difficult task had been thrown on the counsel for the defence in consequence of the mass of evidence with which he had had to deal. Counsel had conducted that defence with a skill and ability which had been rarely equalled, and never excelled, in his experience. The case they had to deal with was that of Matilda Clover, who died on the morning of October 21st. It was alleged that she was wilfully poisoned by the administration of strychnine and that the prisoner was the murderer. There were several questions the jury would have to decide. Firstly, did Matilda Clover die of strychnine poison? If they decided that poison was wilfully administered to her, was it done with the intent to kill or do her grievous bodily harm? As to that, the learned counsel for the defence had prudently offered no observations, for it almost stood to reason that

DR. NEIL CREAM, WHOLESALE POISONER

if one gave deliberately a fatal dose of poison, there could be but one intent. Then the third and all-important question was, did the evidence prove that the poison was administered by the prisoner at the bar? If it were not administered by him, they were not inquiring as to who else could have done it. Did the evidence reasonably satisfy them with the same reasonable satisfaction which they would desire in any important matter in their own private affairs? It was not to be expected that in every case there could be mathematical proof of the commission of a crime. It often happened, as in this case, that no eye-witness of the crime could be called.

In the course of the case a long argument had been heard by him as to whether evidence of the three or four other deaths could be offered. He had come to the conclusion that it was impossible to keep separate the various cases, or rather that it was impossible to exclude the evidence offered on the subject. If the circumstances of one case legally and legitimately threw light on the other, evidence on both might be given. But the only issue they were trying was the death of the girl Clover, and the evidence offered in the other cases was simply as corroboration. His lordship then went into the details of the testimony given by the various witnesses. They had distinct evidence that on October 9th the girl Clover was seen to enter her home with Cream. This was testified to by two girls named Masters and May, and they both knew the prisoner well. There was not the slightest reason for casting any doubt on the veracity of these two witnesses.

The evidence of the witness Rose was that she saw Clover on October 20th, the evening before her death, enter her home with a man who answered the description of Cream. The girl was seized with a severe illness in which she had spasms of convulsions and would then for a short time be free. When she was free from pain she could talk rationally with those around her. The Attorney-

General had truly remarked that, if the girl had died from strychnine poisoning, the only person who could possibly have known of that fact was the person who poisoned her, for not the very slightest suspicion was aroused that she had been murdered till April of the following year. But long before that the prisoner had written to Dr. Broadbent suggesting to him that the girl had died, not of intemperance, as every one else thought, but of poisoning. No one knew that strychnine had been administered but the person who had administered it. The great importance of this letter was pointed out by the Judge. The conclusion of the Attorney-General that the prisoner had given the poison was beyond a doubt if they believed that this was a letter written by the prisoner—and his counsel had not disputed it—that on November 28th, when there was no suspicion of poison, the prisoner wrote to Dr. Broadbent that Clover had died from poison. His lordship pointed out to the jury that Dr. Stevenson was a gentleman of great scientific attainments, of vast experience, and untiring perseverance in discovering the truth of all matters entrusted to him. No one in the world would doubt this. He had been for years employed by the Government of the day in making all the most important inquiries which in the public interest they had thought right should be made. He had exhumed the body, made an exhaustive analysis, had found no natural cause for death, but had found evidence of strychnine. Did they, looking at the evidence, come to the conclusion that the prisoner was the person who committed the diabolical crime of poisoning Clover ? If the jury were not satisfied, the prisoner was entitled to be acquitted. If they were satisfied that he did commit the crime, it was their duty to say so fearlessly.

The jury after an absence of twelve minutes returned a verdict of guilty. The Judge then sentenced the prisoner to death in the usual terms.

The Times, in a leading article published on the day of

DR. NEIL CREAM, WHOLESALE POISONER

the report of the conviction of Cream, says, " From one familiar plea for leaving this man unhanged we have been fortunately saved by his own acts. Nobody in his senses can contend that Neil is mad, at all events in any sense that can possibly be twisted into an excuse for his crime. The series of letters which he wrote after the perpetration of the murders shows that they were committed with ample knowledge of the nature and quality of the acts done, with ample knowledge that they were punishable with death, and with an object which is perfectly intelligible. . . . In no instance were his acts of a kind to suggest the smallest doubt of his entire sanity. He is simply a cold-blooded villain, who took four human lives and attempted a fifth for the purpose of making money by his crimes."

With the greatest respect for this expression of opinion, there can be no doubt that there is very grave reason for claiming that Neil Cream was insane, and this awful series of crimes was just as much the work of a lunatic as, for instance, were those of the Whitechapel murderer. This opinion does not imply that the punishment meted out to Cream was not the right and proper one.

THE MURDER OF M'DONALD BY DR. SMITH, OF ABERDEENSHIRE

A VERY callous murder for the sake of pecuniary gain, and that for the sum of £2,000 only, was committed by a medical man, Dr. Smith, living in the old village of St. Fergus, in the north of Aberdeenshire, in 1853. It is difficult to imagine an educated professional man carrying out this cold-blooded, carefully planned crime for such a paltry advantage. Though he was not convicted, there can be little doubt of his guilt, and had it not been for the charge of the presiding Judge to the jury, the doctor would certainly not have escaped the just punishment of his crime.

The trial took place at the High Court of Justiciary at Edinburgh in April, 1854, before the Lord Justice Clerk, Lord Cowan and Lord Handyside. A few months earlier the prisoner had been brought to trial, but this was interrupted by the illness of a juryman.

The charge was that of murdering William M'Donald, a farm-servant, at Burnside, in the parish of St. Fergus, on Saturday, November 19th, 1853. Dr Smith pleaded not guilty.

Robert M'Donald, a brother of the murdered man, told the Court that William had been looking out for a farm to rent, and had had frequent meetings with Dr. Smith. On the evening of November 19th the deceased left home at 4 p.m., saying he had an appointment with Dr. Smith at about six o'clock. As on the next morning William had not returned, witness went to look for him. He found him lying dead in a ditch in a field belonging to Dr. Smith. There was a wound on the right cheek and a little blood on the face. There was a pistol lying near the body.

Witness went to the house of Dr. Smith, but did not find him at home. Shortly afterwards the doctor was seen coming towards the place where the dead man lay. On seeing the body Dr. Smith held up his hands, calling out, "God preserve us." The doctor said that the deceased had shot himself, but witness did not agree with this. His brother had no reason to commit suicide, and he had never seen any firearms in his possession.

Witnesses deposed to selling Dr. Smith a revolver (like that found by the side of M'Donald), and also gunpowder and percussion caps.

James Hutchinson, agent for the Northern Insurance Company, was asked questions regarding a life insurance proposal effected in 1852 on the life of M'Donald for £499 for five years. Witness wrote to Dr. Smith wishing to know what pecuniary interest he had in the life of M'Donald, as, if he had none, the insurance would be illegal. Dr. Smith answered that the nature of the proposal depended upon a third party from whom he expected something, and that he would send M'Donald to be examined. Later an insurance was effected on the life of deceased, the interest being in Dr. Smith. The conditions of insurance included a clause in which it was stated that the policy would not be invalidated in the event of death by suicide, if the policy were taken by a third party for valuable consideration. M'Donald seemed to know very little about why he was taking out this insurance. He said, "The doctor is a fine chield, and I have aye done as he bade me do."

Henry Dickie gave evidence of a very similar transaction, the amount this time being £999 19s. This insurance was effected in 1852. The same condition as to suicide was contained in the policy.

Alexander Robertson also testified that a third insurance was effected by Dr. Smith on the life of the deceased for £500. The conditions were the same as in the other two cases.

Two medical men gave evidence. Dr. Comrie, surgeon, of Peterhead, stated that he had examined the body of the deceased and the place in the ditch where it was found. There was blood on the outside of the ditch, to the left of where the body had been lying. There was very little water in the ditch. The bottom consisted of long grass and soft decayed matter. There was no appearance of a struggle. Death must have been instantaneous. The pistol must have been discharged at a very close range, for the face was much blackened with powder. He could not say whether the wound might not have been inflicted by the deceased's own hand. If the shot had been fired by another person, he must have been walking alongside the deceased. The position of the body as found was a remarkable one had deceased shot himself. If he had done this whilst standing, it was very improbable that the body would have assumed the position in which it lay. He could not account for the blood which was found on the side of the ditch, if the deceased had committed suicide. He saw the pistol lying beside the body. It seemed to correspond with the bullet found in the head of the dead man.

In cross-examination witness said that the appearances did not present materials to form an opinion as to whether it was or was not a case of suicide. His impression was that, had deceased been shot by another person, his body must have been laid in the ditch in the way it was found. It would not have been difficult to do so. Had the body been rolled over the edge of the ditch, it might have assumed that position.

Dr. Gordon, a surgeon in the Royal Navy, corroborated the evidence of Dr. Comrie. He thought the pistol was discharged at a distance of about a foot from the head, and he did not think a suicide could have fired at such a distance.

Evidence was given by various people as to the movements of Dr. Smith on the night of M'Donald's death.

James Pirrie, a farmer, of St. Fergus, said he was called upon by Dr. Smith on the Sunday morning to come and see the body of William M'Donald. Witness was conducted by the prisoner to the spot where it was lying. There they saw Robert M'Donald, standing weeping by the body of his brother, which was lying in the ditch. There was a pistol wound on the face and the mark of blood and powder. Dr. Smith picked up the pistol and said, " That's the thing that's done it." He said perhaps the pistol might have gone off by accident. William said he did not think that was possible, for the shot was a good and close one. He thought so from the appearance of the powder about the wound. Dr. Smith said there had not been a ball in the pistol; there had only been wadding. He gave no reason for saying that.

The Rev. Alexander Moir, Free Church minister at St. Fergus, said that Dr. Smith came to him on Sunday morning and told him that the body of William had been found, and asked him to go to Burnside to break the news to the relatives. Dr. Smith said, in reply to a question by the witness, that M'Donald had committed suicide. He said there had been quarrels in the family. On the next day Dr. Smith called at the manse. He said he was disappointed with the widow, who had expressed the view that her son had been murdered. Witness said it seemed to him there was something which required explanation, and he should like to have the matter looked into. He asked Dr. Smith, " Where were you on Saturday night ? " Dr. Smith mentioned several places where he had been. Witness then remarked that, if it were a strange hand which had done the deed, it was curious they should have looked for the man where they did, as it was a lonely and little-used road.

Mr. White, a surveyor, was questioned as to distances mentioned by the various witnesses. He said that from the back of Dr. Smith's house to the place where the body was found was not far, about three minutes' walk.

The prisoner had made three declarations, and these were put in as evidence. He stated that on Sunday, the day of M'Donald's death, at nine in the morning, Robert M'Donald had come to the house and said that his brother had been found lying dead. He (the doctor) was not at home, and no word had been left as to where the body was. He went out, and as he passed the house of James Pirrie he called for him. They saw Robert not far away, and on reaching him they saw lying on the ground a small pistol. He (the doctor) had never seen it before that Sunday morning. He examined the wound in the face of the dead man, and came to the conclusion that it had been caused by small shot and not by a bullet, and that it was not the cause of death, as it was not in a vital part. He thought M'Donald had met his end by drowning, as there were two or three inches of water in the ditch. He had had no appointment with the deceased. He then gave a detailed account of his movements on the night of the death. He had not effected any insurances on the life of the dead man, but although he himself had not done this, it had been carried out by the late William Milne, his uncle, for his (the doctor's) benefit. Milne desired him to get this done and gave him the money for it. He carried out the insurances by the request of William Milne. He was not sure if he had the policies. There were three of them, but he did not know the conditions. He did not know the sums assured were to be paid to him in the event of the death of M'Donald. He did not expect to get the money on these policies in consequence of the death being due, as he was convinced, to suicide. The prisoner in a second statement said he had bought a pistol two years ago, but had broken it. When shown a parcel of gunpowder, he said he remembered he had bought a small amount from M'Leod, the merchant, with which to make up an ointment. He used a good deal for this purpose. A fortnight ago a girl named Reid got some ointment made up with gunpowder from him.

Counsel for the prosecution in his final speech argued that the deceased had not committed suicide, that the prisoner had definite motives for wishing the death of M'Donald, and that the close proximity of the spot where the body was found to the places where the prisoner had been on the night of the death rendered the account of his movements and the times which he had sworn to of little importance.

Prisoner's counsel admitted the existence of motive, but reasoned that, if the prisoner had committed the murder, he must have made up his mind to carry out this crime before the insurances were effected, and this the evidence given distinctly disproved. There was not the slightest proof, direct or indirect, to connect the prisoner with the deed.

The Lord Justice Clerk, in his summing up to the jury, said, if this were a case of murder, it was one of the most atrocious which had ever been before the Court. He himself thought the evidence was not sufficient either to convict the prisoner or even to substantiate the allegation that a murder had been committed. He, however, could not relieve the jury of their duty, and the responsibility of forming an opinion on the innocence or guilt of the prisoner rested with them.

The jury were absent only ten minutes, which is remarkable in a murder case, and especially considering the fact that the verdict returned was that of " Not proven " by a majority. The Lord Justice Clerk asked whether the difference of opinion was as to " Not proven " or " Not guilty," to which the foreman replied that it was between " Guilty " and " Not proven."

There was considerable indignation at the result of the trial, as the opinion of the general public was that there was no doubt as to the guilt of the prisoner. Considering the summing up of the presiding Judge, it is rather remarkable that the verdict was even so far against the prisoner as " Not proven."

DR. CRIPPEN'S TRIAL

THE trial of Dr. Hawley Harvey Crippen for the murder of his wife Cora, commonly known by her stage name of Belle Elmore, was opened at the Old Bailey on Tuesday, October 18th, 1910, before the Lord Chief Justice of England. The case was quite a *cause célèbre*, enormous crowds collecting in the neighbourhood of the court to watch the arrival of the various counsel and witnesses engaged. Mr. R. D. Muir, Mr. Travers Humphreys and Mr. Oddie appeared for the Crown, whilst Mr. A. Tobin, K.C., Mr. Huntly Jenkins and Mr. Roome appeared for the prisoner. Dr. Crippen pleaded " Not guilty."

Mr. Muir in opening the case stated that Crippen had been married about eighteen years to the deceased, and that, so far as appearances went, the two seemed to be on the best of terms. According to the prisoner's account, he had not been cohabiting with his wife for about four years, but had been carrying on an intrigue with a woman, Ethel Le Neve, who had been in his service as a typist. At the end of January, 1910, the financial position of the prisoner, who had been engaged in a quack medicine business, known as " Munyon's Remedies," became serious. It was quite certain that at this time Crippen was badly in need of money. The position was this. He was in love with Ethel Le Neve, he had no affection for his wife, he wanted to establish closer relations with his late typist, and he had not the money to allow him to do so. If his wife died, he would at once come into a sum of money from her estate.

On January 31st a Mr. and Mrs. Martinetti spent the evening at the house of Crippen and could testify to the good relations on which they appeared to be at that time

If, therefore, she should from then disappear, who would suspect that the loving husband was in any way concerned in this? From that date she did, as a matter of fact, disappear, never again to be heard of. She left behind her everything she would have left if she had died—money, jewels, furs, clothes, home and husband. The prisoner acted as if he had made up his mind that she would not reappear and began to convert her property into money. He invented a tissue of lies to account for her disappearance, telling her friends that she had gone for a trip to America, and later, to account for her failure to return, he announced that he had had a telegram with the news of her death. He sent an advertisement to the *Era*, the theatrical paper, notifying her death, and even went so far as to tell the friends that she had been cremated and that the ashes were being sent over to him. Inquiries from those interested as to details of her disappearance, as, for instance, the name of the ship she had sailed by, were so unsatisfactorily answered that suspicions were aroused, and as a result Chief Inspector Dew called to see Crippen. He confessed that his previous tale was untrue, and that the actual facts were that he and his wife had had a little quarrel on the night of the Martinettis' visit, and that she had run away the next day; he believed that she had gone to an old lover named Miller.

Directly after making this statement to Inspector Dew, Crippen took to flight. If his tale was true, why should he have fled? The answer to this question would be found in the fact that in a cellar of the house from which Belle Elmore was supposed to have run away were found human remains, and it would be for the jury to say whose remains these were. On July 14th these remains were carefully examined where they lay in the cellar by Mr. Pepper, the eminent surgeon, and by Dr. Marshall, the police surgeon, and having been examined so that these gentlemen were able to speak to the position of things as then existing, these human remains and some other things that were found with them were removed to the mortuary, and there they were subjected to a critical examination. The remains were headless, limbless, and boneless, and the sex could not be certainly determined on anatomical grounds. But some Hinde's curlers with human hair in them and some feminine undergarments might be said to indicate that the remains were those of a woman. On the other hand, there were also in that grave with the remains some piece of a man's pyjama jacket and a large handkerchief, which was probably not a woman's. The identification was almost impossible, but there were certain indications. The human hair in the Hinde's curlers was naturally a dark brown, and it had been bleached to a lighter colour. Belle Elmore's hair was a dark brown, and she was in the habit of bleaching it to a lighter colour. These facts were undoubtedly true of many other women besides Belle Elmore. The undergarments had been seen by some of Belle Elmore's friends, and they were such as Belle Elmore was in the habit of wearing, but they were also such as many besides Belle Elmore would wear. One piece of flesh had been identified as coming from the lower part of the abdominal wall, and it had upon it an old scar. Belle Elmore, as a fact, was operated upon in that region in 1892 or 1893, and the scar remained upon her body up to the time of her death and was seen by two persons. The place of burial was significant. It was in the house occupied by Crippen and his wife, and by nobody else, and was the house where she was last seen alive. Upon these facts it was for the jury to say whether they were satisfied that the remains were those of Belle Elmore. Another question which the jury would have to consider seriously was, Who put the remains where they were found ? In endeavouring to answer that question they would ask themselves, who but Crippen had the opportunity to put them there if the surgeons were accurate as to the date of burial, some period not less than four months and not more than eight months ? Belle Elmore disappeared five and a half months before her remains were found. The remains were mutilated in a way which indicated to the skilled mind of the surgeon that the person who did it had some acquaintance with anatomy. Crippen had a very good degree; he had practised in America and had studied at London hospitals. The placing of the remains in the hole in the cellar was an operation which required considerable time and freedom from observation. Crippen was alone in the house for some time after the disappearance of Belle Elmore, and he only had any opportunity of burying her remains.

Crippen fled, but was arrested in American waters on the boat, the *Montrose*, in which he had sailed, news of his whereabouts having been given by wireless. He was found disguised. Ethel Le Neve, who was with him, was dressed as a young man. Mr. Muir said he would sum up the case so far against Crippen. There was the motive to get rid of his wife in order that he might live with Ethel Le Neve. There was the total disappearance of Belle Elmore and the fact that Crippen was the only person who professed to be able to account for her disappearance. His first tale was admittedly untrue; his second was followed by his immediate flight. There were the human remains found in the cellar, the pyjama jacket found with them, the remains mutilated by some one familiar with anatomy. Could it be doubted that the remains were those of Belle Elmore, or that Crippen was the person who placed them in the cellar ?

But there was another important fact to which their attention must be directed. At the post-mortem no natural cause of death could be discovered, but on analysis of the viscera by Dr. Willcox a poison, hyoscine, was found, and in sufficient quantity to show that over $\frac{1}{2}$ grain had been taken, and from the distribution in the body it was clear that it must have been taken by the mouth. Hyoscine was a preparation used in medicine, but not very frequently, and was given in doses of $\frac{1}{200}$ to $\frac{1}{100}$ of a grain, and a fatal dose would be from $\frac{1}{4}$ to $\frac{1}{2}$ grain. The taste was easily disguised by tea and similar drinks. Who gave her this poison ? Crippen had obtained from Messrs. Lewis and Burrows, chemists, in January, 5 grains of this substance. When signing the poison book, he had made false statements, saying the drug was required by Munyon's, whereas Munyon's made no preparation containing hyoscine.

The jury must keep in mind these questions. What had become of Belle Elmore ? Whose remains were those in the cellar ? If they were those of Belle Elmore, what was the explanation of their presence ?

Mr. Pepper and Dr. Spilsbury both gave evidence that they believed there was no doubt as to the presence of scar tissue in the piece of flesh from the cellar, and this piece was part of the abdominal wall. Dr. Marshall, divisional police surgeon for Kentish Town, said in his examination of the remains he could find no trace of any natural cause for death. He thought the remains had been in the ground for several months.

Dr. Willcox said he had found enough hyoscine in the remains to prove fatal. He was subjected to a long and searching cross-examination by Mr. Tobin, but his evidence remained unshaken. Dr. Luff, scientific adviser to the Home Office, corroborated the evidence given by Dr. Willcox.

William Chilver, a buyer for Messrs. Jones Brothers, Holloway, said the pyjama coat exhibited (which had been found with the remains in the cellar) was sold on January 5th, 1909, and it matched the odd pair of pyjama trousers which had been found in the house of Dr. Crippen.

This was a complete refutation to the contention of the prisoner that the remains had been buried in the cellar before the commencement of his tenancy.

DR. CRIPPEN'S TRIAL 175

The defence had a hard case to answer. Mr. Tobin did all that could be done for his client, but there never was any doubt as to the verdict. Counsel opened the case for the prisoner by saying that directly he sat down Dr. Crippen would go into the witness-box and tell his tale. He would be followed by medical men of good positions and the highest qualifications who would speak on the length of time the remains might have been buried. They would criticise the evidence for the Crown, and discuss whether the piece of skin came from the abdomen of any person at all. One of them was a man of the highest reputation as a microscopist in the medical profession, and he and others would give conclusive reasons why the mark on the piece of skin was not a scar at all. If there were doubt whether the piece of skin came from any one's abdomen, and if there were doubt as to whether there was a scar or no, then it afforded no evidence whatever that the remains were those of Belle Elmore. They would be followed by an expert on poisons of high reputation, who would give them his reasons why the alkaloid found in the remains might not have been a vegetable alkaloid introduced into the body during life, but might be an animal alkaloid produced by the ordinary process of putrefaction in a dead body.

Mr. Tobin explained Crippen's campaign of lies as due to his desire to avoid a scandal. He believed his wife had run away with an old lover, and he wished to prevent this becoming the subject of public discussion. His flight was easily explicable. It was the panic of a man who found himself under suspicion, and who determined to escape while there was an opportunity. Any one might do this.

Counsel dealt at length with the medical aspect of the case. The jury had to be satisfied as to the sex of the remains. Could the jury on the evidence produced say that there was anything to prove that the remains belonged to either sex? If they had any doubt about that,

Crippen was by law entitled to a verdict of not guilty. Taking the remains by themselves, the Crown witnesses had said it was impossible on anatomical grounds to say whether they were those of a man or a woman. If the mark on the skin was the result of an operation—and he disputed this—why should it not be the result of an operation on a man? The clothing found with the remains was absolutely no evidence as to the sex; it left the matter open. As to the contention of the Crown that Crippen had the anatomical knowledge to cut up the remains as they had been cut, he contended that the prisoner had never performed any operations and had never dissected a body. Referring to the piece of skin with the alleged scar on it, counsel first argued that it had not been proved that this came from the lower part of the abdomen at all, and if it did not it had no bearing on Belle Elmore's operation, and, secondly, that the presence of scar tissue had not been established. The last point he would deal with was the poison. On January 19th Dr. Crippen obtained 5 grains of hyoscine hydrobromide. He need not have signed the poison book at all, but he openly left the record of his purchase and his name at a shop where he was known. He bought the drug to reduce it to a liquid and to use it in the tiny tabloids he prepared for patients. Doctors did not seem to use hyoscine in England, but he supposed American ways were different. Was the alkaloid found in the remains hyoscine? Dr. Willcox said there was not enough of it to use for what he said would be the most certain test of all to ascertain which mydriatic vegetable alkaloid it was. As Dr. Willcox did not apply this test, he asked the jury to say that the matter remained in far too much doubt whether, even if this was a vegetable alkaloid at all, it was hyoscine rather than hyoscyamine or atropine. He would go farther and ask the jury to say there was not enough to enable a man to determine whether the alkaloid found in the body was vegetable introduced during life or animal produced after death by the natural processes of decomposition.

At the conclusion of Mr. Tobin's speech Crippen at once entered the witness-box. He said he was forty-eight years of age and was a doctor of medicine of Cleveland Homœopathic Hospital. He believed the disappearance of his wife was accounted for by the fact that she had gone to her lover, Bruce Miller, and he had told all the falsehoods in connection with this matter to save any public scandal. With regard to the drug hyoscine, he was familiar with it, having first used it at the Royal Bethlem Hospital for the Insane. It was employed very frequently in America, especially in the treatment of the insane.

His cross-examination, which lasted about three hours, was undertaken by Mr. Muir :—

On the early morning of February 1st you were left alone in your house with your wife ?—Yes.

She was alive ?—Yes.

And well ?—Yes.

Do you know of any person in the world who has seen her alive since ?—No.

Do you know of any person in the world who has ever had a letter from her since ?—No.

Do you know of any person in the world who can prove any fact showing she ever left that house alive ?—No. I told Mr. Dew exactly all the facts.

Mr. Muir pointed out that it was most important for the defence that he (Crippen) should be able to mention somebody who had seen Belle Elmore alive after the Martinettis left. Could he give any one ? Had he made any inquiries of the shipping companies, of the cabmen on the rank near the house, of the tradesmen who left goods at the house, or of any one else ? Crippen acknowledged he had made no inquiries at all.

Medical evidence was then called on behalf of the prisoner.

Mr. Turnbull, M.D., B.S., Oxford, Director of the Pathological Institute at the London Hospital, said that he had conducted a very large number of post-mortems. He had examined the piece of flesh from the remains, and he was able to say that there could not possibly be any scar tissue in it. The mark was caused by the folding of the skin and pressure on it. The piece of flesh probably came from the lower part of the wall of the abdomen.

Dr. Reginald Wall, assistant physician at Brompton Hospital for Consumption, said he had examined the piece of skin both with the naked eye and with the microscope, and in his opinion it was not scar tissue.

Dr. Alexander Wynter Blyth was the last witness for the defence. When cross-examined by Mr. Muir he was asked whether it was possible to differentiate between vegetable and animal mydriatic alkaloids. Witness replied that he thought some of them were so nearly identical that it was possible to make a mistake.

Mr. Muir read an extract from a book on poisons written by witness, in 1895, in which the following appeared: " Further search has conclusively shown that at present no ptomaine is known which so closely resembles a vegetable poison as to be likely in skilled hands to cause confusion."

Mr. Muir. That is quite correct, is it not ?—Not absolutely. I have somewhat altered my opinion since then.

Have you published that altered opinion ?—No.

When did you alter your opinion ?—I have altered it lately, during this month, in reading up the various foreign papers on the subject.

For the purposes of this case ?—In connection with this case.

The Lord Chief Justice. That is for the purposes of this case.

Mr. Muir. For the purposes of this case, then, you have altered your opinion.

DR. CRIPPEN'S TRIAL

Mr. Tobin in his final speech to the jury on behalf of his client again reviewed the evidence given against the prisoner in the light of that on his behalf. Dr. Crippen had said in answer to Mr. Muir that he knew of none who had seen or heard from Belle Elmore after February 1st. The law did not cast on Dr. Crippen the burden of finding out where his wife might be, or whether she were alive or not, whether she were in some foreign country, or whether she had joined some man or not. Dr. Crippen had said that on February 1st Le Neve had slept with him at Hilldrop Crescent. Was it conceivable that a few hours before Le Neve slept in that house Dr. Crippen would have taken his wife's life, buried the flesh and skin in a hole in the cellar floor, and done away with the head, hands, feet and bones? He had been at work all day, and what time had he in which to do all this? The jury must remember strange things had happened in legal history. A man had been convicted of murder, had been hanged, and afterwards the supposed victim had appeared alive. This was a case which they would all remember to their dying day, and if in the course of time—not for the first time in history—Belle Elmore should in very truth appear again, what then?

The question of poison had also to be proved beyond the possibility of doubt. It was unfortunate that before Dr. Willcox had found hyoscine he had heard that Dr. Crippen had bought some of that poison. Counsel would not say more than that. The point was whether the gummy substance which Dr. Willcox had found was a vegetable alkaloid, obtained from a plant, or an animal alkaloid, produced after death by the natural process of decomposition. Were they sure that scientific men had got to the bottom of things? Only eight years ago it was thought that the chemical formulæ of atropine, hyoscine and hyoscyamine were the same. It was now proved they were not. Were they satisfied beyond all doubt that science had reached its limit?

Concluding his address, Mr. Tobin said, " Gentlemen, the materials are before you now. My lord holds the scales of justice even. It is for you to say which way those scales shall come down. My only anxiety is this: lest by any want of vigilance or care in this case, by any omission on my part, I have done anything that might imperil this man's life. But this I do want to say: I want to acknowledge—and I should be ungenerous if I did not—the loyal help given to me and the wise suggestions made to me not only in court, but for long hours out of court, by my two colleagues, Mr. Huntly Jenkins and Mr. Roome, and all those who collected the material to enable me to present the case for the prisoner. I do not plead for mercy. Not at all. There is only one anxiety which oppresses me, and that anxiety is that you should have the will-power, because you need it—you need all the will-power a man could have—to enable you to expel the prejudice which must have been instilled into your minds by reason of his lies, by reason of his folly, and beyond that by reason of so much that has appeared in the columns of the papers. You need the will-power to expel all that prejudice. All I plead for is that you give the verdict with minds unclouded by any preconceived prejudices. What I do demand, and what I have the right to demand, is that you should never forget that greatest principle of all in English justice—that great principle of the benefit of the doubt. That is not a principle to be ignored, you know. That is a principle to be jealously guarded and to be sacredly preserved by every juror, whatever the case may be. Each of you, let me remind you, is separately responsible for the verdict which you jointly give, each of you individually. Not one of you must yield his opinion to that of the others unless his reason and his conscience dictate to him that he should so yield. Not one of you can shelve his responsibility. Each of you is responsible for his verdict to his conscience and his God.

Mr. Muir replied for the Crown. In his review of the case, he made special reference to the medical evidence and had some scathing observations to make on that produced for the defence. He pointed out that it had been disputed by counsel for the defence, at the opening of the trial, that the piece of flesh exhibited was part of the abdominal wall at all, and it was suggested to the jury that the medical evidence would leave their minds in such doubt that they would be bound to acquit the prisoner. The evidence on this part of the case could be summarised in a few sentences. Mr. Pepper, a surgeon of the greatest experience, who had himself performed hundreds of operations, had seen a healed scar caused by his own operations which was just such a scar as this. Dr. Willcox, a surgeon of great experience, and Dr. Marshall, the police surgeon, all saw the piece when it was fresh ; they agreed that it was a scar. On the other hand, there was the evidence of Dr. Turnbull and Dr. Wall, who at first said the piece of flesh did not come from the abdominal wall at all, but from the buttocks, and who had now been obliged to admit in the witness-box that they were absolutely mistaken. Those were the two men who did not scruple to give a report after a twenty minutes' examination of a piece of the human body to the effect that three of their distinguished colleagues had been talking nonsense in the witness-box on oath. Now they had recantations in the witness-box, recantations and confessions of incapacity or the grossest carelessness and rashness. And these two men who had so recanted and so confessed were the two men on whose evidence the jury were asked to say that Mr. Pepper, with his vast experience, and Dr. Willcox, acting for the Home Office, and who had probably conducted more inquiries than any other living man except perhaps Dr. Luff, were absolutely mistaken. The mistakes Dr. Turnbull made were these. He was wrong as to the part of the body from which the flesh came, he was wrong as to its not having the characteristics of aponeurosis upon the abdominal wall, he was wrong as to the absence of the tendon, and he was wrong as to the absence of the transverse muscles. All these mistakes he had to confess in the witness-box. It was for the jury to judge between the evidence for the Crown and that for the defence.

Scientific witnesses sometimes made sorry spectacles of themselves in the witness-box, but was there ever a sorrier sight than had been presented by Dr. Wynter Blyth, who said that since he had been instructed in the case he had altered his opinion from that expressed in his previous writings?

The Lord Chief Justice in his summing up reviewed all the evidence very closely. He devoted some considerable amount of time to the two very important medical questions involved, namely, the examination of the piece of flesh and the analysis of the remains for poison. With regard to the first, he said he wished to remind the jury what the dispute was. Mr. Pepper said the piece of flesh undoubtedly came from the abdomen. At the police court Dr. Turnbull and Dr. Wall had said that the piece did not come from the abdominal wall at all, and they made this statement with great confidence because they said there was no trace of the aponeurosis which should have been there if it belonged to the abdomen. Now, in this court these two witnesses did not suggest any part of the body to which it could belong but the abdomen. Therefore they had got the evidence of the prosecution, acquiesced in by the defence, that this piece of flesh did come from the abdomen. In the police court the scar was not of importance, for the case was that the piece of flesh was not from the abdomen at all, and therefore it was immaterial whether there was a scar or no, as the abdomen was the only part of the body on which Belle Elmore had a scar. But yesterday the defence developed the theory that the tissue alleged to be scar by the prosecution was nothing of the kind. Under the microscope

DR. CRIPPEN'S TRIAL

there were seen one sebaceous gland and four or five hair follicles. The prosecution said it was not uncommon for a small fragment of epidermis to be included in scar tissue. Dr. Turnbull said he had never known of this, but had read of it. They had a further examination yesterday in the presence of prisoner's counsel, and there was one remarkable piece of evidence given and not contradicted by Dr. Turnbull, although he did not say he assented to it. Mr. Pepper said, " You can see under the magnifying glass in that scar the irregular line of the knife from top to bottom." If that were so they need not trouble much more about it. What they had to deal with was a mark which resembled a scar, sworn by the witnesses for the Crown to be to the best of their belief a scar, sworn by the witnesses for the defence to be not a scar at all, but caused by a fold. If they came to the conclusion that this flesh was from the abdomen, that the mark was a scar, that it was put into the grave with hair on hair curlers dyed in the way Cora Crippen dyed her hair, and with the pyjamas and the other garments, it was for them to say whether they had any doubt that it was the body of Cora Crippen.

The Judge referred in great detail to the evidence of poisoning. He remarked that Mr. Tobin had suggested that it was unfortunate that Dr. Willcox knew before he had made his analysis that Crippen had purchased hyoscine. When people were conducting an examination by analysis, he did not think it right to suggest that it was unfortunate that it was known that poison had been purchased. If they were satisfied with the evidence of the doctor, they ought not to come to the conclusion that he was influenced one single bit. He had sworn he was not. He had examined the remains, and that had taken him something like three weeks. He had found a vegetable alkaloid. The doctor had said, " As far as my medical knowledge goes, and as far as every book produced at the present time goes, Vitali's test, which is to find out whether an alkaloid is a vegetable or animal alkaloid, is only operative in the three vegetable alkaloids atropine, hyoscine and hyoscyamine." There was no animal alkaloid which would respond to Vitali's test. Then the doctor said he had to distinguish between the three vegetable alkaloids. There was not enough to try the heat test, so he had used the bromide test. If there had been atropine or hyoscyamine, there would have been crystals produced, but this did not happen, and a gummy matter was found. This was evidence of hyoscine. He had also found that the poison paralysed the pupil. Dr. Luff said that the tests applied by Dr. Willcox were the best that could be used.

Mr. Wynter Blyth agreed that Vitali's test distinguished vegetable from animal alkaloids as far as present knowledge was concerned, but he thought it would be found that there were some animal alkaloids which might give the same result. The jury had got to ask themselves whether there was any doubt that Dr. Willcox and Dr. Luff were right. Dr. Willcox had found hyoscine in the body, as much as $\frac{1}{2}$ grain. Nobody denied that such a dose should not be given to any living being. Was there any doubt that the woman was poisoned by hyoscine?

The jury, after a short absence, returned a verdict of wilful murder against Crippen, and the Judge said he agreed that the evidence was perfectly convincing to any reasonable being.

The trial was conducted throughout with the care and skill which is synonymous with English justice. The speeches on both sides were fair and moderate. The only feature of regret in connection with the case was the exhibition of vulgar and morbid curiosity by the public, especially the band of fashionable women who crowded the court daily.

A notable feature of the trial was the marked progress which had been made of late years in the science of toxicology and the high stage which medical jurisprudence had reached. If the medical evidence in this trial is compared with that, for instance, in the celebrated Palmer murder case, a very noteworthy advance will be seen. Crippen was caught in his flight by means of wireless telegraphy, the first instance in which this then new discovery was utilised for the apprehension of a criminal fleeing from justice.

The Court of Criminal Appeal heard the appeal of Crippen, but, in spite of an eloquent and learned address by Mr. Tobin, Mr. Justice Darling, voicing the decision of the Court, said that they considered that there was ample evidence to support the verdict of the jury, and on all the points taken the appeal failed.

Ethel Le Neve was tried as an accessory to the murder of Cora Crippen on October 25th, the result being an acquittal.

The usual petition was signed by the usual type which is always ready to ask for mercy for the most brutal criminal, and always forgets the poor wretched victim, but happily it did not alter the course of justice. A remarkable incident in connection with the case occurred at Cambridge, where an old soldier, noted for his eccentricity, offered to be hanged in place of Crippen. His offer was not accepted.

A MEDICAL LIBEL

A REMARKABLE and fortunately unusual libel action between two medical men practising at Rotherhithe was heard in the Court of Common Pleas, before Mr. Justice Vaughan, in the year 1839. Dr. Charles Ventris Field was the plaintiff, and Dr. Austin the defendant. Dr. Field had been in practice in Rotherhithe for about eighteen years, whilst Dr. Austin was comparatively a new-comer, having been only four years in the neighbourhood. He had however been appointed medical officer to the Rotherhithe Guardians, and this was probably the *fons et origo mali*.

In 1838 an anonymous letter had been sent to the Poor Law Commissioners to the effect that a woman named Daly, who was about to have a child, had failed to receive proper care and attention from the medical officer of the guardians, namely, Dr. Austin. The board of guardians, instead of consigning this anonymous communication to its proper place, the waste-paper basket, decided to hold a court of inquiry into the allegations, with the result that they decided that there was no ground for the complaint and stated they were quite satisfied with their medical officer. The letter appeared to have been written by an illiterate person, but Dr. Austin believed it to be the work of his colleague, Dr. Field, and, without making any communication to him, wrote libellous letters to members of the Board and to others, including the clergy of the parish. This circular letter was as follows: " Sir,—You have probably heard that a complaint was made to the Poor Law Commissioners against me, as parochial surgeon, for neglect of duty; but, as I fear that the result of the inquiry into the truth of the charge and the name of the reporter of it may not be so generally known as the complaint itself, I presume to forward an account of it to you." There followed a *résumé* of the proceedings and the result, and the letter continued thus: "Now, sir, with respect to the individual who has considered himself called on to make this attempt to do me a serious injury in your estimation and that of my fellow-parishioners, of whom, I may say, it is of great consequence to me that I should have the good opinion, you will naturally ask if any act or acts of mine warrant such treatment. I distinctly answer, No. In fact, my silence in the case of a murderous operation performed by him on a Mrs. Mason, in Staple's Rents, has been the means of screening him probably from criminal proceedings, certainly from universal disgust and the opprobrium of every medical man, nor is this a solitary instance of his malpractice. Of his character I should say that he was shunned and avoided by every medical man as a dangerous, ignorant, presuming fool and cowardly poltroon. This animal answers to the name of Charles Ventris Field, and he lives in Paradise Row."

Dr. Austin had sent one of these circulars to Dr. Field, with a covering letter as follows: " In all my transactions I like to act openly and gentlemanly, and not to do things sneakingly like you. I have therefore enclosed the copy of a letter which I have sent to each member of the board of guardians concerning your late handsome treatment of me. Your obedient servant Edward V. Austin."

The defendant made no denial of the publication of this libel. He pleaded in justification that there were expressions in the anonymous letter which induced him to believe that the plaintiff had written it. Respecting the charge that Dr. Field had performed a murderous operation on Mrs. Elizabeth Mason, he alleged that this was true, that the woman had died as a result of this operation, and that, had Dr. Field been prosecuted for this, he would perhaps have been convicted of felony and manslaughter, and as proof that this was not a solitary instance of malpractice he gave five other instances, all midwifery cases, in which he claimed the plaintiff had exhibited gross want of skill and attention. One of these, however, had happened fourteen years previously, and it did not appear that there could be much foundation for the allegation, for the woman had again employed Dr. Field in the following year. Finally, as a justification that the term "cowardly poltroon" was right for him to use, he instanced that the plaintiff was insulted by one of his colleagues and that this was not resented.

Several eminent medical men, including Sir Benjamin Brodie, gave evidence for the plaintiff.

Dr. Barry, who had been an assistant of Dr. Field for four years, said plaintiff had had a very extensive experience in midwifery. He remembered the case of Mrs. Mason. In May, 1835, he went to her with Dr. Field. Her abdomen was very considerably enlarged, and they considered she was suffering from an ovarian cyst which required tapping. Mrs. Mason had had this operation performed before by Dr. Field, and this had given her much relief. She thought more of Dr. Field's skill than of that of others in the neighbourhood. The operation was performed quite properly, and just as witness had seen it done since in hospitals. The instrument was inserted a little below the navel. Not much fluid came out—about two ounces of a brown viscid substance. There was no difference in the operation or in the fluid which came out from what he had seen in hospital. He had seen four similar cases, in all of which the patient died. One of the operations was performed by Mr. Liston, surgeon at University College Hospital.

Sir Benjamin Brodie said that in ovarian dropsy the fluid varied very much in appearance, sometimes resembling coffee grounds. Tapping was the proper procedure if the patient were in danger of dying from suffocation, and only the doctor in attendance could properly decide that question. If the case were left, it ended in death. He had only known one recover without operation, that of a young lady who was thrown from her horse, and this accident fortunately ruptured the sac of the tumour. Age was no bar to operation. The removal of a few pints of fluid afforded relief, but the withdrawal of two ounces would be useless. Care must be exercised in performing the operation, otherwise the colon might be pierced and fatal results ensue.

The other medical witnesses agreed with the evidence given by Sir Benjamin Brodie.

The defendant then called his witnesses to justify his accusations. The nurse who had attended Mrs. Mason said that the swelling of the abdomen had been coming on for some long time and was causing obstruction of the intestines. At the post-mortem on Mrs. Mason witness had observed that the colon was punctured. (It is very unusual for a nurse to attend an autopsy on a patient, and certainly very rarely would counsel allow her to give expert evidence on a matter of this nature.) Mrs. Jane Smith deposed that she had sent for Dr. Field to attend her in her confinement, that he had come, and then told her he would not be wanted for some long time ; she had sent for him again, as she was taken very ill. He had delivered her with forceps ; she had felt as if she were being torn to pieces, and the child had a cut over its right eye. She was ill for some years after her baby was born.

Sarah M'Ivor, a monthly nurse, said she attended a Mrs. Clockworthy in her confinement. Dr. Field was sent for. It was a long, lingering labour, and the child was born with its head very much mutilated. There were many incisions on the head and neck. She had not seen any instruments used. Mrs. Clockworthy did very well, and expressed herself as very satisfied with Dr. Field. She would have had him again, but the distance of the house to which she had removed was too great. (This witness does not appear to have done the case of the defendant much good. Her evidence was rather in favour of the plaintiff.)

Another nurse said she had attended a Mrs. Bright. Dr. Field was sent for; he only remained in the room half an hour. He said he wanted to go to a lady who was to give him three guineas. Witness said she hoped he would not leave as the birth was so near. She was sent out of the room. When she returned in three minutes, the child was born. The cheek of the child was cut, and there was a deep wound in the forehead. The next day Dr. Field called, and was told the child was very much cut. He said he had scratched him with his thumb-nail. Afterwards, when charged with using an instrument, he acknowledged this was so. The child in question was alive and in good health.

William Jefford, a lighterman, deposed that his wife had had eleven children and that Dr. Field had attended her in two of her confinements. The first child lived six hours; the second was born dead. It was cut about the neck. Witness asked Dr. Field how it was that his wife had such bad times. The doctor replied he did not know, but he did not care about killing a hundred such things to save the woman. The wife of witness had had two children before Dr. Field attended her, and both were born dead.

Dr. Ashwell, physician to Guy's Hospital and Lecturer on Midwifery, said the position of the colon depended on the state of the bowels, and a careful doctor would make inquiries on that matter before he proceeded to tap a patient. The average practitioner should be able to distinguish whether abdominal distension was due to the state of the bowels or to an ovarian cyst. He himself would not perform the operation of tapping unless the distension caused great difficulty of breathing With a person of the age of seventy the wounding of the colon might produce death in a very short time. He thought generally that the use of instruments for labour should not cause laceration of the child, but it might happen accidentally. He would not say that instruments might not have been properly used in the cases to which reference had been made.

Several other leading medical men attached to hospitals in London gave similar evidence, and some of the professional men living in the neighbourhood of Rotherhithe, who were called by the defendant, said that they had asked the plaintiff to assist them in difficult cases, and they could not say that he had been shunned by the doctors in the neighbourhood. Again, these witnesses seem to have helped the plaintiff rather than the defendant, although called by the latter.

Dr. Murdock, a medical man practising in Bermondsey, said he had had a personal quarrel with Dr. Field. He believed Dr. Field was considered an ignorant and dangerous man in the neighbourhood. Dr. Field had spoken disrespectfully about witness's professional skill, and he had put his hand on Field's shoulder and pushed him with his knee, but he had not struck him. Plaintiff sent a lawyer the next day, but witness had refused to give a written apology, and he heard nothing further of the matter. Plaintiff told him that he often used instruments in order to save time.

Mr. Waller, a relieving officer, said the plaintiff had told him that the defendant had been guilty of gross neglect, that he was at home at the time he had refused to attend Mrs. Daly, and that, if the case were not investigated, the Commissioners should hear of it, and witness would certainly be dismissed.

In summing up Mr. Justice Vaughan said that, as the defendant admitted he was the author of the defamatory publication which was the subject of the action, the jury would be saved a great deal of trouble. All they had to consider was whether the plea of justification was made out. If these pleas were not substantially borne out by the evidence, they must find for the plaintiff.

The jury found for the plaintiff, giving him damages to the extent of £100.

For the credit of the medical profession, one is glad to be able to say that such discreditable quarrels between professional brethren are most unusual. A letter like that written by Dr. Austin to Dr. Field is a very unsavoury production, and it is difficult to imagine that an educated gentleman could have written it.

DR. SMETHURST'S LUCKY ESCAPE

THE case of Dr. Smethurst, who practised in London, presents several points of interest. The doctor was a married man of about fifty, his wife being some twenty years older. In 1859, whilst living in a boarding-house in Bayswater, he met a young lady named Bankes, who was twenty-eight years of age, and had a moderate competency of her own; in addition she had further expectations. She was looking for a " mate," and soon such an intimacy sprang up between the doctor and Miss Bankes that the proprietress of the establishment asked the young lady to leave. This she did, and shortly after the doctor and the young lady went through the marriage service in Battersea Church. The action of Mrs. Smethurst throughout the whole affair is very difficult to understand, but it is fairly certain that she was a consenting party to this so-called marriage and still remained on friendly terms with her husband. After the sham ceremony Dr. Smethurst and his new " wife " went to live at Richmond. It was not long before she was taken ill, and Dr. Julius, a well-known medical man in the neighbourhood, was called in. Greatly to his surprise, all his treatment failed to benefit her, and he became suspicious. Naturally, he was very loth to mention this to any one, and therefore, without saying anything of his doubts, Dr. Julius asked his partner, Dr. Bird, to look after the patient for a few days. At the end of this time both the doctors were convinced that she was being poisoned. The sister of Miss Bankes, who visited her at this time, was so shocked at her appearance that she requested that further advice should be taken. A well-known physician was called in, and immediately and independently he came to the same conclusion as the other doctors, and that was that poison was being used. Some of the vomit was obtained by artifice and analysed, and in this Professor Taylor found arsenic. On this evidence a warrant was applied for, and the husband arrested. However, strange as it may seem, the magistrate, after hearing the evidence and after Smethurst had stated that his absence would kill his wife, considered there was not enough justification to commit him, and released him. He was able to return home without any of his movements being under supervision. Miss Bankes died the next day.

The first trial was rendered abortive by the illness of a juryman. This occurred on the second day, and after an examination by the medical witnesses present, and by the surgeon of Newgate, it was announced that the juryman was so ill that it was unlikely that he would be in a condition to resume his duties for some days. The case was accordingly postponed till the next sessions. At this trial Lord Chief Baron Pollock presided, Mr. Serjeant Ballantine prosecuted, and Mr. Serjeant Parry defended the prisoner.

Smethurst was a man of small stature and of insignificant appearance, with a reddish brown moustache. He was probably considerably older than he admitted.

The landlady of the house in which Dr. Smethurst and his wife lodged gave evidence that the doctor alone looked after his wife, on the plea that he was too poor to afford help. (This was not a fact. He was not short of money. He had just received £70 in dividends for his wife.) The witness prepared her food, but the doctor always carried it up himself or received it at the door from her. No one but the prisoner administered either food or medicine to the deceased.

A solicitor proved that during Miss Bankes' illness, shortly before her death, he had drawn up a will at the request of the doctor, and in this will everything was left to the so-called husband. It was signed by Miss Bankes in her maiden name.

The first point which arises in connection with these facts is whether they show any motive for the terrible crime of murder by poisoning. The doctor stood to gain very little from a monetary point of view. Miss Bankes had under £2,000 to leave (she had made a will bequeathing this to the doctor), but she had had during life the interest in £5,000, an income which Smethurst might hope to enjoy, and which, of course, ceased at her death, so that on balance, especially as he had no particular financial embarrassment, there seems on this score hardly sufficient reason for the crime. Much more probable as a motive were the facts that Miss Bankes was pregnant and that the doctor had no desire to render himself liable for the upbringing of a child, or to risk a prosecution for bigamy should she discover he was married.

The medical evidence in this case was of the very utmost importance. Unfortunately, as in almost every example where any professional opinion is involved, the experts were totally at variance and absolutely contradictory. Dr. Julius stated that, whatever was the complaint of Miss Bankes, his efforts to cure her were frustrated by the administration of some irritant poison. " I tried a variety of remedies ; whatever was given, the result was the same. No medicine produced any of the effects I expected in arresting the disease. The symptoms continued the same after every medicine. . . . I thought there was something being administered which had a tendency to keep up the irritation of the stomach and bowels, and now I am unable to account in any other way for the continued irritation. In consequence of this opinion, I requested my partner, Mr. Bird, to see her, and I left him to form an unbiassed opinion." Neither witness nor Mr. Bird had been allowed to be alone with their patient at any of their visits.

Mr. Bird said, " I formed an opinion that some irritant

was being administered that counteracted the medicine we were giving. I had a conversation about it with Dr. Julius. . . . He asked me my opinion of the case before he told me his own."

Dr. Todd, who had been called in consultation, and was physician to King's College Hospital, said, " I was very strongly impressed with the opinion that she was suffering from some irritant poison. It was by my desire that part of a motion was obtained " (for analysis).

The three doctors who had seen her alive and attended her were all convinced that she was being poisoned. In fact, so strongly were they of this opinion that two of them actually went before a magistrate in order to obtain the arrest of Dr. Smethurst.

Mr. Barwell, who made the post-mortem, stated that the appearances found (inflammation, ulceration and sloughing in the intestinal canal) were not consistent with any form of disease except the administration of some irritant poison. Dr. Wilks, Dr. Babington, Dr. Taylor and Dr. Copland all agreed with this evidence. This was a formidable collection of expert opinion as to the cause of death.

Medical evidence to contradict this was, of course, forthcoming. It was argued that the symptoms were not those of chronic poisoning ; there were inconsistencies between the symptoms noted and those of poisoning by either arsenic or antimony, for several were absent. All the symptoms observed could be explained on the hypothesis that death was due to some natural disease.

Convulsions and tremor, inflammation of eyes and nose, and skin eruption, which should be present, were all absent. This was not like metallic poisoning and negatived the view of the prosecution.

Strangely enough, all the medical witnesses, both for the Crown and for the defence, acknowledged they had never seen a case of chronic arsenical poisoning.

The medical evidence, then, came to this. That for the

DR. SMETHURST'S LUCKY ESCAPE

defence did not really negative the allegations of the prosecution, who had alleged irritant poison. The defence said that whilst there was a general resemblance of the signs to those of irritants administered, yet symptoms which would be expected if there were poison were absent.

Serjeant Parry, for the prisoner, attributed death to dysentery following pregnancy, and the medical witnesses called by the prisoner all said the symptoms were consistent with this, but all, with the exception of Dr. Richardson, agreed that in this country dysentery was a rare disease.

The three doctors who had attended her independently came to the conclusion, on clinical evidence, that she was suffering from irritant poisoning, and eight other doctors who had had submitted to them the symptoms, treatment and post-mortem appearances also formed the same opinion. The symptoms which Serjeant Parry alleged should have been present and were not, were not invariably concomitants of irritant poison. The argument of the defence would, of course, apply to any case of poisoning. In none are all the symptoms always observed.

The analytical and chemical evidence had a very important bearing on the case. Dr. Taylor, the celebrated expert on toxicology, deposed that he had found arsenic in a motion passed by the murdered woman before her death, and also that he had discovered antimony in the viscera. His analysis was at once questioned and his credit assailed by the defence. He had undoubtedly made a mistake.

The error which Professor Taylor made arose as follows. After the death of Miss Bankes it was discovered that the medicines sent in by the doctors were nearly untouched; there was one bottle filled with a colourless liquid, which aroused suspicion. Arsenic had already been discovered in the body, and this bottle was at once suspected as the possible source of the poison. Taylor tested this by Reinsch's method. This test consists of mixing a little hydrochloric acid with the liquid to be examined and then putting into the mixture a piece of copper gauze, which at once becomes black if arsenic is present. Taylor tried this test three times, but each time the gauze dissolved. A fourth test was successful, a piece of the copper gauze remaining undissolved and becoming black. The Professor when before the magistrate stated that he had discovered arsenic, but omitted to mention the difficulties he had encountered. The remaining part of the colourless liquid was later on analysed by a different method, and found to contain no arsenic, but was simply a solution of chlorate of potash. Dr. Taylor found that the arsenic which he had believed was contained in the solution was actually due to impurities in the copper gauze he had used. It is due to him to say that it was a doubt in his own mind which was the cause of the discovery of the mistake, and this was disclosed at the trial. He said that after Dr. Odling and he had given their evidence at the magistrate's court as to having found arsenic in the bottle they thought it possible some mistake had been made, and they had therefore made other experiments to satisfy themselves. Seventy-seven tests were made with the same copper gauze, and in seventy-six of them no arsenic was found.

It was argued that, as the arsenic which Dr. Taylor had found in the solution had actually been introduced by himself in his reagents, what value could be placed on the rest of his investigations? Might he not just as well have made the same mistake in his analysis of the excretions of the deceased?

Three chemical witnesses appeared for the defence: Dr. Richardson, Mr. Rogers, and Dr. Thudicum. Dr. Richardson said that it was quite impossible that a person should die of arsenic poison and yet none be found in the tissues. The prosecution replied that, if no arsenic had been administered for the last few days of the illness of Miss Bankes, she still might have died of the after-effects of this irritant, although the arsenic previously administered would by this time have been eliminated from the body.

With regard to the antimony which Dr. Taylor had found in the intestines, very little contra-evidence was offered by the defence. Dr. Richardson said he would have expected to find some in the liver. Mr. Rogers, who acknowledged that he was a chemist and not a pathologist, agreed. There was then the positive evidence of Dr. Taylor, who had found the antimony, against the vague opinion that it should also have been present in the liver. It was also alleged that whatever antimony was found in the body was derived from the bismuth mixture which Miss Bankes had taken, for antimony is frequently contained as an impurity in bismuth.

The reliability of the chemical experts of the defence was questioned. They were all connected with the Grosvenor School of Medicine, and might be expected to be friends and colleagues, and therefore likely each to support the opinion of the others. Two of them had been witnesses in the trial of Palmer, shortly before, in which Dr. Richardson had given it as his opinion that the victim of Palmer had died of angina pectoris, and not of strychnine poison. It was hinted that the two witnesses were in the habit of giving evidence to assist prisoners.

Dr. Girdwood, Mr. Edwards and Dr. Tyler Smith, gentlemen of extensive experience in cases of pregnancy, stated that the early stages of this condition were frequently accompanied by purging, vomiting and burning sensations. The symptoms in this case were not inconsistent with their observations in other cases. They thought the death of the deceased was occasioned by exhaustion produced by continued purging and sickness from natural causes. Dr. Smith said that in cases of pregnancy accompanied by vomiting and purging it was very common for the patient to feel a burning sensation in the stomach, and the mouth would become sore. He had seen cases where the symptoms had been so similar to those which would have resulted from the administration of poison that the evacuations of the patient had been submitted to a chemist.

Mr. Serjeant Parry made all use possible of the points in favour of his client, but his brilliant defence was without avail. He pointed out that the theory of the prosecution that the arsenic had been carried off by the chlorate of potash was foolish. It was merely the offspring of a fertile brain to account for what was felt to be an overwhelming difficulty in the way of the prosecution, namely, the absence of any arsenic in the body of the deceased. He naturally made the very utmost of the unfortunate mistake of Dr. Taylor. He reminded them that Dr. Taylor when originally examined had stated distinctly and positively, without any reservation, that he had discovered arsenic in a bottle in the possession of the prisoner. If this had been a fact, it would have been almost conclusive evidence against the prisoner; and if the mistake had never been found out, upon that fact alone the prisoner would have gone to the scaffold perfectly innocent probably of the crime for which his life was sacrificed. He could not avoid saying it was almost a miraculous interposition that the blunder had been discovered. Would they not pause before they gave effect to the medical testimony after that extraordinary fact? Dr. Taylor, no doubt, believed he was right, but was it not clear that he was wrong? The question then was, What reliance ought to be placed on evidence of this description when a fellow-creature's life was at stake? The same test was applied to the evacuation as was applied to the bottle of chlorate of potash, and how were they to tell that there had not been a mistake with one as well as the other?

Serjeant Ballantine referred to the fact that the prisoner had definitely stated that the deceased was not pregnant when he knew this statement to be untrue. It

DR. SMETHURST'S LUCKY ESCAPE

made it important from the point of view of the prisoner that his wife should be got out of the way. The direct evidence of the able practitioners who had seen the deceased during life must outweigh the theories of scientific men who only knew the case by hearsay. Then, with regard to the will, he would ask them why the prisoner should have induced this unhappy lady to make a will by which she bequeathed him all the property she possessed in the world when, supposing she was only suffering from a bowel complaint, there was no reason to suppose her death was imminent, and whether that proceeding could be reconciled with any other supposition than that the prisoner knew perfectly well that the complaint would be fatal? Could they go into the details of the sick-chamber, could they reflect that the prisoner had performed all the painful offices that must be required during a period of three weeks when he had plenty of money to employ nurses and proper persons to attend on the deceased, without asking themselves whether the prisoner could have acted thus unless he had some extraordinary motive in view? The error made by Dr. Taylor was such as any one might have made and reflected no discredit on him. It formed no part of the present case, for it had not only been communicated to the prisoner as soon as discovered, but he himself had stated it to the jury in his opening.

The summing up of the Lord Chief Baron was a very full one, occupying nearly nine hours. The first question to which the jury had to devote themselves was whether the deceased died by poison, and if she had, was it administered by the prisoner? The conduct of the prisoner at this time was matter for very serious consideration. At the very period when the unhappy woman was lying on her deathbed, and when, according to the prisoner's own statement, she was in such a condition as not to be able to bear the excitement of seeing her own sister, he took into her bedroom on a Sunday an entire stranger, an attorney, and there a will prepared by himself was read over to the unhappy woman, who executed it under circumstances of degradation. His lordship then proceeded to comment upon the medical evidence. In reference to the point urged in favour of the prisoner, that no poison had been found in his possession, it was pointed out that he had had ample time to dispose of any he might have had before his arrest. The medical witnesses called for the defence thought the symptoms of this case inconsistent with slow arsenical poisoning, and that, had arsenic or antimony been the cause of death, some portion of those substances would have been found in the body. These statements, however, were the opinions of scientific men, the result of reading and study, and the jury would have to consider how far they weighed against the evidence of the doctors who had seen and attended the patient during life. The medical men first called in found themselves baffled by the disease; the medicines not only did not alleviate the symptoms, but they did not produce their proper effects. The doctors therefore came to the conclusion that something was being administered which was poisoning her. Counsel for the prisoner had made much of the mistake of Dr. Taylor in one of his tests and had asked them to dismiss the evidence of this witness entirely from consideration. His lordship did not agree with this. The failure of Dr. Taylor's analysis in one instance arose from a new and hitherto unknown fact in science, and did not in any way invalidate the testimony. He did not agree with the learned counsel for the prisoner that the real question for the jury was to consider which set of medical witnesses were entitled to credence. The medical evidence was, of course, of great importance, but the jury must in addition look to all the other facts, and particularly to the conduct of the prisoner and to his motives for committing the crime. They must, after all, be guided by those rules of common sense that would operate upon the minds of reasonable men with regard to the more important actions of their lives, and even supposing there were no medical evidence at all in the case, they would still have a very grave question to decide with reference to the guilt or innocence of the prisoner.

The jury after a very short deliberation found the prisoner guilty. The learned Judge expressed his agreement with the finding, and sentenced the prisoner to death. Dr. Smethurst exclaimed : " I declare Dr. Julius to be my murderer. I declare I am innocent before God."

The case was of such an unusual and exciting nature that it would have attracted a great amount of interest at any time, but taking place as it did when Parliament was not sitting and other news was scarce, it aroused an immense amount of public attention. A heated controversy took place in the papers, some of these making themselves champions of the prisoner, stating that they were convinced that he was innocent, and demanding a reversal of the verdict. Sir George Lewis, the Home Secretary, was inundated with letters, petitions and communications of all kinds, some of them sensible, some of them utter rubbish. He forwarded all these various documents bearing on the matter to the Judge who had tried Smethurst, and the Chief Baron, after a full consideration of the papers, made the following report: " The medical communications which have since reached you put the matter in a very different light, and tend very strongly to show that the medical part of the inquiry did not go to the jury in so favourable a way as it might, and indeed ought to, have done, and in two respects : (1) that more weight was due to the pregnant condition of Miss Bankes (a fact admitting, after the post-mortem, of no doubt) than was ascribed to it by the medical witnesses for the prosecution ; (2) that, in the opinion of a considerable number of medical men of eminence and experience, the symptoms of the post-mortem appearances were ambiguous, and might be referred either to natural causes or to poison. Many also have gone so far as to say that the symptoms and appearances were inconsistent and incompatible with poison."

On the other side the Lord Chief Baron made reference to disclosures since the trial which in his opinion confirmed the guilt of the prisoner.

The report concluded as follows: " I think there is no communication before you in all or any of the papers I have seen upon which you can rely or act. That from Dr. Baly and Dr. Jenner seemed to me to be the most trustworthy and respectable; but there is an unaccountable but undoubted mistake in it which must be rectified before it can be taken as the basis of any decision. If you have been favourably impressed by any of the documents, so as to entertain the proposition of granting a pardon or of commuting the sentence to a short period of penal servitude, I think it ought to be founded on the judgment of medical and scientific persons selected by yourself for the purpose of considering the effects of the symptoms and appearances and the result of the analysis, and I think, for the prisoner's sake, you ought to have the points arising out of Herepath's letter further inquired into and considered. I forbear to speculate upon facts not ascertained; but if Dr. Taylor had been cross-examined as to this, and had given no satisfactory explanation, the result of the trial might have been quite different."

The allusion to the mistake in the letter of Dr. Baly and Dr. Jenner is as follows: " We would further remark, with regard to the symptoms present, that Dr. Julius appears to have been in attendance on Isabella Bankes before he heard of vomiting as a symptom; this absence of vomiting at the commencement is quite inconsistent with the belief that an irritant poison was the original cause of the disease." If this had been an accurate statement of fact, it would undoubtedly have been an important point in Smethurst's favour, but actually Dr. Julius in his evidence had stated that diarrhœa and vomiting were present from his first visit and continued throughout the illness.

The reference of the Lord Chief Baron to " points arising out of Herepath's letter " was this : Mr. Herepath sent a letter to *The Times* asserting that Dr. Taylor had extracted from the chlorate of potash bottle more arsenic than could have been obtained from the copper gauze. If this were so, the value of Dr. Taylor's evidence would have been diminished, but at the same time it would have shown that the chlorate bottle did contain arsenic, and this, if a fact, would have been fatal to Smethurst.

The Home Secretary, after considering this report, took a most unusual course. He wrote to the Judge, and at the same time sent a copy of the letter to *The Times*, saying that he had considered the recommendation of the Judge and had sent the evidence, the report of the Judge, and all the papers bearing on the medical points of the case to Sir Benjamin Brodie (the celebrated surgeon of St. George's Hospital) ; that Sir Benjamin had reported that the facts, though full of suspicion against Dr. Smethurst, did not afford absolute and complete proof of his guilt. The Home Secretary continued, " After very careful and anxious consideration of all the facts of this very peculiar case, I have come to the conclusion that there is sufficient doubt of the prisoner's guilt to render it my duty to advise the grant to him of a free pardon. . . . The necessity which I have felt for advising Her Majesty to grant a free pardon in this case has not, so it appears to me, risen from any defect in the constitution or proceedings of our criminal tribunals ; it has risen from the imperfection of medical science, and from the fallibility of judgment in an obscure malady even of skilful and experienced practitioners."

Sir George Lewis might truthfully have expressed himself on this point very differently. He might have pointed out that a brutal and deliberate murderer was to escape justice because members of the medical profession by their evidence had made it difficult, if not impossible, to bring home his guilt without doubt.

The report of Sir Benjamin Brodie was a very curious document. It did not confine itself to a consideration of the chemical and medical points, but ranged over the whole of the evidence submitted at the trial. It contained six reasons for thinking Smethurst guilty and eight for doubting his guilt, but these reasons are by no means all medical.

This procedure of the Home Secretary of allowing what practically amounts to an appeal of a murderer against his conviction to be adjudicated on by an eminent surgeon who was no lawyer is probably unique. It could not possibly obtain at the present day with a court of criminal appeal. Had this been in existence at that time, there is every probability that a great scoundrel would not have escaped the justice due to him.

An interesting speculation arises in connection with the bottle of chlorate of potash solution found in the room of Miss Bankes. In a number of the *Lancet* published some seven years before this trial is a letter by Smethurst on the extraction of teeth. On the opposite page is an article by a well-known professor of chemistry in which the tests for arsenic are discussed, the professor stating that the method of Reinsch always failed in the presence of chlorates. Did Smethurst give his wife chlorate of potash in the hope that this might invalidate any test should any analysis be made ? At any rate, the bottle of chlorate of potash saved his life.

After Dr. Smethurst's pardon he was put on trial for bigamy, convicted and given one year's imprisonment. When released, he brought an action in the Probate Court to have the will of Miss Bankes established, and although it was contested by her family, who alleged fraud on the ground that Miss Bankes believed she was the lawful wife of Smethurst, he won his case. We have the remarkable facts that a man who had undoubtedly murdered his wife brought an action and invoked the aid of the law to obtain her property and that he succeeded.

THE TRIAL OF CHARLES BATEMAN, SURGEON, OF LONDON, AT THE OLD BAILEY FOR HIGH TREASON, 1685

AFTER the fight at Sedgemoor in 1685, the last battle worthy of the name fought in England, the Government, not satisfied with the brutal and vindictive treatment of the rebels by the most inhuman judge this country has ever known, namely, Judge Jeffreys, who in the Bloody Assizes had hanged over 300 people and transported 800 more, determined to make a sacrifice of others, including a surgeon in the City named Bateman, although they had had nothing to do with Monmouth's rebellion. Bateman was accused of complicity in the Rye House Plot two years previously, but, whatever part he had taken in the affair, it is certain he was not one of the leading conspirators. The malignity with which so humble a political opponent, guilty of a relatively slight offence, was hounded, whilst other traitors of much higher position and much more criminal were left, is partly explained at least by the fact that Bateman had rendered assistance to Titus Oates after that wretched being had been flogged at Newgate. Dr. Bateman had also attended Lord Shaftesbury professionally and had been a zealous advocate of the Exclusion Bill, a Bill to prevent the Duke of York succeeding to the throne.

Dr. Bateman, when brought to the Old Bailey, protested against the way in which he had been treated. He had been a close prisoner for ten weeks, his health was undermined, and he had had no notice of his trial, and was therefore quite unprepared with his defence. The Court allowed him a few hours for preparation, and also permitted him on account of his health to have his son assist him.

It must be remembered that trials for treason and other political offences were conducted very differently in the seventeenth century, and the procedure told very hardly on the accused. For instance, the prisoner was denied a sight of his indictment and did not know what his offence was till he actually appeared at the bar. The Crown had the power to force witnesses to attend; the prisoner had no such power, and if witnesses of their own free will came forward to speak for him, they could not be sworn, and therefore the jury did not regard their testimony as of the same value as that of one who had taken a solemn oath. The Crown had the services of the best lawyers and the most skilful advocates, but none could appear for the prisoner. However ignorant or illiterate he might be, he must defend himself. This gross unfairness to the accused applied to others charged with non-political crimes, such as larceny, but did not cause so much hardship in these cases, as it was especially in charges of treason and similar crimes that the vindictive spirit of persecution was shown by the Government. It was not till the end of the reign of William and Mary that this oppressive law was altered.

The indictment was long and vague: "That Charles Bateman, late of the parish of St. Dunstan in the West, in the ward of Farringdon Without, London, surgeon, as a false traitor against the most illustrious and excellent prince Charles the Second, late King of England, Scotland, France and Ireland, defender of the faith and his natural lord, not having the fear of God in his heart, nor weighing the duty of his allegiance, but being moved and seduced by the instigation of the devil, the cordial love and true, due and natural obedience which a true and faithful subject of our late lord the king towards him should, and of right ought to, bear, altogether withdrawing and practising, and with all his strength intending the peace and common tranquillity of this kingdom to disquiet and disturb, and war and rebellion against our late lord the king, within this kingdom to stir up, move and procure, and the government of our late lord the king of this kingdom to subvert, and our said late lord the king from the stile, title, honour, and kingly name of the imperial crown of this kingdom to depose and deprive, and our said late lord the king to death and final destruction to bring and put, the 30th day of May in the 35th year of his reign and divers other days and times, as well before as afterwards, at the parish and ward aforesaid, falsely, maliciously, devilishly and traitorously with divers other rebels and traitors to the Jurors unknown, did conspire, compass, imagine and intend our said late lord the king, then his supreme and natural lord, not only of his kingly state, title, power, and government of his kingdom of England to deprive and depose, but also our said late lord the king to kill, and to death bring and put, and the ancient government of this kingdom to change, alter and subvert, and a miserable slaughter among the subjects of our said late lord the king to cause and procure, and insurrection and rebellion against our said late lord the king to procure and assist. And the same most wicked treasons and traitorous conspiracies, compassings, imaginations, and purposes aforesaid to effect, and bring to pass, he the said Charles Bateman, as a false traitor, then and there, (to wit) the said 30th day of May in the 35th year aforesaid, and divers other days and times, as well before as afterwards, at the parish and ward aforesaid, falsely, unlawfully, and most wickedly and traitorously, did promise and undertake to the said other false rebels and traitors then and there being present that he the said Charles Bateman would be assisting and aiding in the taking and apprehending of the person of our late lord the king, and in taking and seizing the city of London, and the Tower of London, the Savoy, and the Royal Palace of White-hall, against the duty of his allegiance, against the peace etc., and against the form of the statute in this case made and provided, etc."

The Crown had retained the services of Mr. Phipps, Mr. Serjeant Selby and Mr. Charles Molloy. James Keeling was put into the witness-box first and gave general evidence of the Rye House Plot, but none against Bateman, and after the latter had pointed out to the Judge that this did not affect the charge against him (Bateman) in any way the Court agreed, and told the jury that Keeling's evidence did not affect the prisoner in particular.

Thomas Lee then swore that Bateman had agreed to take part in the plot and was to be one of the leaders for seizing the City, the Tower, the Savoy, Whitehall, and the person of Charles II.

Richard Goodenough gave similar evidence; but all these men were of infamous character, and were swearing for their own lives. None of them had yet got their pardon for the part they had taken in the plot. The rope was, so to speak, round their own necks. Various witnesses were called for the defence, but their evidence had no very direct bearing on the case. The Lord Chief Justice appears to have summed up very fairly. (A remark such as this would be superfluous, in fact, insulting, to a judge of the present day, but is a tribute which could rarely be paid to a Stuart judge.) Just before the jury retired Miss Bateman asked the Recorder to hear another witness in her father's favour, a witness she had only just been able to find. The Judge at first refused, but after some of the jury had expressed a wish to have this fresh witness called, permission was given. However, in spite of the new testimony, the jury found Bateman guilty. Then Mr. Recorder, after exhorting the prisoner not to flatter himself that there would be any reprieve, and thereby delay the repentance necessary for his future happiness, pronounced sentence " that he should return to the place from whence he came, from thence be drawn to the place of execution, there to be hanged by the neck, and whilst alive be cut down, and his bowels to be taken out and burnt, his head to be severed from his body, and his body divided into four parts, and that his head and quarters be disposed at the pleasure of the king." He was executed at Tyburn according to the sentence.

In the reign of William III. Sir John Hawles, Solicitor-General, published a pamphlet, entitled "Remarks on the Trials of . . . Charles Bateman," in which he pointed out the grossly unfair way in which certain of those accused of complicity in the Popish and the Rye House Plots were treated. He remarked that his pamphlet was only for the purpose of considering how far the proceedings in capital matters of late years had been regular or irregular; he did not argue whether the accused were guilty or not guilty, but simply the legal question of whether the evidence produced at the trials was sufficient proof of guilt, and if of sufficient proof, what crimes it proved against the accused.

Reviewing the trial of Dr. Bateman, the Solicitor-General pointed out that he was the last to conclude the tragedy of these vindictive prosecutions, and that he was so distracted in court that he was allowed to have his son to defend him. The witness Keeling gave evidence of the plot generally, but none against Bateman. Lee and Goodenough did swear that the surgeon was mixed up in the plot, but Baker, a witness for the prisoner, swore that Lee had tried to bribe him (Baker) to insinuate himself into the prisoner's confidence and discuss State affairs. If he did this, Lee promised he would make Baker a great man. Upon this evidence Bateman was found guilty. Against Goodenough's evidence there was this to be said, that he was pardoned, but so far only as to qualify him to be a witness, though not a very credible one, with the fear of punishment for what he had lately done hanging over his head. Witnesses such as Goodenough "hunted like cormorants, with halters about their necks." He next asked why had Lee waited three years after the Rye House Plot before he had brought any charge against

Bateman. It was a foolish story to say that Goodenough could not be got hold of before, and that the testimony of a single witness was not sufficient; though a single witness was not sufficient to convict a man of high treason, yet the testimony of one person was enough to commit a person accused, and upon conviction on the evidence of a single witness to make him a prisoner for life. " In 1683, when the words were pretended to be spoken, Bateman had not been spared if accused; and though it be a good reason for the Court to have given why they did not proceed against the prisoner till that time, because there were not two witnesses against him, yet it was no reason for Lee why he did not accuse the prisoner before that time, especially he having been several times before that time examined, not only of what he knew, but of what persons he knew concerned; but, to say truth, Lee, in the trial, did not proceed to answer the objection, but the Court, in the manner before, endeavoured to answer it for him. The last matter observable in this trial was the permitting Bateman's son to make his father's defence, which was an extraordinary unparalleled favour: it was the first and last time that, or anything like it, had been done; the lord Russel's lady, indeed, was permitted to make notes at the trial for her lord, but he only was permitted to make use of them. Fitzharris's wife, when she but whispered her husband or but told him what jurors he should challenge, and what not, was severely corrected, and threatened to be thrust out of court, for doing it in prejudice to the king. In Colledge's trial, he was told that persons that advised a prisoner in treason, even before a trial, were guilty of a high misdemeanour: nay, a solicitor had been indicted of high treason for it; and therefore nothing can excuse the allowing the prisoner counsel in matter of fact, as was done in this case (it is not material whether the son was a barrister-at-law or not), but the weakness of the prisoner, who to all appearance was moped mad."

These observations of the Solicitor-General show very clearly the great necessity of a reform in the law and procedure concerning trials for high treason, a matter which has been referred to above, and a reform which, as was mentioned, was carried out in the reign of William and Mary.

The Solicitor-General then proceeded to make some comments on the question of lunatics and crime, which are particularly interesting at the present time:—

"But the Court, by excusing their favour on that account, incurred a worse censure, for nothing is more certain law than that a person who falls mad after a crime supposed to be committed shall not be tried for it, and if he falls mad after judgement he shall not be executed, though I do not think the reason given for the law in that point will maintain it, which is, that the end of punishment is the striking terror into others, but the execution of a madman hath not that effect, which is not true, for the terror to the living is equal whether the person be mad or in his senses; and that is the reason of breaking the person executed for treason, and exposing his quarters, which is done rather to deter the living than for punishing the dead. But the true reason for the law I think to be this: a person of *non sana memoria*, and a lunatick during his lunacy, is by an act of God disabled to make his just defence. There may be circumstances lying in his private knowledge, which would prove his innocency, of which he can have no advantage, because not known to the persons who shall take upon them his defence, and that is the reason many civil actions die with the persons against whom they lay in their life times, and that is the reason why in criminal matters persons by ordinary course of law cannot be convicted after their deaths. . . . I know it will be objected that if this matter of *non sana memoria* should be permitted to put off a trial or stay execution, all malefactors will pretend to be so. But I say there is a great difference between pretence and realities, and *sana* and *non sana memoria* hath been often tryed in capital matters, and the prisoners have reaped so little benefit by their pretences, it being always discovered, that we rarely hear of it. In this case the prisoner might have been tried as well absent as present, according to that repealed statute, for any advantage he did or could reap by being present; and it seems very probable the Court thought him distempered, for if he was of sane memory, his son ought not to have been permitted to make his father's defence : if he was distempered, he ought not to have been tried, much less executed. And this person being the last man as far as I can remember, or can find by the printed trials, who suffered from the plot of high treason first set on foot by Fitzharris, and carried on against Colledge, and the other persone herein mentioned, and the design stopping here, I think fit to end my remarks on the proceedings of all capital matters with him."

THE BRIGHTON MURDER

IN the long list of medical poisoners the name of Dr. Alfred William Warder will always be a very prominent one. His career is a little difficult to follow, for he was a pronounced wanderer. He practised in London, living at Chelsea, then at Uxbridge (during which time he was Lecturer on Medical Jurisprudence at the Grosvenor School, attached to St. George's Hospital), at Ottery St. Mary, Devonshire (where his first wife died), at Ithels, at Wotton-under-Edge, Gloucestershire, and at Penzance. He was a widower for the second time when he met Miss Ethel Branwell, sister of Dr. Branwell, of Brighton. After a very rapid courtship a secret marriage took place. Mrs. Warder was thirty-six years old, her husband some ten years more. Soon after the wedding Dr. and Mrs. Warder came to Brighton for a visit, staying in rooms in Bedford Square. She was in excellent health when she left London, but soon after her arrival in Brighton she was taken ill, and her brother, Dr. Branwell, called in Dr. Taafe, a well-known local medical man, to attend her. The illness terminated fatally, and Dr. Taafe, who could not diagnose any natural cause for death, asked for a post-mortem. After this procedure had been carried out Dr. Taafe refused a death certificate, and an inquest was held. This was conducted by the borough coroner, Mr. David Black, at the Olive Branch Inn, Silwood Street, in July, 1866.

Dr. Taafe, who was a very highly qualified practitioner, holding the degrees of M.D. and M.S. of London University, was the principal witness. He said that about five weeks before the death of Mrs. Warder he was called in to attend her by Dr. Branwell. She complained of constant pain in the bladder. Dr. Warder gave witness a history

THE BRIGHTON MURDER 217

of hysteria in his wife. He told him that he was administering to the patient twenty-drop doses of Fleming's tincture of aconite for her bladder trouble. (The British Pharmaceutical Codex describes this substance as a remedy for external use only, and as an extremely powerful application.) Witness objected both to the aconite and to the dose, ordered it to be discontinued, and gave instead a mixture which contained henbane and opium. These did the patient good. Some time later Dr. Warder told witness that Mrs. Warder had got tired of these medicines and could not take them. This was said in the presence of his wife. Witness never saw Mrs. Warder except with her husband. Witness could not understand why she did not get well. His suspicions were aroused, but Mrs. Warder was so devoted to, and had such confidence in, her husband, and he appeared so attached to her, that witness did not mention these suspicions. On seeing the patient a few days before her death he was so struck with her appearance that he told the husband that he intended to ask Dr. Branwell to agree to call in another doctor to assist him. He saw Dr. Branwell and mentioned this to him, and also suggested that a nurse should be sent in, and that the patient should be in sole charge of this nurse, not even her husband seeing her. The next day he was informed that Mrs. Warder had died. He then saw Dr. Branwell and told him how puzzled he was, and though he would not raise a suspicion against any one unjustly, yet he could not understand the death. Dr. Branwell said he, too, was uneasy in his mind as to the cause of his sister's illness. He and witness then went to see Dr. Warder and told him they wanted a post-mortem, and to this he offered no objection. The next day witness, with the help of Dr. Withers More and of Mr. Jowers, made an autopsy; Dr. Warder was also present. They could find no natural cause of death. Some two weeks before the patient died the idea came to witness that she might have had something improper given to her, but, as she got so much better, he dismissed it from his mind. Later, when she again became bad, the suspicion recurred. He did not mention this to any one during the life of Mrs. Warder, but he fully intended to do so to the second doctor whom he wished to call in. The three doctors who conducted the post-mortem decided that the best thing they could do would be to take the viscera to Dr. Alfred Swayne Taylor, the toxicologist, for analysis. In reply to Mr. Stuckey, who watched the case on behalf of Dr. Branwell, witness said he could not find symptoms during life consistent with any natural disease, and his medicines did not act as he expected they would.

Dr. Withers More, physician to the Sussex County Hospital, and Mr. Frederick Jowers, surgeon to the same hospital, said they had not seen the patient during life, but they confirmed Dr. Taafe's account of the findings at the autopsy.

Dr. Taylor, of Guy's Hospital, said he had made an analysis of the viscera and their contents. He had examined them very carefully for inorganic poisons, such as arsenic, antimony or mercury, and found none, nor could he find any trace by analysis of morphia, strychnia, aconitine or other alkaloids. Some of the extract made from the viscera was tested physiologically by inserting it into a wound in the neck of a rabbit. After five hours no bad effects were observed, although in a control experiment some aconite similarly injected into another rabbit killed it in a very short time. The results of his examination, then, were (1) that the viscera examined presented no cause of natural death; (2) that no poison had been detected. He did not consider this finding was inconsistent with death from aconite poisoning. If the patient had had small doses given at short intervals, and had had none for a few hours before death, he would not be able to find it in the contents of the stomach.

The evidence of Dr. Taafe was then read over to Dr.

THE BRIGHTON MURDER 219

Taylor, after which he said he had no doubt that the death of Mrs. Warder was due to poisoning by aconite.

Dr. Samuel Wilks, Lecturer on Medicine at Guy's Hospital, who had assisted Dr. Taylor, expressed a similar opinion.

Dr. Taylor mentioned to the coroner that Dr. Warder was one of the band of men from the Grosvenor School who had given evidence in the celebrated Palmer poisoning case with the object of proving Palmer's innocence, evidence which had called forth some very scathing remarks from the learned Judge who had tried the case, on the importance of medical witnesses remembering that they were scientific experts to help the Court and not advocates for the defence.

The coroner then summed up very briefly, and the jury returned a verdict " that the deceased Ellen Vivian Warder, died from the effects of aconite administered wilfully and of malice aforethought by her late husband, Alfred William Warder." (The doctor had committed suicide between the death of his wife and the inquest.)

Dr. Warder's two previous wives died under similar suspicious circumstances, one in 1863 and the other in 1865. There is very little doubt that he was responsible for their deaths. His first wife, who had lived apart from him, died a few weeks after she had returned to him, and his second wife, whose life he had insured, died eight months after her marriage, with similar symptoms to those shown by Mrs. Warder.

Dr. Warder, who had been present at the post-mortem on his wife and who was also at her funeral, was served with a subpœna to attend the inquest, which had been adjourned for the analysis of the viscera by Dr. Taylor. Although under great suspicion, there was no warrant issued, but the Chief Constable had the doctor watched of which fact he was well aware. He determined to anticipate the hangman. He had already made his preparations. The day before the inquest was held he wrote to Miss

Gunning, the sister of his first wife, disposing of his property. Although watched by the police, he went to London, probably for the purpose of securing the prussic acid with which he ended his life. He knew it would arouse suspicion if he bought it in the town. He returned to Brighton and late at night went to the Bedford Hotel and engaged a room. The next day, as he did not come down, his room was entered, and he was found dead in bed.

Dr. Warder showed some good feeling at the last moment, as the following letter, addressed to his landlady in Bedford Square, proves:—

"MY DEAR MISS LANDSELL,—You have already suffered enough through me and mine, and another death in your house would, of course, be worse. When you receive this, have the kindness to telegraph to Miss Gunning, to whom you will give up what I have left at your house. I have left on the table the cash for the bills and £3 in addition as some compensation.

"Believe me, yours truly,
"A. W. WARDER."

An inquest was held; and Dr. Pickford, of Cavendish Place, Brighton, said that on a table near the bed he found a bottle of prussic acid, from which, if the bottle had been full originally, four teaspoonsful were missing. He also found some opium pills in the pocket of the dead man. Dr. Pickford at the close of his evidence asked the coroner if he might, in the interests of science, make a post-mortem on the body of Dr. Warder. It was not absolutely necessary, as the cause of death was so clear, but it would be helpful to future cases if he were allowed to do this. The coroner said he had no power to order a post-mortem, but he thought it was very advisable it should be done, and were he a medical man he should act on his own authority.

As the inquest was nearing its end, a solicitor entered the room and said he had come to watch the case in the interests of Miss Gunning. It had been represented to him that members of the family of Dr. Warder had exhibited insanity, and that the deceased had at times acted like a madman. He asked for an adjournment in order that he might bring evidence on this point.

The coroner, in answer to this application said, supposing the jury were about to find a verdict of *felo-de-se*, which he thought they must do upon the evidence as it now stood, the body would have to be buried in a certain way within twenty-four hours and at night. If, therefore, he agreed to the suggestion of Mr. Eland, unless the adjournment was for a very short period only, the law would be defeated. Mr. Black then ordered the room to be cleared so that he and the jury might consult together on the matter. Upon reassembling he said that the jury and he had carefully considered the question, and had come to the definite conclusion that, in face of the evidence, there was no doubt that the deceased was perfectly sane when he committed the crime, but they would agree to adjourn till the next day in order that Dr. Pickford might make a post-mortem and ascertain the condition of the brain of Dr. Warder. If nothing abnormal were found, the jury would return a verdict of *felo-de-se*. If anything wrong were discovered with the brain of Dr. Warder, he could not say what the jury might do. On the following day Dr. Pickford, who in the meanwhile had made the autopsy, said that he, assisted by Dr. Taafe, Dr. Hall, Dr. Withers More and Mr. Jowers, had examined the body of Dr. Warder. The brain was found to be in every way perfectly normal. Dr. Taafe was asked if during life he had observed any signs of mental trouble in the deceased. He said he had never seen even the slightest symptoms of insanity in Dr. Warder. He was, on the contrary, a most cool and collected man. A juror asked whether Dr. Warder had expressed any surprise when told the death certificate was refused. Dr. Taafe: Well, he didn't express any surprise, but expostulated and asked me for my reasons. I said I would not give any reasons then, but preferred deferring them. On the morning of my making the post-mortem he touched me on the shoulder and asked me again if I would give him a certificate, and I said I must consider it. On the day after I had seen Dr. Taylor I saw Dr. Warder with Mr. Stuckey, and again he asked me if I could give him a certificate of the cause of death, and I then informed him I could not give him a certificate that death was from natural causes, for the simple reason that I didn't know what to insert in the certificate. Mr. Stuckey asked him what he considered was the cause of death, and instead of answering Mr. Stuckey he turned to me and said, " Don't you think the appearances of the brain and kidney sufficient to account for death ? " I said, " No, I do not." He then asked me what my opinion was, and I said I must reserve that.

The jury, after a short deliberation, returned a verdict of *felo-de-se*. The body was buried at half-past ten the same night without any ceremony. It was conveyed to the parochial cemetery in a hearse, accompanied by a few policemen and a straggling crowd of about a hundred vulgar, morbid sightseers. The body was very rapidly lowered into an unconsecrated grave, the whole proceeding occupying but a few minutes. Thus sadly ended the career of a doctor whose talents, had they been directed in right courses, would undoubtedly have taken him to a very high position in his profession.

MISCELLANEOUS CASES

THE unusual incident of a medical student committing a serious assault on his examiner is illustrated in the case of Charles Wadham Wyndham Penruddock, who was charged with assaulting Mr. Thomas Hardy, a surgeon, with intent to maim and disable him. On December 22nd, 1836, Penruddock went to the Apothecaries' Hall to be examined in the usual way, the examiners present being Mr. Hardy, Mr. Este, Mr. Randall, and Dr. Merriman. Only quite ordinary questions were asked, but Penruddock seemed totally unable to answer many of them, and was obviously not well up in his subjects. Mr. Este asked him a question, and as no answer was given, Mr. Randall more or less repeated what Mr. Este had said with some explanation of what was meant, to make it more clear to the candidate. Very rudely he remarked, " How the devil can I answer if you all badger me with questions ? " No notice was taken of this impertinence. Mr. Este put several more questions, but again Penruddock could not answer, so the examiner attempted to help the student by partially giving the replies himself. Mr. Hardy interposed, saying they must really ascertain the fitness of the candidate before they passed him. By this time it seems to have become clear to Penruddock that his chances of getting through were not very great so he told his examiners that even at school he had not been good at answering queries. It was pointed out to him that there was no other way of ascertaining a candidate's knowledge except by that of question and answer, and that the examiners had no wish to be hard on him. They intended to treat him quite fairly. Penruddock then suggested that he knew his anatomy well and wished to be tested in that, but it was pointed out that that was no part of the examination, and he must show his competency in the proper subjects of the test, *i.e.*, chemistry, materia medica and therapeutics, before he could pass. The reply of Penruddock was that it did not matter a farthing to him financially whether he passed or not, and he added viciously, " I will not be disgraced in the eyes of my family by such a set of fellows as you are. I would rather die first and would swing for it." The examiners had borne his insolence with exemplary, too exemplary, patience. He repaid them by a ferocious attack, saying to Mr. Hardy, " You are one of those who have been hard on me," and drawing a life preserver loaded with lead, struck him a very violent blow on the head. Mr. Hardy was stunned, and the other examiners in attempting to stop Penruddock received severe injuries. He was given into charge, and on him was found a bottle of gin, the consumption of some of the contents of which was no doubt the cause of his violent outbreak.

The defence set up by the prisoner was that he had only hit the examiner with his knuckles, and not with the life preserver. Penruddock was a member of a very respected family in the west of England, and was described as a young man of a particularly kind and gentle disposition. Dr. Seymour and other well-known people gave him a most excellent character, and he was acquitted. He was later charged with a common assault on Mr. Hardy. He pleaded guilty, was sentenced to twelve months' imprisonment and bound over to keep the peace.

It is difficult to imagine such an occurrence taking place at an examination at the present time.

Dr. Willobycki, of Polish birth, who had left his country owing to political troubles, and settled in Scotland, started to practise in Edinburgh. Here he soon developed a very good connection. He commenced his career of crime by robbing a patient named Darling of £4,000. He offered to invest this money, but instead of doing this he appropriated the amount to his own use.

He paid the interest, and when Darling died, he continued this to the heirs, Darling's sisters, Margaret and Isabella. Margaret soon became seriously ill and wished to leave her share to a nephew. This would have entailed the discovery of the doctor's crime, so Isabella was persuaded by Willobycki to write out a will (her writing resembling her sister's), and the dying Margaret to sign it. However, the peculiar interest of the fashionable doctor in this working class family excited a good deal of remark, and finally the police investigated the whole matter. Dr. Willobycki was arrested, and fashionable Edinburgh swarmed to the court to witness his trial. He was sentenced to fourteen years' penal servitude.

During the time of the Commonwealth amusements and sports were not regarded with much favour. Even to-day football played in the main street of a town is frowned upon by the police, but the following indictment of an unfortunate member of our profession in the time of Cromwell would cause a good deal of astonishment to a sitting magistrate :—

"Kent. Before the justices of the peace it was presented that at Maidstone, in the county aforesaid, John Bishop, of Maidstone aforesaid, apothecary, with force and arms did wilfully and in a violent and boisterous manner run to and fro, and kick up and down in the common highway and street within the said town and county, called the High Street, a certain ball of leather, commonly called a football, unto the great annoyance and incumbrance of the said common highway, and to the great disquiet and disturbance of the good people of this commonwealth passing and travelling in and through the same, and in contempt of the laws, etc., and to the evil example of others, and against the public peace, which indictment the Lord Protector, etc., caused to come before him."

A ponderous charge for a minor offence!

A daring attempt by a doctor to save a convicted criminal from the gallows was made in the year 1880. A man named Charles Shurety was tried for the murder of a child and found guilty. At ten minutes to eight on the day of Shurety's execution the governor of Newgate was just about to leave his office to proceed to the condemned cell when a warder handed him an official-looking letter. On opening this, to his astonishment, he saw that it was from the Home Secretary, ordering the postponement of the execution. At first he was about to act on this instruction, but on second thoughts he had his doubts as to the genuineness of the letter. Why had the Home Secretary delayed so late? Why was the letter delivered in the curious manner it had been? Of course, the Minister might have discovered facts at the last moment in favour of the convict, and might have scribbled the order on the nearest sheet of notepaper. It was only two minutes to eight, and the governor had to decide at once. If the letter were genuine and he permitted the execution to go on, he might be disastrously involved, if the letter were a forgery, it would be an equally serious matter were he to postpone the execution. It was a terribly anxious moment. "We are waiting, sir," said the head warder. "Very well," replied the governor, and the execution took place. The letter *was* a forgery; and it was found to have been cleverly carried out by a doctor, a member of a noted family. It was an attempt to help a convicted murderer for whom he had great sympathy. The doctor was sentenced to a year's imprisonment, and to pay a fine of £50.

The first instance of which I can find any record of a medical man pleading privilege in a court of law is that of Mr. Cæsar Hawkins in the case of the Duchess of Kingston in 1766, charged with bigamy. He was called as a witness in the case.

Q. Mr. Hawkins, are you acquainted with the prisoner at the bar, and how long have you been so?

A. A great many years, I believe about thirty.

Q. Are you acquainted with the present Lord Bristol, and how long have you been so?

A. I have had the honour of knowing the Earl of Bristol nearly as many.

Q. Do you know of any intercourse between my Lord Bristol and the lady at the bar?

A. Of an intercourse, certainly; of an acquaintance, undoubtedly.

Q. Do you know from the parties of any marriage between them?

A. I do not know how far anything that has come before me in a confidential trust in my profession should be disclosed consistent with my professional honour.

This question was repeated.

Counsel. I trust your lordships will see nothing in my question that can betray confidential trust or dishonour Mr. Hawkins in giving it. My question is simply whether Mr. Hawkins knows from the parties of any marriage between them.

Lord High Steward. The question that was asked by counsel at the bar is "whether the witness knew from any information of either of the two parties that they were married." The witness objects to it whether he is to answer any questions that are inconsistent with his professional honour. Your lordships are to determine whether the question put by counsel at the bar shall be asked.

Lord Mansfield. I suppose Mr. Hawkins means to demur to the question upon the ground that it came to his knowledge some way from his being employed as a surgeon for one or both of the parties, and I take for granted, if Mr. Hawkins understands that it is your lordships' opinion that he has no privilege on that account to excuse himself from giving the answer, that then, under the authority of your lordships' judgment, he will submit to answer it; therefore to save your lordships the trouble of an adjournment, if no lord differs in opinion, but thinks that a surgeon has no privilege to avoid giving evidence in a court of justice, but is bound by the law of the land to do it (if any of your lordships think he has such a privilege, it will be a matter to be debated elsewhere), if all your lordships acquiesce, Mr. Hawkins will understand that it is your judgment and opinion that a surgeon has no privilege, where it is a material question in a civil or criminal cause to know whether parties were married or whether a child was born, to say that his introduction to the parties was in the course of his profession, and in that way he came to the knowledge of it. I take it for granted that, if Mr. Hawkins understands that, it is a satisfaction to him and a clear justification to all the world. If a surgeon was voluntarily to reveal these secrets, to be sure he would be guilty of a breach of honour and of great indiscretion, but to give that information in a court of justice which by the law of the land he is bound to do will never be imputed to him as any indiscretion whatever.

Mr. Hawkins then answered the question.

The ruling of Lord Mansfield was undoubtedly correct law, and is exactly as held by judges of to-day. It is, in addition to being legal, sound common sense.

THE CASE OF DR. JOSEPH COLLIER

PROCEEDINGS ON THE TRIAL OF AN INDICTMENT AGAINST DR. JOSEPH COLLIER FOR A CONSPIRACY TO OVERTHROW THE CONSTITUTION AND GOVERNMENT AND TO AID AND ASSIST THE FRENCH (BEING THE KING'S ENEMIES) IN CASE THEY SHOULD INVADE THIS KINGDOM. TRIED AT LANCASTER BEFORE THE HON. JOHN HEATH, ONE OF THE JUSTICES OF HIS MAJESTY'S COURT OF COMMON PLEAS, APRIL 2ND, 1794

WHEN the unrest and upheaval caused by the French Revolution at the end of the eighteenth century spread to neighbouring countries, including England, George III. declared war against the French nation. In Britain there was a good deal of dissatisfaction with the political situation, and large numbers of the advanced thinkers were agitating for various reforms, especially for the removal of the disabilities under which the religious sects outside the Established Church laboured. An attempt was made to repeal the Test Act, but this failed and was made the occasion of great rejoicings by the Tory party. In Manchester the demonstrations were very pronounced, and there was formed a society called the Church and King Club, whose members met to celebrate what they were pleased to call the glorious decision of the House of Commons in rejecting the prayer of their Dissenting brethren. As a result the advocates of repeal formed themselves in 1792 into the Reformation Society, to pursue their aims for political freedom. A good deal of sympathy was felt and expressed by the democratic party in England for the efforts of the French nation in its struggle for liberty, a sympathy which rapidly evaporated when the excesses of the Revolution became pronounced.

The trial of Dr. Collier and others at Lancaster on the charge of conspiracy in 1794 was directly due to the political unrest in England, an unrest which had spread from the neighbouring country of France. Counsel engaged in the trial were—for the Crown, Mr. Law (Attorney-General for the County Palatine of Lancaster), Mr. Wood, Mr. Topping, Mr. Johnson, and Mr. James; for the defendants, the celebrated Hon. Thomas Erskine, Mr. Serjeant Cockell, Mr. Chambre, Mr. Lloyd, and Mr. Felix Vaughan. The prisoners were accused of conspiring together for the purpose of assisting the French should they land in England, and of drilling with firearms to prepare for the opportunity of assisting the enemies of the King.

Mr. Law, in his opening statement to the jury, pointed out that it was about the close of the year 1792 that the French nation thought fit to hold out to all nations on the globe, or rather to the discontented subjects of all those nations, an encouragement to confederate and combine together for the purpose of subverting all regular established authority amongst them, by a decree of the French nation of November 17th, 1792, which was the source and origin of the Reformation Society and other mischievous societies. The French nation in convention pledged to the discontented inhabitants of other countries its protection and assistance in case they should be disposed to innovate and change the form of government under which they had hitherto lived. Under the influence of this fostering encouragement, and meaning to avail themselves of the protection and assistance thus held out to them, this and other dangerous societies sprang up, and spread themselves within the bosom of this realm. It was about the period which followed close upon the promulgation of this detestable decree that the Society, ten members of which were on trial, was formed. The vigilance of those to whom the administration of justice and the immediate care of the police of the country was primarily entrusted had already prevented or dispersed every numerous assembly of persons which resorted to public houses for such purposes; it became therefore necessary for persons thus disposed to assemble themselves, if at all, within the walls of some private mansion. At the rooms of this Society, meeting in such a private house, it was contended the conspirators were guilty of the heinous offence of reading the works of Thomas Paine. Here they devised their plans for overthrowing the Constitution; here they dared to speak disrespectfully of royalty.

To the present generation most of the speech for the prosecution would appear rather nonsensical, with its narrow-mindedness, its awe of the great of the earth, and its political bigotry.

The only witness produced to prove the charge of conspiracy was a man named Thomas Dunn, a weaver, of Manchester, who had been arrested as one of the members of the Society, but released to give evidence against his former associates. After swearing to the effect outlined by Mr. Law in his address to the Court, he was subjected to a very severe cross-examination by Mr. Erskine, with very little effect at this stage of the trial.

Mr. Erskine then made a very powerful, eloquent and able speech for the defence, in the course of which he pointed out that the sole evidence of conspiracy was that of "a common soldier, or rather a common vagabond discharged as unfit to be a soldier, of a wretch lost to all reverence for God and religion, who avows that he has none for either." He showed the Court that the town of Manchester had long been extremely divided in religious and civil opinions. "Gentlemen, you all know that there have been for centuries past in this country various sects of Christians, worshipping God in different forms and holding a diversity of religious opinions; and that the law has for a long season deprived numerous classes even of His Majesty's Protestant subjects of privileges which it confers upon the rest of the public, setting, as it were, a mark upon them, and keeping them below the level of the community by shutting them out from offices of trust and confidence in the country. Whether these laws be wise or unwise, whether they ought to be continued or abolished, are questions for the Legislature, and not for us; but thus much I am warranted in saying, that it is the undoubted privilege of every man or class of man in England to petition Parliament for the removal of any system or law which either actually does aggrieve or which is thought to be a grievance. Impressed with the sense of this inherent privilege, this very constitutional Society, which is supposed by my learned friend the Attorney-General to have started up on the breaking out of the war with France for the purpose of destroying the Constitution—this very Society owed its birth to the assertion of this indisputable birthright of Englishmen, which the authors of this prosecution most rashly thought proper to stigmatise and resist. It is well known that in 1790 the Dissenters in the different parts of the kingdom were solicitous to bring before Parliament their application to put an end for ever to all divisions upon religious subjects, and to make us all, what I look forward yet to see, one harmonious body, living like one family together. It is also well remembered with what zeal and eloquence that great question was managed in the House of Commons by Mr. Fox, and the large majority with which the repeal of the Test Acts was rejected. It seems therefore strange that the period of this rejection should be considered as an era either of danger to the Church or of religious triumph to Christians: nevertheless a large body of gentlemen and others at Manchester, whose motives I am far from wishing to scrutinise or condemn, considered this very wish of the Dissenters as injurious to their rights and as dangerous to the Church and State; they published advertisements expressive of these sentiments, and the rejection of the Bill in the Commons produced a society styled the Church and King Club, which met for the first time to celebrate what they called the glorious decision of the House of Commons in rejecting the prayer of their Dissenting brethren." He pointed out to the Court that the publicans, probably directed by the magistrates, had thought fit to shut up their houses, open by immemorial law to all the King's subjects, to all the gentlemen and tradesmen of the town who did not belong to the Church and King Club. Mr. Walker, one of the leaders of the Society, then opened his house to the members of the Constitutional Society, at a time when they must otherwise have been compelled, by the action of the publicans, to meet in the streets.

Mr. Erskine then produced a large number of witnesses, many of them men of high reputation in Manchester; the result of their combined testimony was so strong that Mr. Law, the Attorney-General, made this observation: " I know the character of several of the gentlemen who have been examined, particularly Mr. Jones; I cannot expect one witness alone, unconfirmed, to stand against the testimony of these witnesses; I ought not to expect it."

Mr. Justice Heath. You act very properly, Mr. Law.

The jury immediately gave their verdict, not guilty.

Application was at once made for the arrest of Dunn for perjury, and this was carried out. He was tried at the autumn assizes in 1794, found guilty, and sentenced to two years' imprisonment and to be stood in the pillory.

In the present day it is impossible to imagine that any Government would be so foolish as to institute a prosecution such as this. For many generations our country has allowed the fullest freedom to all for the discussion of political matters and political differences without interference, and the *raison d'être* of the Reformation Society was clearly the advocacy of what in these days would be called ordinary progressive views. An attempt on the part of the Government to suppress such a society could result in nothing but discredit to the ruling powers. It must be remembered in considering the political situation in 1794 that Pitt, who had declared war against France the previous year, had induced Parliament to pass many repressive and reactionary measures (*e.g.*, the Traitorous Correspondence Act, the Suspension of the Habeas Corpus Act, etc.), and reform had become more impossible than ever. It was said that Frenchmen had so abused their liberty that Englishmen were deprived of theirs. During this period of political panic, so unlike our country's habit and happily of only short duration, many prosecutions for sedition and treason were undertaken, some of them successful, some of them, as in Dr. Collier's case, unsuccessful. But sanity soon returned to our politicians, and this country gradually recovered confidence in itself. Persecution for political opinions became a thing of the past for good and all.

PALMER THE POISONER

THE trial of William Palmer, a general practitioner, of Rugeley, in Staffordshire, for the murder of his friend Cook, took place in May, 1856, at the Old Bailey. So great was the feeling against him in his native county that the Government, in order to avoid the influence of this prejudice, introduced and carried rapidly through Parliament a measure (the Trial of Offences Act) by which the Court of Queen's Bench, the chief court of criminal jurisdiction, was empowered to order that certain offenders should be tried at the Central Criminal Court. The case of Palmer was, under this Act, ordered to be heard there. The experienced Lord Chief Justice (Lord Campbell) himself presided, assisted by Baron Alderson, from the Court of Exchequer, and Justice Cresswell, from the Common Pleas. The interest taken in the case was so unusual that the arrangements for the trial threw a great burden on the City of London. Considerable difficulty was experienced in finding the requisite accommodation. Twelve days were occupied with the hearing, and it is doubtful if any trial of this nature has excited more interest both among lawyers and the general public, or produced more books, articles and pamphlets, each with its own particular view of the matter.

The prisoner, who was described in the calendar as William Palmer, 31, surgeon, of a superior degree of instruction, was a short, fat man, with nothing in his expression which indicated cunning or cruelty or any hardened temperament.

There appeared for the Crown the Attorney-General, Mr. Edwin James, Q.C., Mr. Bodkin, Mr. Welsby, and

Mr. Huddlestone, whilst the prisoner was represented by Mr. Serjeant Shee, Mr. Groove, Q.C., Mr. Gray and Mr. Kenealy.

The charge against Palmer was that he had murdered by poison his intimate friend Cook on November 21st, 1855, at Rugeley, in Staffordshire. Palmer (who had received his medical education at St. Bartholomew's), though engaged in general practice, gave a good deal of his time to sport, especially horse-racing, his friend Cook also having the same proclivities. They both attended a race meeting at Shrewsbury on November 13th, and eight days later Cook died at the Talbot Arms Hotel, Rugeley, under circumstances which pointed very strongly to poison. Suspicion was aroused against Palmer, who was arrested and accused of murder.

The evidence given at this trial is worth careful examination, especially on the medical aspect of the case. It must again be pointed out that the science of toxicology had not by any means reached its present advanced state, and that our knowledge of poisons and the tests for their detection was not nearly as complete as it is at the present day.

Palmer was at the time of Cook's death, and had been for some time previously, in financial difficulties. In 1853 he was involved in various bill transactions, but by the death of his wife a year later he received £13,000 from insurance companies with which he had taken out policies on her life, and this enabled him to clear himself of his liabilities. (He was indicted for the murder of his wife, and also of his brother Walter, and true bills were found in both these cases by the Grand Jury, but as he was convicted in Cook's case, the others were dropped.) He was constantly in money difficulties and as constantly resorted to shady and dishonest means to relieve himself. He took out a policy on the life of his brother Walter for £13,000. Walter died. The company refused to pay, for suspicion was aroused that something was wrong. At the time of the Shrewsbury races Palmer was being pressed for the payment of £20,000 due on forged acceptances. He was in desperate circumstances, with ruin, disgrace, and punishment staring him in the face, which could only be averted by means of money, and, according to the allegations of the prosecution, Palmer took advantage of his friendship with Cook, who, as the result of the Shrewsbury races, had won a good deal, something like £2,000, to murder him.

From November 13th, the day of the races, till the time of his death, Cook was several times taken ill, generally with bouts of vomiting, each time after partaking of some food or drink which Palmer either gave him or prepared for him.

Palmer sent for Mr. Bamford, a doctor nearly eighty years old, telling him Cook had been taking too much to drink ; but Mr. Bamford was unable to find any evidence of this when he examined the patient. Two days later Palmer wrote to Mr. Jones, an apothecary and an intimate friend of Cook, asking him to come over, as the latter was confined to bed with a severe bilious attack combined with diarrhœa. Up to this time there is no suggestion of the administration of strychnine, but it was alleged that the various articles of food given to Cook by Palmer contained antimony. The symptoms from which Cook suffered were consistent with the administration of this poison.

On Monday, two days before the death of Cook, Palmer went to the house of Mr. Salt, a surgeon, and saw there Newton, Mr. Salt's assistant, obtaining from him 3 grains of strychnine. Mr. Bamford, who was still attending Cook, visited him on the Monday evening and brought some pills, which were left on the dressing table. Palmer called in later and sat in the room where the pills were, and could therefore have substituted poisoned pills if he wished. Palmer produced a witness to contradict this piece of evidence, but the Attorney-General in cross-examination proved this witness to be such a rogue that no credit could be attached to his testimony. In the middle of the night Cook had a severe attack of some sort. He screamed violently; his head and neck and whole body jumped and jerked. His hand was stiff, and he had great difficulty in swallowing. The next day he was much better; on the same day Palmer purchased from a local druggist 2 drachms of prussic acid, 2 drachms of Batley's solution (this contains opium), and 6 grains of strychnine. It seems he was determined to take no chances; some of the poisons must surely act. On this afternoon Mr. Jones, the apothecary and friend of Cook, arrived. Palmer, Mr. Bamford and Mr. Jones held a consultation, some pills were decided upon, and Mr. Bamford made them up. Palmer took them home to Cook (who by this time was well and comfortable, with no diarrhœa or vomiting), and urged him to take the pills. He was reluctant to do this and at first refused, but later consented. He was at once sick, and soon after was taken seriously ill. He became dreadfully convulsed and died in a few minutes. The body was twisted to the shape of a bow, and would have rested on head and heels if placed on its back. The limbs were stiff.

Shortly before Cook's death Palmer had forged the name of his friend to a cheque, and there was no doubt he appropriated considerable sums of money belonging to his dead companion. It was clear that the doctor had a double object in getting rid of Cook : he dreaded the discovery of his forgery, and he badly wanted Cook's ready money, of which there was a very considerable sum at hand, won at Shrewsbury races. Mr. Stephens, Cook's stepfather, became very suspicious, and made no secret of his belief that there had been foul play.

The chemical and medical evidence in this case is very interesting, and most important in its bearing on Palmer's guilt. The post-mortem was conducted by Dr. Harland, and there were also present Mr. Devonshire, a medical student, Mr. Newton, Dr. Salt's assistant, and Palmer himself. On what grounds he could have been allowed admittance to the autopsy it is impossible to imagine, under suspicion as he was. His behaviour both before, during and after the examination of the body aroused comment. Newton said that Palmer had recently asked what dose of strychnine would kill a dog, and was told 1 grain. He then wanted to know whether it would be found in the stomach and what would be the appearance of that organ after death. Newton told him there would be nothing special in the appearance of the stomach, and he did not think any strychnine would be found in it.

Mr. Devonshire conducted the autopsy, under the direction of Dr. Harland, and it does not seem that he exercised the care so essential in a case of this nature. The stomach was ruptured, and it was necessary to tie it up at both ends with string. It was turned inside out, and was thrown with what came from it into a jar. Whilst this was being done Palmer, who was standing behind, pushed up against the workers so much that Dr. Harland remonstrated with him. The jar, with its contents, was covered with parchment, tied down and sealed by Dr. Harland. It was then put on one side, and Dr. Harland, happening to look round in a moment, saw the jar was gone. He at once called out, "Where is the jar?" The prisoner was seen with it in his hand and making for the door. The jar was at once obtained, and it was seen that there were two slits in the parchment. After this the prisoner was very anxious to know what was to happen to it. Finding that Dr. Harland, who was a magistrate and a well-known practitioner, was about to remove it, Palmer objected on the ground that it might be tampered with and something added. However, it was taken to Mr. Freer, a surgeon of the town, and was afterwards sealed tightly. Palmer discovered that the jar was to go to London for the purpose of analysis, and that it was to be taken in a fly to the station and later sent by train to its destination. Palmer went to the post-boy and said, " I am told that they are going to take the jar with them; they have no business to take it; I do not know what they may put into it. Could you not manage to upset the fly and break the jar? I will give you ten pounds to do it." The driver indignantly refused to carry out this suggestion.

The autopsy seems to have been most laxly carried out. It is impossible to imagine anything of the kind occurring in a present-day case.

The proceedings in connection with the inquest strike one as most unusual. Palmer induced the postmaster at Rugeley to open a letter from Dr. Taylor containing the result of the analysis of the viscera, and just before the inquiry the coroner, Mr. Ward, received a present of a codfish, a barrel of oysters, a turkey and a brace of pheasants, certainly the materials for a very pleasant dinner, but hardly what one would expect an officer of the law to accept from a man who might be sent for trial on a murder charge as the result of this officer's investigation. The postmaster was sentenced to a term of imprisonment for his conduct, and Lord Campbell, at the trial at the Old Bailey, remarked in severe terms on the conduct of the coroner.

Among the belongings of Palmer was a book on medicine, with marginal notes on strychnine.

These facts prove, firstly, that Palmer had a very strong motive to get rid of Cook, for he was in urgent need of a large sum of money and would be able to obtain this if he could get rid of Cook; further, he had an additional reason for the removal, for he had forged his name and was certain of discovery if Cook lived. The facts also clearly show that Palmer had plenty of opportunities of giving poison, and that he had purchased several varieties, for which he had no legitimate use.

At the trial evidence was produced to show that Cook had died from strychnine poisoning and that antimony had been given to him, this substance being found in the body.

The medical witnesses for the prosecution, Sir Benjamin Brodie, Mr. Curling, Dr. Todd, Mr. Daniel and Mr. Solly, gave evidence that he had died of tetanus. Now tetanus at that time was a designation used for several conditions in addition to the disease now known by that name. It was divided into three classes: (1) idiopathic tetanus, or tetanus for which no cause was known; (2) traumatic tetanus, or tetanus following a wound; and (3) tetanus caused by strychnine and similar drugs. All the witnesses agreed that though the exciting causes of tetanus varied, the symptoms produced were much the same. This is not a proposition to which present-day medical science would agree. The medical question then was this: Did Cook die of tetanus ? If so, of what variety ? Mr. Curling defined tetanus as a spasmodic contraction of the muscles, and all the witnesses, whether for the Crown or the defence, said that Cook had had these spasmodic contractions, and all may therefore be said to be in agreement that tetanus (as then defined) was the cause of death. The controversy was rather as to the particular form of which he died.

Mr. Curling was asked, " Were the symptoms consistent with any form of traumatic tetanus which has ever come under your knowledge or observation ? " and his answer was " No."

Q. What distinguished them from the cases of traumatic tetanus which you have described ?

A. There was the sudden onset of the fatal symptoms. In all cases that have fallen under my notice the disease has been preceded by the milder symptoms of tetanus.

Q. Gradually progressing to their complete development and death ?

A. Yes.

He also stated that the sudden onset and very rapid

course of the spasms was not consistent with either idiopathic or traumatic tetanus.

Sir Benjamin Brodie gave evidence that although the spasmodic muscular contractions were like those of traumatic tetanus, yet the course of the symptoms was entirely different. " The symptoms of traumatic tetanus always begin, as far as I have seen, very gradually, the stiffness of the lower jaw being, I believe, the symptom first complained of : at least, so it has been in my experience ; then the contraction of the muscles of the back is always a later symptom, generally much later ; the muscles of the extremities are affected in a much less degree than those of the neck and trunk except in some cases where the injury has been in a limb and an early symptom has been a contraction of the muscles of that limb. . . . The ordinary tetanus rarely runs its course in less than two or three days, and often is protracted to a much longer period." Six other medical witnesses supported generally this testimony.

The evidence of Dr. Alfred Taylor, who was the most important of the witnesses for the prosecution, occupied nearly a whole day, and he was subjected to the most searching and repeated cross-examination. He admitted that he had not found any strychnine in the body of Cook. He said he had poisoned four rabbits with strychnine, and from two of these he had been unable to recover any strychnine. He had found antimony in the viscera sent to him from the body of Cook. Dr. Owen Rees, Lecturer on Materia Medica at Guy's Hospital, confirmed Dr. Taylor's evidence in all particulars.

The prosecution contended that the deceased was killed by strychnine ; the defence, on the other hand, contended that several of the symptoms were inconsistent with strychnine poisoning, and that all the symptoms could be explained on other grounds.

The great argument used on behalf of the prisoner was that no strychnine had been discovered by the analysis of the viscera. Dr. Taylor accounted for the failure to find the poison on the ground that the stomach had had its contents spilled, that it had been cut right open, and its inner surface found rubbing against other viscera. This made the conditions most unfavourable for detecting any poison it might have contained. The defence argued that, whilst they agreed it might have made it more hard to find any strychnine, it would not have destroyed any evidence there might be; it would merely have increased the difficulty of detection. (Mr. Justice Hawkins in his memoirs makes the astonishing misstatement that at the time of the Palmer trial there was no test for strychnine known.) Dr. Taylor argued that strychnine must be absorbed from the stomach to the blood before it could exert its characteristic effect on the nervous system, and in the event of moderate quantities only being administered, the whole of it would pass from the stomach, and therefore the test would fail. The amount in the blood or nervous system, although sufficient to produce a fatal result, would be so small as to render the test for it invalid. (This would not apply at the present day, with its ultra-refined methods of detecting the smallest quantity of this alkaloid.)

For the defence there appeared Mr. Nunneley, Mr. Herepath, Mr. Rogers, Dr. Letheby and Mr. Wrightson, and these experts all contradicted Dr. Taylor (who was then regarded as one of the leading toxicologists in the country), saying it was quite possible to detect the presence of strychnine in any body into which it had been introduced, even though the tissues examined contained the most minute quantity. Mr. Herepath claimed he could detect one fifty-thousandth part of a grain if it were unmixed with organic matter. But this evidence was not really vital to the case, for all it proved was, not that there was no strychnine on Cook's body, but that Dr. Taylor should have found it if there were any present. All Dr. Taylor attempted to prove on behalf of the Crown was that he had discovered antimony in the body, that he had not discovered strychnine, but that the clinical evidence of those who had witnessed Cook's last illness made him believe that strychnine poisoning was the cause of death. This placed the counsel for the prisoner on the horns of a dilemma. If they attacked Dr. Taylor's credit as an expert (and they did this very vigorously) for the purpose of showing that his opinion that Cook died of strychnine poisoning was unreliable, it would be difficult to belaud him as a skilful chemist and to claim that he had helped to prove the prisoner's innocence by finding no strychnine. The position was hopeless. To admit he was a skilful and credible witness was to admit the guilt of the accused; to deny Dr. Taylor's skill was to do away with the value of the evidence of their own experts. The defence therefore admitted his ability, but accused him of bad faith.

Another point raised, though in a rather feeble way, was that some of the symptoms observed were inconsistent with strychnine poisoning, but these alleged inconsistencies were all satisfactorily explained, and this position was not maintained with any vigour by prisoner's counsel. They rather attempted to show that the symptoms described were consistent with other causes than strychnine. One suggestion made was that it was a case of traumatic tetanus caused by syphilitic ulcers; but there were no syphilitic ulcers, no expert witness for the defence claimed that he thought the case was one of traumatic tetanus, and finally several doctors experienced in syphilis said they had never heard of this disease producing tetanus.

Among the many other theories propounded by the defence as to the cause of death was that of Mr. Nunneley, who suggested general convulsions, though he acknowledged that he was unable to quote any case of this condition which was not associated with loss of consciousness. Dr. McDonald, of Garnkirk, attributed the fatal result to "epileptic convulsions with tetanic complications," whatever that may be. His evidence was very difficult for the average mind to follow. He gave the most extraordinary reasons for the fit. It might have been due to sexual excitement (Cook had been ill in bed for nearly a week before his death), and he actually said in the box that sexual intercourse might produce a convulsion after an interval of a fortnight. It is evidence of this ridiculous nature which brings so much discredit on our profession in the courts. The cross-examination of these witnesses was a masterly piece of forensic work. When they left the box, it must have been with feelings of great relief for their exit and of regret that they had ever entered it.

Mr. Partridge was called to testify that the cause of death was arachnitis (inflammation of the membrane covering the spinal cord), but he willingly admitted that he did not think this was the actual cause, and when asked whether the symptoms described were consistent with strychnine poisoning, he answered, "Quite."

Perhaps the most fantastic of the many theories and of the many witnesses for the defence was seen when Dr. Richardson was sworn and declared that Cook might have died from angina pectoris, for the symptoms of this disease and of strychnine poisoning were so similar that he would have great difficulty in distinguishing them. If this were actually the measure of Dr. Richardson's medical capacities, he was certainly unfit to be on the register.

Dr. Swayne Taylor in his work on poisons has some stringent comments to make on the facility with which medical witnesses can be procured to bolster up any case.

Mr. Serjeant Shee then addressed the Court in defence of the prisoner. He argued that it would be impossible to convict his client unless it could be clearly shown that there was a very definite motive for such an act. No such motive had been proved against Palmer. Counsel laid very great stress on the fact that strychnine had not been found in the viscera of the murdered man. If he had died from this poison, he had died within two hours of the administration of a very strong dose. He died within twenty minutes of the convulsions seen after the administration of this dose, and there was not the least reason to suppose that between the taking of the dose of poison, if any had been taken, and the paroxysm in which he died, there had been any dilution of it in the stomach or any loss of it by vomiting. Never were there circumstances more favourable for the detection of a poison, unless there was nothing at all in the science of toxicology. There was not the slightest doubt that no strychnine was found. Whatever might be thought of Dr. Taylor, of his judgment, and of his discretion, there was no doubt whatever that he was a skilful chemist. He and Dr. Rees had done everything possible to detect the presence of strychnine, but, in spite of their skill, they had failed.

"I tell you exactly what the case for the defence will be as to the point that strychnine was not found in Mr. Cook's body. Let me state it as fairly as I can. The gentlemen who have come to the conclusion that strychnine may have been there, though they did not find it, have arrived at that conclusion by experiments of a very partial kind indeed. They contend that the poison of strychnia is of that nature that when once it has done its fatal work and become absorbed into the system it ceases to be the thing which it was when it was taken into the system: it becomes decomposed, its elements separated from each other, and therefore no longer capable of responding to the tests which according to them would certainly detect the presence of undecomposed strychnine; that is their case. They account for the fact that it was not found, and for their still retaining the belief that it destroyed Mr. Cook, by that hypothesis. Now it is only an hypothesis; there is no foundation for it in experiment; it is not supported by the evidence of any eminent toxicologist but themselves; Dr. Taylor does not propound that theory in his book, and when we recollect that his knowledge on the matter consists— good humane man—in having poisoned five rabbits twenty-five years ago and five since this question of the guilt or innocence of Palmer arose, his opinion, I think, unsupported by the opinion of others, cannot have much weight with you." (Mr. Serjeant Shee, who, for the sake of making a small point against Dr. Taylor, aimed this gibe at him as regards his cruelty, at the end of his address, offered to prove one of his contentions by having " some morning before the Court sits a reasonable number of animals brought into one of the yards of the building, so that the jury should see them die by strychnia and form an opinion for themselves." This was of course refused by Lord Campbell.) Counsel then intimated that he would call many medical men of the highest repute, who would state their utter renunciation of Dr. Taylor's theory. This evidence would satisfy them that the only possible conclusion at which they could arrive was that, as no strychnine had been found in Cook's body, there never had been any there to find.

Counsel then referred to the fact that the Prince of Wales Insurance Company, in which Walter Palmer, brother of the prisoner, was insured, had refused to pay over the insurance money. Just before the death of Cook prisoner knew that he was the object of suspicion as regards this matter, but he acted as if he thought it was the most unfounded and unwarrantable suspicion, putting the policy in the hands of a lawyer to enforce payment. The company met this by insinuations and inquiries which were of a nature to destroy the character of prisoner, and to bring around his head suspicion of another murder. Now, if anything happened to Cook as the result of foul play, Palmer had not the slightest chance of getting the £13,000 insurance money from the company, and this £13,000 was the only means Palmer had of extricating himself from his financial difficulties.

Mr. Shee again referred to the evidence of Dr. Taylor. At the inquest he had said that, as he had found antimony in Cook's body, this poison might have been the cause of death. Then, when he had heard the evidence of some of the other witnesses, he had had the incredible imprudence to state on oath before the jury that he believed the pills given to Cook might have contained strychnine, and that Cook might have been poisoned by it. This opinion, once delivered, was irrevocable. By it Dr. Taylor's reputation was staked against Palmer's life.

The reply of the Attorney-General was a very able analysis of the evidence, and especially of the most important part of that evidence, that given by the medical men. He remarked that it had been suggested that Cook died from idiopathic tetanus. Idiopathic tetanus proceeding from what? It was said that Cook was a delicate man with a weak chest and a bad throat, and subject to excitement, and that, putting all these things together, if he took cold he might get idiopathic tetanus. "I cannot help saying that it seems to me that it is a scandal upon a learned, a distinguished and a liberal profession that men should come forward and put forward such speculations as these, perverting the facts and drawing from them sophistical and unwarranted conclusions, with the view of deceiving a jury. I have the greatest respect for science—no man can have more—but I cannot repress my indignation and abhorrence when I see it thus perverted and prostituted to the purposes of a particular cause in a court of justice. . . . Gentlemen, I venture upon the evidence to assert boldly that the cases of idiopathic tetanus and traumatic or what I may call natural tetanus are marked by clear and distinct characteristics, distinguishing them from tetanus produced by strychnine; and I say that the tetanus which accompanied Mr. Cook's death is not referable to either of those forms of tetanus.

You have upon that point the evidence of witnesses of the highest competency and of the most unquestionable integrity; and upon their evidence I am quite satisfied you can come to no other conclusion but that this was not a case either of idiopathic or traumatic tetanus." The Attorney-General then referred to the attempts to account for the symptoms on other grounds than tetanus. "There was first the theory of general convulsions. Mr. Nunneley was asked whether he had ever seen a case in which death arising from general convulsions had not ended in the unconsciousness of the patient before death. His reply was No, but he had read of one in a book. He quoted Dr. Copland, a very eminent medical man, but was Dr. Copland produced as a witness? No. Why? Because it is so much easier to call together from the east and from the west practitioners of more or less obscurity instead of men of authority.

"Then there was the suggestion that Cook died from inflammation of the membranes of the spinal cord. Mr. Partridge," whom the Attorney-General referred to as "not only a man of great eminence, but a man of the highest honour and the most perfect veracity;" (in forensic language this means that the evidence given by Mr. Partridge was of assistance to the Attorney-General's case)—"Mr. Partridge was called to prove Cook died of arachnitis. When his attention was called to the symptoms of Cook, he candidly admitted that he was not prepared to assert that arachnitis was the cause of death."

He next referred to the gentleman who came all the way from Scotland to inform them that Cook died of epilepsy, who when asked if he had ever known a case of epilepsy which had caused the death of a patient without loss of consciousness replied that he never had, but he had read in a book of such a case. "Is there anything to make you think that this was epilepsy?" "Well, it may have been epilepsy, because I do not know what else to ascribe it to." All this evidence, remarked the Attorney-

General, was most speculative and without any shadow of foundation.

"Nevertheless, gentlemen, on the other hand, the case is not without its difficulties; and I will not shrink from the discussion of them nor from the candid recognition of those difficulties so far as in reality they exist. Strychnia was not found in this body, and we have it, no doubt, upon strong evidence, that in a variety of experiments which have been tried upon the bodies of animals killed by strychnia, strychnia has been detected by tests which science places at the disposition of scientific men. If strychnia had been found, of course there would have been no difficulty, and we should have had none of the ingenious theories which gentlemen from a variety of parts have been brought forward to propound in the court. The question for your consideration is, whether the absence of its detection leads conclusively to the view that this death could not have been caused by the administration of that poison. Now, in the first place, under what circumstances was the examination made of which Dr. Taylor and Dr. Rees have spoken? They tell you that when the stomach of this man was brought to them for the purpose of analysis it was presented to them under the most unfavourable circumstances. They say that its contents had been lost and that they had no opportunity of experiment upon them. It is very true that those who put up the jar make a statement somewhat different. They say that the contents of the stomach were emptied into the jar, but there appears, at all events (I will put it no higher than accident) by accident, to have been some spilling of the contents; and there is, I think, the clearest and most undeniable evidence of very considerable bungling in the way in which the stomach was cut and the way in which it was emptied in the jar. It was cut from end to end, says Dr. Taylor. It was tied up at both ends. It had been turned inside out into the contents of the intestines, and lay there in a mass of feculent matter and was therefore in a condition the most unsatisfactory for analysis and experiment. It was very true that the witnesses upon the other side—Mr. Nunneley, Mr. Herepath, and Dr. Letheby—say that, no matter how contaminated or how mixed with impurities, they would have been able to ascertain the presence of strychnine in the stomach, if strychnia ever had been there. I own I should have more confidence in the testimony of these witnesses if their partiality and partisanship had not been so much marked as they are. I should have more confidence in Mr. Herepath if he had not been constrained to admit to me a fact which had come to my knowledge, that he has again and again asserted that this case was a case of poisoning by strychnine, but that Dr. Taylor had not known how to find it out ; he admits that this is a statement he has made again and again."

Mr. Serjeant Shee. It was in the newspapers, he said.

The Attorney-General. He did not venture to say that the newspaper statement in any way differed from the fact which he admitted in this court. I have seen this gentleman not merely contenting himself with coming forward, when called upon for the purpose of justice, to state that which he knew as a matter of science or experiment, but I have seen him mixing himself up as a thoroughgoing partisan in this case, advising my learned friend, suggesting question upon question, and that on behalf of a man whom he has again and again asserted he believed to be a poisoner by strychnine.

On the eleventh day of the trial the Lord Chief Justice commenced his summing up, which occupied many hours. After a review of the whole of the evidence, he concluded as follows : " Gentlemen, the case is now in your hands; and, unless upon the part of the prosecution a clear conviction has been brought to your minds of the guilt of the prisoner, it is your duty to acquit him. You are not to proceed even upon a strong suspicion : there must be the strongest conviction in your minds that he was guilty of the offence ; and if there be any reasonable doubt remaining in your mind, you will give him the benefit of that doubt ; but if you come to a clear conviction that he was guilty, you will not be deterred from doing your duty by any considerations such as have been suggested to you. You will remember the oath which you have taken, and you will act accordingly. Gentlemen, I have performed my task ; you have now to discharge yours, and may God direct you to a right finding."

During the summing up the Judge made this comment on the medical evidence produced by the defence : " With regard to the witnesses on the part of the prisoner, there were gentlemen whose object was to procure an acquittal for the prisoner. It is in my opinion indispensable to the administration of justice that a witness should not be turned into an advocate nor an advocate into a witness."

The result of the trial could never for a moment have been in doubt. The jury convicted Palmer of the murder. The Lord Chief Justice said that his two colleagues and himself had no doubt whatever that the verdict was a right one. " The case is attended with such circumstances of aggravation that I do not dare to touch upon them. Whether it is the first and only offence which you have committed is certainly known only to God and your own conscience. It is seldom that such a familiarity with the means of death should be shown without long experience, but for this offence of which you have been found guilty your life is forfeited. You must prepare to die ; and I trust that, as you can expect no mercy in this world, you will by repentance of your crimes seek to obtain mercy from Almighty God. The Act of Parliament under which you have been tried and under which you have been brought to the bar of this Court at your own request gives leave to the Court that the sentence under such circumstances should be executed either within the jurisdiction of the Central Criminal Court or in the county where the offence was committed. We think that for the sake of example the sentence ought to be executed in the county of Stafford."

Sir James Stephen, who was one of our most celebrated criminal lawyers and who was present throughout the greater part of the case, makes some very interesting comments on the conduct of the trial of Palmer :—

"It is impossible to give an adequate idea of the manner in which it exhibited in its very best and strongest light the good side of English criminal procedure. No more horrible villain than Palmer ever stood in the dock. The prejudice against him was so strong that it was considered necessary to pass an Act of Parliament to authorise his trial in London. He was actually indicted for the murder of his wife and for that of his brother, and it was commonly reported at the time that he had murdered many other persons. . . . No one of these matters was introduced or referred to except so far as it bore upon the case of Cook. . . . A study of the case will show, first, that evidence could not be more condensed, more complete, more closely directed to the very point at issue ; secondly, that the subjection of all witnesses, and especially of all skilled witnesses, to the most rigorous cross-examination is absolutely essential to the trustworthiness of their evidence. The closeness and the skill with which the various witnesses, especially those for the defence, were cross-examined and compelled to admit that they could not really distinguish the symptoms of Cook from those of poisoning by strychnine was such an illustration of the efficiency of cross-examination as is rarely afforded. The defence was by far the least impressive part of the trial, but that was mainly because there was in reality nothing to say. It was impossible to suggest any innocent explanation of Palmer's conduct. It was proved to demonstration that he was in dire need of money in order to avoid a prosecution for forgery, that he had robbed his friend of all he had by a series of devices which he must instantly have discovered if he had lived, that he had provided himself with the means of committing the murder just before Cook's death, and that he could neither produce the poison he had bought nor suggest any innocent reason for buying it. There must have been some mystery in the case which was never discovered. Palmer, at and before his execution, was repeatedly pressed to say whether he was guilty or not, and was told that every one would believe him to admit his guilt if he did not emphatically deny it. He would only say Cook was not poisoned with strychnine, and I have reason to know he was anxious that Dr. Herepath should examine the body for strychnine, though aware that he said he could detect the fifty-thousandth part of a grain. He may have discovered some way of administering it which would render discovery impossible, but it is difficult to doubt that he used it, for if not, why did he buy it ? "

Sir Henry Hawkins, in his reminiscences, narrates the following interesting story in connection with the Palmer trial. Sir Henry was travelling from London to Norwich shortly after the execution of Palmer and overheard a conversation between two fellow-travellers who were evidently bookmakers returning from the races. One of the men, named Kirby, a rough, good-natured sort of fellow, began talking on the almost universal subject, the recent murder.

" Bill," said Kirby, " I knowed that there Palmer. Did you ? "

" No," said Bill, " don't know as ever I did."

" Well, I had dealings with him, and a nice sort of fellow he was, only nobody never could get any money from him." After a pause he continued : " Well, he owed me a matter of five-and-twenty pound, and I wrote, I suppose, a dozen letters to him, perhaps more ; but it was no good, so at last I sent him a stinger. I knowed what to say to him, for I had 'eeard a bit from the ostler at the public-house where I stopped. He told me as Palmer persuaded him to let him insure his life, which the fool did, and next time he see Palmer the doctor gave him a drink that nearly made old Sam kick the bucket there and then. After I sent the letter Palmer asked me to come over one day, and he'd settle with me. So over I goes, and when I gets to his house was asked into a little room, and left there by myself for a goodish while. On the table was a decanter of sherry wine and a glass. I was putty thirsty, of course, but I didn't touch the wine. Howsomever, there it was to help myself if I'd a mind to. Presently in comes the doctor with a pleasant smile, a friendly shake of the hand, and a ' Very glad to see you, Kirby. How are you getting on, Kirby? A glass o' sherry, Kirby? It will do you good after your walk."

" 'I shall be glad to have one, Mr. Palmer, if you'll join me,' I ses, for a thought come to me about Sam the ostler.

" 'No,' he says, 'thank 'ee, Kirby I never drink sherry.'

" 'No more don't I, Mr. Palmer,' I ses; and then I asked him if it was agreeable to pay what he owed.

" 'No,' says he, ' Kirby, it is not quite agreeable at present, but are you quite sure you won't take a glass of sherry, Kirby?'

" 'Quite, sir,' I says, ' thank 'ee all the same. I ain't no sherry-drinker, Mr. Palmer.'

" 'What will you take?' says he. ' You must have something.'

" 'No, sir, thank 'ee. My little account's all I want.'

" 'Well, if you won't take anything,' he says, ' you may as well have a look round my little farm. I've got some nice little pigs to show you.'

" Well, when we got to the sty there was as nice a farrer as you could see.

" ' I'll tell you what it is, Kirby,' says he: ' you've been very good letting that little account of ours stand over, and I'll make you a present of one of these sucking-pigs, and my cook shall send him over all ready for roasting.'

"' No, thank 'ee, sir,' I ses again ; ' I ain't come for no pigs.' I worn't goin' to have his damned sherry and poisoned pig."

Sir Henry firmly believed that Palmer meant to get rid of Kirby as he had got rid of his other victims. Palmer talked freely about his case whilst waiting execution, and said that all through the trial he expected an acquittal, and even after the Judge's terrible summing up hope did not desert him. "But," he added, "when the jury returned into court, and I saw the cocked-up nose of the perky little foreman, I knew it was gooser with me."

Major Talford, the governor of the gaol where Palmer was hanged, tells how on the morning of the execution the path from the condemned cell to the gallows being wet and muddy, Palmer minced along like a delicate school-girl, picking his way and avoiding the puddles. He was particularly anxious not to get his feet wet.

During the trial, whilst Lord Chief Justice Campbell was examining an expert doctor, so as to test his evidence, which was in favour of Palmer, the prisoner wrote on a slip of paper, which he handed down to his junior counsel, Mr. John Gray, these words : " I should like to give just such a dose to that old devil," meaning Campbell.

On the morning of the execution the gaol was surrounded by thousands of eager spectators, many of whom had taken up their stations the preceding evening, and had patiently endured the discomforts of a dark and rainy night. The wretched man had slept his last sleep quietly, and when in the morning the chaplain had entered his cell he declared himself quite prepared. He was asked by the sheriff whether he acknowledged the justice of his sentence. " No, sir, I do not ; I go to the scaffold a murdered man."

The chaplain of the gaol, the Rev. Mr. Goodacre,

PALMER THE POISONER

relates that Palmer, when he had given up hope of any reprieve, said he had not poisoned Cook by strychnia, and when further exhorted to confess openly he replied, "If it is necessary to confess this murder, I ought to confess the others; I mean my wife and brother." When the chaplain specifically asked him to definitely confess, Palmer made no reply.

Some twenty years after the murder Palmer's mother, who was a woman of low character, visited Rugeley, and when asked if the notorious poisoner were her son, at once acknowledged she was Mrs. Palmer. "I had seven children, and my saintly Bill was the best of the lot, and they hanged him."

Dr. Alfred Swayne Taylor, who was at this time recognised as the leading expert on toxicology, made some severe strictures on medical witnesses who, to use his phrase, "trade in evidence," strictures which, I am bound to confess, would be equally applicable to-day:—

"That the prisoner was guilty of the foul crime of murdering his friend no one who views the whole case apart from prejudice can entertain a reasonable doubt. A distinguished German writer, who has commented on this trial, expresses his astonishment that any professional men could be found in England who could stand forward and publicly state on oath that the symptoms under which Cook died might be explained by any form of nervous disease, epilepsy or angina pectoris. It argues but little for the knowledge or moral feelings of medical witnesses and must shake the confidence of the public, as it has already done to a great extent, in the trustworthiness of medical opinions. Such must be the result when scientific witnesses accept briefs for a defence; when they go into a witness-box believing one thing and endeavour to lead a jury by their testimony to believe another; when they make themselves advocates and deal in scientific subtleties, instead of keeping to the plain truth. Such men should be marked by the public, and their efforts at endeavouring to confer impunity on the foulest crimes and to procure the acquittal of the most atrocious criminals should be duly noted. The chemical defenders of the culprit Tawell on the ' apple-pip ' theory were in the foremost rank to defend the culprit Palmer. Fortunately for society, their efforts did not prove successful in either case." (Tawell was charged with the murder of a woman by means of prussic acid. Dr. Letheby gave evidence for the prisoner, and said that the odour in the stomach might be caused by apple pips, and counsel gravely put this fantastic suggestion forward. Serjeant Ballantine comments on this, and remarks that the opinion of professional witnesses should be listened to with respect, but adopted with great caution. Can one wonder ?)

THE RESURRECTION MEN

BEFORE the passing of the Anatomy Act in 1832 it was very difficult to procure dead bodies in a legitimate manner, for the purpose of dissection and the teaching of anatomy. A regular trade, carried on by men who desecrated graveyards and were known as "resurrection men," arose. When Hunter, the celebrated anatomist, was at the height of his practice, he had an anatomical theatre behind his house in Windmill Street, where he demonstrated on "resurrected" bodies to his pupils. So many stolen subjects were brought here, and so great was the outcry against the practice, that on more than one occasion mobs of infuriated people endeavoured to pull the house down. Body-stealing was, of course, illegal, but the price obtained for the corpses was sufficiently high to induce the "resurrection men" to continue their abominable trade. As a matter of fact, no very serious effort was made to stop the traffic, for it was recognised that a supply of subjects was absolutely necessary if surgeons were to continue to be properly trained. A monthly paper in its issue for March, 1776, says, "The remains of more than twenty dead bodies were discovered in a shed in Tottenham Court Road, supposed to have been deposited there by traders to the surgeons, of whom there is one, it is said, in the Borough, who makes an open profession of dealing in dead bodies, and is well known by the name of 'The Resurrectionist.'"

An incident which occurred in December, 1777, led to the arrest of two men for body-snatching, but although a very great public outcry arose over this affair, it was not till some thirty-five years later, mainly as the result of the revelations of the Burke and Hare trial, that the

Anatomy Act was passed. The two men arrested for body-stealing were named Holmes and Williams. Holmes was a grave-digger at St. George's, Bloomsbury, and Williams was his assistant. They made an attempt to steal the body of a Mrs. Sainsbury, who had been buried in the churchyard, but they were detected in the act before they had secured the corpse. The husband, as an example to evildoers of this nature, determined to prosecute, hateful as it was to his feelings. The grave-digger and his assistant were convicted on the clearest evidence and were each sentenced to six months' imprisonment, and to be whipped twice on their bare backs from Holborn to St. Giles's, a distance of half a mile. This sentence was duly carried out, amidst crowds of approving spectators.

But this horrible business of body-snatching was by no means the worst evil caused by the lack of sufficient subjects for the teaching of anatomy. There is no doubt that a very large number of people were deliberately murdered for the price for which their bodies could be sold. The notorious Burke and Hare case, which is perhaps one of the most cold-blooded of crimes possible to imagine, is an example of this. The scene of the atrocious deeds of these two men was Edinburgh, and the date was the year 1828. At this time the city authorities became alarmed at the frequent disappearance of members of the poorer classes, such as tramps, Irish haymakers, beggars, people of deficient intellect, all in the class who might be supposed to inhabit the poorest quarters of the town, and concerning whom there was very little prospect of inquiries being instituted.

The actual discovery of the origin of these wholesale murders was due to the disappearance of an old Irish beggar woman, named Mary Campbell. She had been seen for some time in the same neighbourhood, and then was suddenly missed. Unlike the many others who had vanished, she happened to have friends who insisted on the police making inquiries as to her fate. It was suggested that her body might be found in one of the anatomy rooms of the Edinburgh medical schools, and a search of these places led to the discovery of her remains in the dissecting room of Dr. Knox, one of the many well-known anatomists of the town. Investigations were conducted, and a thorough examination of the body was carried out. The doctors had no doubt that death was due to suffocation. Murder had been committed, and the body disposed of to the school. The investigation was then proceeded with for the purpose of discovering the individual from whom the body had been bought. It must be noted that, as all this occurred before the passing of the first Anatomy Act, there was no method authorised by law for the provision of subjects for dissection, except on the occasions on which a criminal was executed, and his body handed over to the surgeons for "anatomising." Beyond this there was no legal means of obtaining bodies. Therefore the supply so essential for the purpose of instruction of medical students (this especially was necessary in Edinburgh, then, as now, so noted for its medical schools) was very uncertain. The porters who procured the bodies were very lax in their inquiries as to the sources of the subjects offered to them, and accepted any explanation, however ridiculous, from those who sold such subjects. It was known that, as a rule, the bodies had been dug up from the graveyards; but no idea of murder entered the minds of the majority of those concerned. During the Napoleonic war the study of anatomy had been much neglected (for students were rushed through their course in order to get them as soon as possible into the army), and therefore not a great quantity of bodies was required, but immediately the war was over the normal course of study was resumed, and large numbers of students joined the hospitals. This resulted in a large demand for subjects. The price paid had been four guineas for every body, but as the demand increased the price was raised, for the difficulty of procuring corpses and the risk of detection and punishment increased, and consequently six, eight and even sixteen guineas became the usual amount demanded.

All sorts of devices were resorted to in order to procure subjects. The unclaimed bodies of people dying in workhouses and hospitals were readily given up by the authorities to bogus relatives, for the parish thus avoided the expense of the burial. Undertakers' assistants actually buried empty coffins, and sold the bodies they should have placed in graves. In short, every device for obtaining a supply of bodies for sale was resorted to by these unscrupulous criminals. Even thus the demand could not be satisfied, and there is no doubt that the very high prices given, the easy acceptance of any story as to how the bodies had been obtained, the infrequency of detection, led directly to the terrible series of crimes of which those of Burke and Hare were perhaps the worst examples.

Paterson, the porter at Dr. Knox's school, was able to tell the police that he had bought this body, that of Mary Campbell, and many others, from two men named Burke and Hare. On October 31st they had come to the dissecting room and told him they had at their house a subject for the doctor. Paterson had often been to their house in Tanner's Close, and when he went there on this occasion he saw a heap of straw under the table, and was told the body was there. There were two women present who went under the names of the wives of Burke and Hare. The body was paid for and delivered at the dissecting room that night, packed in a tea-chest. When Paterson looked at the body it was clear to him that it had never been buried.

He saw Burke again in one of Dr. Knox's rooms in Surgeons' Square, along with Hare, Mr. Jones (who was Dr. Knox's assistant), and the doctor himself. He heard either Burke or Hare say that they had a dead body, and witness was instructed by Dr. Knox to receive any package which they might bring. Witness and Mr. Jones were present when Burke and Hare arrived with an old tea-chest. It was put in a cellar, and Dr. Knox was informed of its arrival. He gave witness £5 to divide among them all. The balance was to be paid later after Dr. Knox had inspected the body. On Sunday the police called, and the package was handed over to them. Witness helped in opening the chest. It contained the body of an elderly female, which had no appearance of having been buried. He had seen both Burke and Hare before and knew that the doctor had dealings with them for the procuring of dead bodies. They often brought subjects which he thought had never been buried. He had heard of bodies being brought to Dr. Knox by those anxious to save the expense of a funeral.

The police looked about for any further evidence to determine the manner in which the poor creature had come by her death. A Mr. and Mrs. Grey, a very poverty-stricken couple, who were passing through Edinburgh, told the authorities that they had engaged rooms at Burke's and had seen Mary Campbell go into the house one evening. She appeared to be drunk. The next morning she had disappeared. They were told by Mrs. Burke that Campbell had been rude and had been turned out of the house. They did not somehow believe this, and seeing marks of blood under the table in the kitchen and later the body of Mrs. Campbell, they became terrified, rushed out of the house and on the next day informed the police.

The house of Burke, in Tanner's Close, was well fitted for the purpose to which it had been put. Like so many of the old closes of the town, many of which exist at the present day, this passage was narrow and dark. It contained only one house, and that at the end of the lane. The place had only two rooms, and was situated in a very dark corner. One of the rooms was occupied by Burke and the woman who passed as his wife; the other he let to lodgers. Burke's own living room contained nothing but a wretched bed and a table; the second room was unfurnished. Burke (who nominally was a shoemaker), Hare, and the two reputed wives were all at the house when the police arrived, and were at once arrested. In the rooms were found a large number of blood-stained garments.

The public outcry caused by these revelations was enormous. The medical men of the town, who were looked upon as indirectly responsible for the crimes, were included with the four prisoners in the indignation of the people. Attempts were made to wreck the dissecting rooms, and measures of precaution had to be taken to guard them from injury. There can be no doubt in the mind of any impartial observer that a great portion of this blame was deserved by the doctors, for it is impossible to imagine that they could have been ignorant of the fact that the large number of bodies supplied to them must have been obtained by improper means. No one has suggested that then or at any time the medical profession had the least suspicion that these dreadful murders were being committed in order to supply them with subjects, but that they showed gross carelessness in the matter cannot be denied. Had they exercised only ordinary precautions, these crimes could never have been committed.

The prisoners appeared before the magistrates in Edinburgh, and the four were committed for trial. After the committal and before the trial Hare offered to turn King's evidence provided he and his wife were guaranteed against any proceedings. The magistrates were most loth to allow Hare to escape his just punishment, and it was only after long and frequent consultations of the legal authorities that it was decided to accept the offer. It was thought there was just a possibility that there might be a failure to bring home the guilt of the worst of the band, namely, Burke, without the evidence of Hare, and rather than risk this the offer of Hare was accepted. He then made a statement to the authorities which enabled them to procure conclusive evidence of Burke's guilt.

THE RESURRECTION MEN 265

The trial of this man and his paramour took place on December 23rd, 1829, before the High Court of Justiciary at Edinburgh. The prisoners were accused of several murders, but, on the ground that the evidence of another crime during a trial for a particular murder would prejudice the jury against the prisoners, it was decided to deal only with that of Mary Campbell. This was a care for the criminals which they little deserved.

Indictments a hundred years ago were far more detailed than they are nowadays. The charge against Burke in connection with this particular murder runs thus: " Further, on Friday, the 31st day of October, 1828, or on one or other of the days of that month, or of September immediately preceding, or of November immediately following, within the house then or lately occupied by you the said William Burke, situated in that street of Portsburgh, or Western Portsburgh, in or near Edinburgh, which runs from the Grassmarket of Edinburgh to Main Point, in or near Edinburgh, and on the north side of the said street, and having an access thereto by a trance or passage entering from the street last above libelled, and having also an entrance from a court or back court on the north thereof, the name of which is to the prosecutor unknown, you the said William Burke and Helen M'Dougal did both and each or one or other of you wickedly and feloniously place or lay your bodies or persons or part thereof or the body or person or part thereof of one or other of you over or upon the person or body and face of Madgy, or Margery, or Mary M'Gonegal, or Duffie, or Campbell, or Docherty, then or lately residing in the house of Roderick Stewart or Stuart, then and now or lately labourer and then and now or lately residing in the Pleasance in or near Edinburgh, when she the said Madge, or Margery, or Mary M'Gonegal, or Duffie, or Campbell, or Docherty was lying on the ground, and did by the pressure thereof, and by covering her mouth and the rest of her face with your bodies or persons or the body or person of one or other of you, and by grasping her by the throat, and keeping her mouth and nostrils shut, with your hands, and thereby, or in some other way to the prosecutor unknown, preventing her from breathing, suffocate or strangle her ; and the said Madge, or Margery, or Mary M'Gonegal, or Duffie, or Campbell, or Docherty was thus by the said means, or part thereof, or by some other means or violence, the particulars of which are to the prosecutor unknown, wickedly bereaved of life and murdered by you the said William Burke and you the said Helen M'Dougal or one or either of you ; and this you both and each or one or other of you did with the wicked aforethought intent of disposing of the body of the said Madge, or Margery, or Mary M'Gonegal, or Duffie, or Campbell, or Docherty, when so murdered, to a physician or surgeon, or to some person in the employment of a physician or surgeon, as a subject for dissection, or with some other wicked and felonious intent or purpose to the prosecutor unknown : And you the said William Burke, having been taken before George Tait, Esq., Sheriff substitute of the shire of Edinburgh, you did, in his presence at Edinburgh, emit and subscribe five several declarations," and so on, the whole indictment containing nearly a thousand words. To the non-legal mind, which fails to see why a lawyer must use ten words when one would do very well, it appears that twenty or thirty words could have made very plain the particular charge against Burke.

A man named Noble, a grocer's assistant, proved that on October 31st Burke came to his shop to make some purchases, and whilst he was there Mrs. Campbell entered and asked for some assistance. She said she had come to Edinburgh to look for her son, but had not been able to find him. She was quite destitute. Burke told her he would give her a lodging for the night. The next day Burke called again at the shop and bought an old tea-chest.

Mrs. Black, a lodger at Burke's, said she saw Mrs. Campbell sitting in the room on the night in question. Later she noticed that Mrs. Campbell was drunk, and between ten and eleven at night she heard the sounds of fighting and screaming. In the morning she was told that Mrs. Campbell had been turned out of the house on account of her familiarity with Burke. This evidence was corroborated by several witnesses.

Then Hare, the accomplice, was called. Lord Meadowbank, the Judge who presided at the trial, earnestly besought Hare to speak the truth, and Hare, who was a repulsive-looking ruffian, said he meant to do so, but he was not going to say anything bearing on the murders, except in this particular case of, as he called it, the "old woman."

Hare said he was a native of Ireland and had lived in Scotland about twelve years. He had known Burke for twelve months and lived close by him. Hare was in a public-house in the West Port on the morning of October 31st, when Burke came in, and they had a drink. Hare was asked by Burke to go to his house to see the " shot " he had got to take to the doctor's. Burke said he had taken an old woman off the street and wished the witness to go and see her and see what they were doing. He went to Burke's house, and there he saw Mrs. Campbell doing some washing. In the evening he went to Tanner's Close, and at that time he had no idea that any harm was to be done to the old woman that night. The two wives were present. Burke started a quarrel with him, and they began to fight. He was sure this was done deliberately with the idea of dragging Mrs. Campbell in and so making an excuse to murder her. She grew alarmed and attempted to get out of the house, but was pulled back. Witness pushed her over on the floor intentionally. She got up, but was so drunk that she could not regain her feet. Burke then stood astride her, and laid himself down on her. She gave a cry and moaned a little and

Burke placed his hand over her nose and mouth and remained so for at least ten minutes, not speaking a word. When he got up she was quite dead. Hare all this time was sitting on a chair, doing nothing. When he saw the woman was dead he stripped the body of its clothing, put it in a corner, doubled up, and covered it with straw. The women had run out of the room whilst all this was going on, but came back when it was all over. Burke then went out. The women asked no questions, nor did they make any remarks. When Burke returned he brought with him Paterson, the porter from the dissecting room, who looked at the body. He said it would do well enough, and they were to get a box to put it in to carry to his master's house. In the course of the next day Burke called on him and asked him to help in getting a box. They procured a chest and then forced the body of Mrs. Campbell into it. A porter named M'Culloch assisted them, and on seeing some of the hair of the woman hanging out remarked that it would be a fine thing to have that seen. They delivered the chest to Paterson; it was placed in a cellar, and they then went to see Dr. Knox, who paid Burke and himself £2 7s. 6d. each.

This callous brute was then cross-examined by Mr. Cockburn on behalf of the prisoners. He acknowledged he had frequently been concerned in supplying medical schools with subjects, but had never been a "resurrectionist." He refused to say whether he had taken part in any other murders, or whether he had been present at any other murder in the month of October.

After the Judge had addressed them the jury retired to consider their verdict; Burke was found guilty, but, contrary to every one's expectations, the finding on his paramour was the Scotch one of "Not proven."

There is very little doubt that Burke and his gang had been responsible for thirty or forty murders. After his conviction he became quite talkative. He did not deny that the statements of Hare were accurate, and he acknowledged that he had supplied large numbers of bodies to the surgeons—bodies which he had not dug up, and which consequently were obtained by murder. There was no reason why he should have accused himself of such things unless they were true, and many points corroborated his statement. He lived in a lonely place, dark and difficult of access; there were found in this place a large number of articles of clothing, many of them blood-stained; there had disappeared in Edinburgh many people, all of the class of more or less unfortunates, of whom no inquiry was likely to be made; all these facts were strongly in favour of the truth of Burke's tale.

The state of affairs existing in Edinburgh at this time is well illustrated by the following anecdote, related by Pelham in his "Chronicles of Crime." About six months before the murder of Mrs. Campbell the body of a female was offered by a gang of men (probably Burke and his friends) to the assistant of one of the teachers of anatomy. This man did not know the men who offered the body, but as a subject was badly needed, he said he would take it if, after he had examined the body, it seemed to be a suitable one. He inquired when they would bring the corpse. To this they replied that they had it now, and would bring it round about ten o'clock that night. At that time they brought the body in a sack, and when it was taken out it proved to be that of a female, a woman of the town, fully clothed and with shoes and stockings on. The assistant was startled, and proceeded to examine the body, when, to his astonishment, he found a large depressed fracture of the skull. He at once exclaimed, "You villains, where and how did you get this body?" to which one of them replied with indifference that it was the body of a woman who had been "popped" in a row in Halkerston's Wynd, and that, if the assistant did not choose to take it, they could easily dispose of it elsewhere. He asked them to wait whilst he saw the doctor, meaning to have them detained, but on this they packed up the body and made off.

The first of the many murders of which Burke was guilty, or rather the first which can with more or less certainty be traced to him, is that of a girl named Paterson, about eighteen years old. This girl, with one of her friends, Janet Brown, had been released from Canongate Police Station early in the morning, and from here they went to a house to get some drink, and were met by Burke. Burke gave them some spirits and then persuaded the two girls to go with him to the house of his brother in the Canongate. After they had been in the house some time Burke and his wife began to quarrel and fight, which was their usual procedure when they were about to commit one of their murders. Hare appeared in the middle of the uproar, and Janet Brown, now very much frightened, wanted to leave and take her friend with her. Paterson was lying asleep on the bed, in a more or less drunken state, and was still there when Janet left the house. She came back for her friend some twenty minutes later, and was told she had left. In the afternoon Janet Brown came back again and once more was told that her friend was not there. That afternoon the body of the girl Paterson was sold to the anatomists for £8. So fresh was the body—rigor mortis had not begun to set in—that suspicion was aroused. Burke, always ready with a plausible excuse, said he had bought the body at the house where the girl had died.

But still more atrocious even than this was the murder of a poor idiot, named Wilson. He was quite harmless and was of such a kind-hearted nature that he was generally loved. Accident unhappily threw him into contact with Burke's gang of ruffians. He was met by Burke early one morning in October, 1828, wandering about in his usual aimless manner in the Grassmarket. Burke managed to persuade him to go to the house of Hare, where they gave him drink, which sent him to sleep.

THE RESURRECTION MEN 271

Burke anxiously watching for his opportunity of killing the poor creature, said to Hare, "Shall I do it now?" to which Hare replied, "He is too strong for you yet; you had better let him alone for a while." Both Burke and Hare were afraid of the physical strength which they knew their victim to possess, so they waited a little while, but at length, getting impatient, Burke suddenly threw himself on Wilson and attempted to strangle him. The idiot fought with the tenacity of despair, and had he not had the two brutes to contend with, he would have undoubtedly escaped; but Burke, with the assistance of Hare, eventually overcame the resistance of Wilson and suffocated him, but not before the victim had inflicted a severe injury on him.

Burke after his conviction spoke quite freely of his career. He attributed his entry into crime to the fact that he took to drink and to his association with the most abandoned characters, which so familiarised him with every kind of vice and wickedness that he had become indifferent to it all. He said he had only been engaged in murdering people for two years, and during that time he was sure he had not killed as many as thirty people. The only one who had actually helped in the carrying out of the murders was Hare. The women might have suspected what was going on, but they took no actual part in the acts. The procedure was to make their victims drunk first and then suffocate them by lying on top of them and holding their mouths and noses. Sometimes Burke held the mouth and nose, while Hare lay on top of the victim; sometimes the *rôles* were reversed. The question was put to him as to how he learned or thought of this method of killing his victims; his reply was that he and Hare had often discussed the matter, and together had come to the conclusion that this was the best method. When asked if he had received any encouragement to commit all these dreadful crimes, he said, "Yes. We were frequently told by Paterson that he would take as many bodies as we could get for him. When we got one, he always told us to get more." "To whom were the bodies so murdered sold?" Burke replied that they always took the bodies to the rooms of a doctor, and received their payment there, sometimes from the doctor and sometimes from his assistants. No questions were ever asked as to the way they had become possessed of the bodies. They had nothing to do but take a subject to the rooms and then get their money. There is no reason to doubt that Burke was at this time speaking the truth. No impartial observer can refrain from the comment that it was largely due to the very great laxity of the anatomists that such callous brutes as Burke and Hare were able to carry on their horrible practices. Little wonder that the anger of the people was not limited to the actual murderers!

On January 28th Burke was hanged. An enormous crowd gathered to see his execution. Seats were sold at a high price. As he ascended the platform shouts of fierce execration greeted him, and his last few moments must have been a very terrible ordeal to him. After his body was cut down an unseemly struggle took place among the officials for pieces of the rope with which he had been hanged, shavings from his coffin and other relics. It is difficult to understand the type of mind to which such gruesomeness appeals. The concluding part of the sentence of this unspeakable ruffian was an apt act of retribution. His body was ordered to be handed over to the anatomists for dissection.

Great popular indignation was expressed at the idea that Hare should escape his just punishment. It was felt that he was at least as great a brute as Burke, possibly the worse of the two. Was he to avoid trial and punishment because he had been accepted as King's evidence? This question was carefully considered by the legal advisers of the Crown before Hare was accepted as a witness against Burke; it was thought that as there was a possibility that he might not be convicted unless Hare appeared against him, it would be better to definitely secure the conviction of one of them than run the risk of an acquittal in both cases. Many thought, even if it were not possible to put Hare on trial for the murder of Mrs. Campbell, he should most certainly be charged with some of the many other murders of which he was guilty. The question was argued before the Scotch judges in February, and by a majority of four to two they decided that a pledge had been given to him that if he gave evidence for the Crown against Burke no proceedings should be taken against the witness, and he should be held harmless. He was accordingly released.

The mob was so incensed against the two women concerned in the case that it was with difficulty that they got off with their lives. Mrs. Hare was pursued by them, but managed eventually to escape. Hare himself went by coach to Dumfries, and when he arrived there he was recognised by the crowd and stoned by them. He left the town as soon as he could. His end was a miserable one, but it is impossible for any one to have the slightest feeling of pity for this brutal criminal.

The following extract from the experiences of Serjeant Ballantine, seems to me worth quoting in connection with this subject: "The interests of medical science had created a body of men that have passed into oblivion. Like the ghouls of Eastern story, they haunted graveyards, and lived upon corpses, violating the tomb and gaining a living by supplying the dissecting table with its ghastly subjects. They were called resurrectionists. It occurred to a native of Edinburgh named Burke that an easier and more profitable method might be devised to attain the same end, and he and an accomplice named Hare established a system of assassination. Lads wandering about the streets were little likely to be missed; there were few to inquire for them. They might be half starving, but still their carcases would serve the purpose

of the surgeon's knife; and they must not be spoilt by
external damage, and so these fiends, stealthily crawling
behind them, pressed a pitch plaster over their mouths
and noses, and thus suffocated them. They were then
conveyed to the dissecting room and sold to the anatomists, fetching a good price, as, unlike many stolen from
the grave, the bodies were comely and free from corrup-
tion. There appears to have been strange carelessness
on the part of the recipients: they knew that the class
they were dealing with was infamous, and the appearance
of the subjects ought to have created suspicion (the
principal surgeon engaged in this traffic was obliged to
leave Edinburgh from the feelings excited amongst the
populace), but it is fair to remember that those best able
to form an opinion were not present at the earlier stages
of the transaction. 'To burke' has become a recognised
word in the English language applicable to stopping a
discussion. No one doubts that the study of anatomy,
pursued through the means of dissection of dead bodies,
is most useful in the interests of mankind. No one will
dispute the labour, thought, and skill that have been
exercised in its practice, or the enormous benefits that
have been attained by it; and although there may be a
sensational feeling against it, no real evil is inflicted by
its exercise: and the interests both of science and
humanity fully justify its use. It is now some fifteen
years ago " (Ballantine is writing of 1882) " that a man of
middle height and proportionally stout, clad in one of the
ordinary white smocks worn by labourers, guided by a
dog, and holding in one of his hands a metal saucer,
might be seen slowly perambulating the streets of
London. His sightless eyes, turned upwards, appealed
to the compassion of the passers-by. This man was Hare,
the accomplice of Burke, who had been admitted as
evidence against him. Subsequently to the trial he
obtained employment in another name upon some lime
works. His fellow-labourers found out who he was, and

threw him into one of the pits, the contents of which caused him to lose his sight. There was a woman who was accustomed to join him at the end of the day, and apparently accompany him to wherever he lived. I have often seen these two meet, but never noticed a smile on the face of either of them."

The result of this trial, with its terrible revelations, was to convince the people throughout the country that it was urgently necessary to alter the law in respect to the supply of subjects for the anatomical schools. Very shortly after the execution of Burke Mr. Warburton gave notice of his intention to raise the matter in the House. Rumour undoubtedly exaggerated the evils, bad enough as they were without any additions. Every person who was reported missing was supposed to have been murdered and the body sent to the dissecting room. Alarm was felt everywhere; the papers were full of accounts of people being "burked"; the feeling of insecurity was not limited to any one district, but was general over the country.

The time of Parliament was just then fully occupied by discussions on Catholic emancipation, so it was not till March that Mr. Warburton had any opportunity of bringing his proposals before the House. He moved for leave to introduce a Bill to legalise and regulate the supply of dead bodies for the purpose of dissection. He said he wished first to confer a species of legality on the practice of anatomy, and he proposed to render anatomy lawful both in its practice and as a mode of instruction in all cities or towns where there were schools which conferred degrees in anatomy or where there were hospitals with not less than fifty beds. To overcome the difficulty of procuring subjects, he suggested that they should follow the custom of the French Government in Paris. The overseers of the poor and the governors of hospitals should be allowed to give up for dissection the bodies of persons who died in the hospitals if these bodies were not claimed. He asked that it should not be imagined that he wished to treat the feelings of the poor with the least disrespect, but it was necessary to procure bodies for dissection, and this seemed to him to be one of the best methods that could be devised. These suggestions met with the approval of the House, and a Bill was introduced embodying the main provisions he had outlined. It passed through the House of Commons the same session, but when it reached the Lords many peers objected on the ground that it subjected the bodies of the poor to treatment which would not be applied to the rich. So great was the opposition that the measure was withdrawn. A further stimulus to public opinion was required before the Bill became law. This stimulus was supplied by the abominable murder of an Italian boy in London, the crime being committed for the purpose of selling the body for dissection. John Bishop and Thomas Williams were executed for this. Other cases were discovered in the metropolis. Elizabeth Ross was hanged for the murder of an old woman whose body she attempted to sell to the hospitals. Mr. Warburton again introduced a Bill, which differed in some respects from his original one. By this second Bill the consent of the individual whose body was to be dissected was required to be obtained before his death, otherwise it could not be given by the authorities to the anatomists, and inspectors were to be appointed to see that the Act was properly carried out. After considerable discussion both Houses agreed, and thus the Anatomy Act of 1832 (which was amended in 1871) came into existence.

DR. BASTWICK AND THE STAR CHAMBER

In the reign of Charles I., in 1637, Dr. John Bastwick, a medical practitioner, was put on trial for a seditious libel, the case being heard before the Court of Star Chamber. This court, renowned for its methods of oppression, injustice and tyranny, possessed powers which had slowly and vaguely grown up, and in the time of the Stuarts exercised almost unlimited jurisdiction. Its procedure was created by itself, and was not that of the common law. No jury was employed; it could act on mere rumour; it could apply torture and inflict any punishment except death. It was admirably calculated to support despotism against individual or national liberty. The Long Parliament abolished this court in 1641; and, needless to say, it has never been revived.

The complaint against Dr. Bastwick was that of publishing seditious, schismatic and libellous books against the heads of the Church, the chief offending work being one written in Latin and entitled "Elenchus Religionis Papisticæ." This was construed as an attack on the hierarchy. Religious feelings ran high in the time of the Stuarts. The abominable proceedings of the authorities in their endeavours to punish Dr. Bastwick make one ashamed that such things could be done in the name of religion.

Previous to the hearing an attempt was made by the Crown to charge the defendant with high treason, but this was overruled by the judges.

Dr. Bastwick prepared his answers to the charges brought against him. According to the ruling of the Court, these must be made through his counsel, but owing to the pusillanimity of this lawyer, who, like most of his profession, stood in great fear of the judges of the Star Chamber, Dr. Bastwick claimed the right to defend himself. He argued that it was unjust that a man who was innocent should be convicted through the fear or treachery of his counsel, and in the present case, the charges being matters of Divinity, which were not within the knowledge of counsel, it would be impossible for the defence to be properly conducted unless he (Dr. Bastwick) could deal with the case himself. The Court refused permission, and as the doctor declined to put his answers through his counsel, and persisted in his right to submit them himself, the Court announced that this amounted to a plea of guilty. Dr. Bastwick argued that the judges were not dealing with him fairly, as some of them had not read his book, and that he could not hope to obtain justice from them, as they had determined on his punishment even before his trial. After a short hearing, during which the usual notorious procedure of the Star Chamber, with all its injustice and unfairness, was observed, Dr. Bastwick was pronounced guilty and was condemned to have his ears cut off, to be fined £5,000, and to be perpetually imprisoned at Launceston, in Cornwall. The sentence was carried out, and subsequently he was removed from this prison to one in the Scilly Isles, and his wife was forbidden to land at this place.

Some three years later the whole matter was brought before Parliament and referred to a Committee appointed to inquire into the proceedings of the Star Chamber, and on the report of this Committee the House resolved that the preliminary proceedings of the trial were illegal, the sentence was against the law, and therefore void, and that Dr. Bastwick ought to have reparation for his suffering and be allowed to resume the practice of his profession.

The doctor was released, landing from Scilly at Dover, where he was received with great popular ovations, continued during his journey through Kent to London.

I can find no record as to whether any compensation was made to this unfortunate victim of the Star Chamber.

Lord Clarendon, who was bitterly opposed to Dr. Bastwick on the question of religion, made the following comment on this and two similar cases: " They were three persons most notorious for their declared malice against the government of the Church by bishops in their several books and writings, which they had published to corrupt the people, with circumstances very scandalous, and in language very scurrilous and impudent, which all men thought deserved very exemplary punishment; they were of the three professions which had the most influence on the people, a divine, a common lawyer, and a doctor of physic, none of them of interest or of any esteem with the worthy part of their several professions, having been formerly all looked upon under characters of reproach; yet when they were all sentenced, and for execution of that sentence brought out to be punished as common and signal rogues, exposed upon scaffolds to have their ears cut off, and their faces and foreheads branded with hot irons, . . . men began no more to consider their manners, but the men: and each profession, with anger and indignation enough, thought their education, and degrees, and quality would have secured them from such infamous judgments, and treasured up wrath for the time to come."

Undoubtedly at the time of which I am writing, 1637, the offence of attacking the heads of the Church by writing a book against certain of their views and practices was looked upon as a serious matter, yet even so the illegal and vindictive action of the authorities, of which this case is only one of innumerable instances, makes one wonder how our predecessors submitted for so long a time to the tyranny of the Stuart *régime*.

THE CASE OF DR. ARCHIBALD CAMERON

TRIAL OF DR. ARCHIBALD CAMERON AT THE KING'S BENCH, MAY 17TH, 1753, ON THE ACT OF ATTAINDER PASSED IN THE REIGN OF GEORGE II., FOR PARTICIPATION IN THE REBELLION OF 1745

THE accused was the younger brother of Donald Cameron of Lochiel, the head of the Cameron clan, and son of Evan Cameron, who had taken part in the rising of 1715. Dr. Cameron received the best education Scotland could afford, at first for the Bar, but as this was not congenial to him, he afterwards took to medicine. Dr. Alexander Monro, of Edinburgh, and Dr. Sinclair, both of whom were at this time noted medical men, were his teachers. Cameron later went abroad, studied at Paris and Leyden, and then returned to Scotland, settling at Lochaber, where he set up practice. He was a man who might have made quite a name in his profession had he started in a large town, but not being of an ambitious nature, he preferred to work in the Highlands, where he devoted his talents to the inhabitants of the little town in which he had settled. He soon became most esteemed and popular, and his work among the sick poor rendered him much beloved in the district where he lived.

Dr. Cameron's brother, the chief of the clan, who was a zealous supporter of Prince Charles Edward, after receiving from the Young Pretender an assurance that the French king would send a proper force for his support, set up the Cameronian standard with the motto "Tandem triumphans," and raised a band of 1,200 for the rebel army, although he recognised that the attempt to put a

Stuart on the throne must be abortive. When Donald Cameron raised his force, he sent for his brother Archibald to undertake medical charge of these troops, and although the doctor was most reluctant to agree to this, he at length yielded to the persuasions of his chief and undertook the work, though he positively refused to accept a commission in the rebel army. Dr. Cameron carried out his medical duties most assiduously and humanely during the whole of the time of the advance and retreat of the troops, and this applied both to his own and the enemy wounded.

When the battle of Culloden put an end to the rebellion, and to the hopes of the Young Pretender, he together with Lochiel, the doctor, and others, embarked in a vessel in the harbour of Flota, in the isle of South Uist, and landed at Boulogne after enduring terrible hardships.

Dr. Cameron joined the French army in a medical capacity, at first being attached to the regiment of which his brother was given command, and later to that under Lord Ogilvie. The doctor visited Scotland in 1749 to obtain assistance for himself and his fellow-sufferers abroad. Two years after his return to France he again came back to Scotland. On this second visit the Government heard of his home-coming, and despatched troops to arrest him. By following a small boy, who, it was believed, had knowledge of the whereabouts of the doctor, they were able to trace his hiding-place. He was arrested, sent first to Edinburgh, and then to the Tower. When brought before the King's Bench for trial, the law officers of the Crown demanded that Dr. Cameron should be at once sentenced to death without trial, as he was one of the persons mentioned in the Act of Attainder passed after the 1745 rebellion for the effectual punishment of those concerned in it. The Act mentioned a large number of people by name, including Dr. Cameron, and stated that any of them who did not submit to justice before July, 1746, was attaint of high treason. The inhuman suggestion of the Crown was not carried out.

The prisoner at the bar pleaded that he was led to take a part in the rebellion against his own judgment and inclination by some upon whom his all depended. He still thought he was not unworthy of the mercy of the King, and mentioned some facts which he hoped might entitle him to this mercy. He said he did not offer these things as a defence in point of law, but as facts which he hoped might have some weight in another place, for he was determined to throw himself on His Majesty's mercy.

The Lord Chief Justice then pronounced sentence as follows : " You, Archibald Cameron of Lochiel, in that part of Great Britain called Scotland, must be removed from hence to His Majesty's prison of the Tower of London, from whence you came, and on Tuesday, the seventh of June next, your body to be drawn on a sledge to the place of execution, there to be hanged, but not till you are dead, your bowels to be taken out, your body to be quartered, your head to be cut off and affixed at the King's pleasure, and the Lord have mercy on your soul."

When Dr. Cameron heard the sentence, he made a bow, and his only request was that he might have leave to send for his wife, who, with seven children, entirely depended on him for support. They lived at Lille, in Flanders.

During the interval between his sentence and his execution his wife did everything she could to obtain a pardon for him, but without success. On Thursday, June 7th, at about 10 a.m., he was brought from the Tower, escorted by a party of Horse Guards, and delivered into the custody of the sheriffs of London and Middlesex. He was dressed in a light-coloured coat, red waistcoat and breeches, with a new bag wig. As soon as he was well out of the Tower Gate he was put on a hurdle, to which he was fastened by the executioner. He was drawn through the City to the place of execution, Tyburn, and there helped into the cart. He looked round at the spectators in the houses and balconies and bowed to several friends. He begged the sheriff to allow his body to hang till he was dead before the executioners began any further operations on him, and the sheriff promised he would see that this wish was carried out. The body was accordingly allowed to hang for forty-five minutes.

Dr. Cameron met his hard fate with great courage and perfect resignation. After his body was taken from the gallows the executioner cut off his head and took out his bowels, but did not quarter the body.

The doctor claimed, in some letters written in prison, that he had been instrumental in saving the lives of 300 people in Scotland who were attached to the Hanoverian king, and that he had prevented many excesses of the rebel army. He declared that he was being very hardly treated in being condemned to death so long after the rebellion, but he still acclaimed himself a staunch supporter of the Stuarts. In one of his letters written from prison occur the following words: " I pray God to hasten the restoration of the royal family (without which this miserably divided nation can never enjoy peace and happiness) and that it may please Him to preserve and defend the King, the Prince of Wales and the Duke of York from the power and malice of their enemies, to prosper and reward all my friends and benefactors, and to forgive all my enemies, murderers and false accusers, from the Elector of Hanover and his bloody son down to Samuel Cameron, the basest of their spies, as I freely do from the bottom of my heart."

In a letter from the same place to his son the sentiments expressed are on a much higher plane: " I have no money to leave you as a legacy, but take what is of infinitely more value, viz., above all things, first serve God, next your king, prince, and country; then be always in your duty to your mother, brothers, and sisters; act honourably and honestly by your neighbours; meddle in no party quarrels; but when you are personally wronged, demand justice with coolness, regularity and resolution, without personal reflections; beware of ever speaking to the disadvantage of the absent, even though they should deserve it. I recommend to you, in a particular manner, the care of your health. Observe great moderation in eating, at any rate abstain from heavy and late supper, and, above all, avoid drinking and whoring. Be a good economist of your little money and clothes. Let the company you frequent be rather of your betters than your inferiors."

He was the last victim of the rebellion of 1745 and the last person to suffer death by Act of Attainder in this country. Macaulay, in his History states that Sir John Fenwick, executed in 1697, was the last person to suffer the death penalty in England, under an Act of Attainder, but he is wrong.

At this distance of time, when it is possible to review the case dispassionately, the execution of this doctor, eight years after the rebellion was over and done with, appears to have been a very cruel and vindictive procedure, especially considering the very small and unwilling part he took in the rising.

For participation in the same rebellion Thomas Deacon, aged twenty-two, son of Dr. Deacon, of Manchester, was tried in July, 1746. He and his two brothers had joined the Young Pretender as soon as the rebel army came to Manchester. One of the brothers died in the Pretender's service; the other two, Charles and Thomas, were put on trial. Charles, the younger, was sentenced to death, but reprieved on account of his youth. Thomas, who had received a good education and was destined by his father, the doctor, to follow in his footsteps, was very active in the service of the Young Pretender, and although only twenty-two, had been made a lieutenant-colonel. He was less fortunate. Several witnesses swore that he had taken a prominent part in the rebellion, and of this there could be no doubt, and no witnesses were produced for the defence. He was found guilty, sentenced to death, and executed on Kennington Common on July 30th,

1746, first being hanged and then beheaded, his head preserved in spirits, and sent to be put on the gates of one of the towns through which the rebel army had passed.

It is interesting to remember that in the old days of about one hundred and fifty years ago death was the punishment for nearly all crimes, and not, as to-day, only for murder, treason, piracy with violence, and burning ships of war, dockyards or royal arsenals, and Government stores. For instance, arson, rape, cutting and maiming, returning from transportation, coining, forgery, falsely performing the marriage service, poisoning racehorses, burglary, housebreaking, highway robbery, horse-stealing, and about two hundred other offences were punishable with death.

Various Acts of Parliament which were passed in the nineteenth century, commencing with an Act by which picking pockets was no longer to be punished with death in 1808, gradually abolished capital punishment for offences, so that at the present day there remain for all practical purposes only the crimes of murder and treason which carry the death penalty.

So brutal was the criminal law in the Hanoverian period that those responsible were in the first place, in large numbers of cases, loath to convict, and juries returned verdicts of not guilty in trials in which it was very clear that the prisoner was actually guilty in order that the accused should escape the capital sentence, and secondly, even when convictions had been obtained and the prisoner sentenced to death, the punishment was only carried out in a small percentage of instances. Thus in 1805 350 people were sentenced to death, but sixty-eight only, or less than 20 per cent., paid the final penalty. In 1831 1,601 people were condemned to be executed, but of this number fifty-two, or about 3 per cent. only, were actually hanged. At the present time the number of criminals sentenced to death in this country in a year is about thirty, and of these nearly one half are reprieved.

Mr. Justice Hawkins, speaking of the punishments of a

century ago, states that at the Lincoln Assizes in March, 1818, there were twenty-four prisoners for trial, all for robbery in some form or arson, and of these fourteen were sentenced to death. Crowds were sent to death after every assize and at each session of the Old Bailey. It was considered a rather light calendar if less than a score had the capital sentence passed on them. One of his earliest recollections was that of seeing the body of a youth of seventeen, who had been hanged for setting fire to a stack of corn, being taken home in a cart by his wretched parents.

Sir James Fitzjames Stephen, commenting on the criminal law of England (and there was perhaps no greater authority on this subject than he), says: "All this legislation shows that the early criminal law was extremely severe, that its severity was much increased under the Tudors, but that it varied but little from the time of Elizabeth to the end of the seventeenth century. Before noticing the legislation of the eighteenth century on this subject it will be desirable to sum up what has been said. Towards the end of the seventeenth century the following crimes were excluded from the benefit of clergy, and were thus capital whether the offender could read or not: high treason (which had always been so), petty treason, piracy, murder, arson, burglary, housebreaking and putting in fear, highway robbery, horse-stealing, stealing from the person above the value of a shilling, rape and abduction with intent to marry. In the case of persons who could not read, all felonies, including manslaughter, every kind of theft above the value of a shilling, and all robbery, were capital crimes. It is difficult, if not impossible, to say how this system worked in practice. No statistics as to either convictions or executions were kept then or till long afterwards. A few vague generalities, with here and there a piece of positive evidence, are all that I can at least refer to. I will mention one specimen of each. There are still preserved at Exeter Castle many of the depositions and other records of the courts of quarter sessions held there from the latter part of the reign of Elizabeth. They begin in 1592. From these materials Mr. Hamilton has compiled a ' History of the Quarter Sessions from Elizabeth to Anne.' The following is one result at which he arrives : At the Lent Assizes in 1598 there were 134 prisoners, of whom seventeen were dismissed with the fatal ' S.P.,' it being apparently too much trouble to write ' *sus. per coll.*;' twenty were flogged; one was liberated by special pardon, and fifteen by general pardon; eleven claimed benefit of clergy and were consequently branded and set free, *legunt uruntur et deliberantur*. At the Epiphany Sessions preceding there were sixty-five prisoners, of whom eighteen were hanged. At Easter there were forty-one prisoners, and twelve of them were executed. At the Midsummer Sessions there were thirty-five prisoners, and eight were hanged. At the October Sessions there were twenty-five, of whom only one was hanged. Altogether there were seventy-four persons sentenced to be hanged in one county in a single year, and of these more than one half were condemned at quarter sessions."

Stubbs, in his " Mediæval and Modern History," makes the following interesting remarks : " I believe I could show that the executions for religious causes in England by all sides during all times are not so many as the sentences of death passed in one year of the reign of George III. for one single sort of crime, the forging of bank notes."

Very young children were hanged. Thus a boy of eight years who had set fire to a barn was actually executed, and two young thieves of fourteen had the capital sentence carried out on them in 1791. In 1833, less than a hundred years ago, a boy of nine, convicted of stealing two pennyworth of paint, was sentenced to death, though, for the credit of our country, I am glad to say the brutal sentence was not carried out. It was only in 1908, when the Children Act was passed, that the death sentence for those under sixteen was abolished.

In this country the manner in which the death punishment has been inflicted has for many centuries been by hanging, though in early times beheading was often carried out, both for those in high and those in low positions. To this the only exceptions were in the case of treason, for which the punishment was in women burning alive and in the case of men hanging, drawing (which originally meant dragging along the ground at a horse's tail), and quartering, and in the case of heresy burning was also the penalty. At one time the punishment for poisoning was death by boiling, and this was in a few instances actually carried out, but the law was repealed in the reign of Edward VI. In the reign of George II. an Act was passed which was intended to make the penalty for murder more severe than any other form of capital punishment. This Act provided that a prisoner convicted of murder should be hanged on the next day but one after his sentence. In the interval he was to be fed on bread and water, and after death his body was to be dissected or to be hung in chains at the discretion of the Judge. Usually the sentence was that the body was to be anatomised, but sometimes the alternative punishment, gibbeting, was given. Further Acts were later passed abolishing both these additional punishments, and the body of the murderer is now decently buried in the prison where he is hanged.

In the case of military and naval court martials, death by shooting is the method of execution. Beheading for treason in the case of males is still allowed by the law of the land, to be ordered by the Sovereign, but this procedure has not been put into practice for a very great number of years.

Until the eighteenth century the time of the execution of the death sentence was left to the Judge, who usually ordered it for the next day, sometimes even on the actual day of the judgment. In 1684, after Bothwell Bridge, three hours after sentence was the time fixed for carrying

CASE OF DR. ARCHIBALD CAMERON

it out. Three prisoners found guilty in connection with this rebellion were condemned about three o'clock, carried down to Gallowlee, between Leith and Edinburgh, and hanged at five. Fountainhall, in reference to these hangings, makes the following comments, showing curious lack of ordinary humanity: "It is strange to find this obstinacy have countenancers, for good black coffins followed them down Leith Wynd, and women privily in the night stole their bodies from under the gibbet, and carried them to the gate of Greyfriars Churchyard, with a design to have them buried there; but the Privy Council ordered their corps to be drawn back again to the Gallowlee, and the wright who made their coffins to be inquired after and apprehended, that he might discover who had employed him."

Lord Hale laid it down that the execution of a criminal must be in accordance with the judgment, otherwise the officer varying it would be guilty of felony, if not of murder. "That the Crown may remit part of the judgement is certainly true, and would silence every doubt in the case of high treason at least, if hanging and beheading were ingredients in every judgement for that offence; but in the case of women beheading is no ingredient in the judgement, and yet ladies of distinction have been for many ages past, by warrant from the Crown, beheaded for that offence. The execution in this instance totally varieth from the judgement, and yet I do not know that those executions have been esteemed illegal, nor can I recollect a single instance where a lady of distinction hath been burnt for high treason; and, with regard to those of inferior rank who have been burnt, it is well known that they have generally been strangled at the stake by the executioner before the fire hath reached them, though the letter of the judgement is, that they shall be burnt in the fire till they are dead."

The whole procedure of the carrying out of the last penalty was different in the old days. At the present time it is performed privately and expeditiously, within the precincts of the gaol. The last public execution took place in 1868. I may mention that Tyburn Tree, the gallows on which so many notorious criminals suffered the extreme penalty of the law, stood close by where the Marble Arch now is, and is marked by a stone in the roadway, which all may see. The last execution took place here in 1783. After that Newgate became the site of executions for the London area.

To-day rapidity is carried almost to a fine art. Only about sixty seconds elapse after the executioner enters the cell till the death sentence is completed. In the old days the criminal (or, as was frequently the case, the batch of criminals) was drawn in a cart from Newgate to Tyburn, a considerable distance, through seething crowds of morbid spectators, and he and his companions, one after the other, had the halter adjusted. The condemned had long talks with the executioner or surrounding spectators, and then the cart in which the prisoners stood was moved on and the wretched people left hanging, to die of strangulation. This often took quite a considerable time. Occasionally the executioner had pity and hung on to the legs of his victim, thus shortening the death struggle. Cases are recorded in which bodies cut down after hanging have been revived by the efforts of their friends. To-day the death factor is not strangulation. The sudden jerk of the fall causes a dislocation or a fracture of the cervical vertebræ, and instant death from injury to the medulla. The knot of the rope is adjusted to fit under the chin, as in this way it has been found by experience that the dislocation is more certainly caused.

Even with the perfected modern arrangements, terrible mishaps will sometimes occur. In the Babbacombe murder case three attempts were made to release the trap, and all failed. The governor of the gaol then stopped the execution, and the man was subsequently reprieved.

CASE OF DR. ARCHIBALD CAMERON

Any hitch in procedure, is, however, a very rare event, a modern execution being carried out in almost every instance in as rapid and merciful a way as such a terrible thing can be.

Examples of resuscitation after death by hanging are recorded, of which the following is an example: Patrick Ledmond was hanged for a street robbery on February 24th, 1767. He had been suspended for twenty-eight minutes, when he was rescued by the mob and carried to an appointed place, where a surgeon was in attendance, who performed the operation of what was called bronchotomy, but was in reality tracheotomy. In less than six hours this produced the desired effect, and the criminal was restored to life.

An interesting legal problem arose. He had been condemned to hang by the neck till he was dead; but he was still alive, and therefore his sentence had not been carried out. Endeavours were made to procure a pardon, but there is no record of the result. Let us hope it was satisfactory.

A less successful experiment was the following: George Foster was executed for murder in 1803. After his body had hung the usual time it was cut down and removed to a house close by where Professor Aldin, with Mr. Carpue and other medical men, subjected the corpse to galvanism, then recently discovered. Violent muscular contractures were obtained, but this was the only result as regards the corpse. Mr. Pass, the Beadle of the Surgeons' Company, was so terrified that he died of fright.

The following case illustrates a ghastly tragedy which occurred at an execution in Edinburgh in 1818. The drop stuck and the prisoner remained half suspended for about five minutes, when the enraged mob, whose sympathies were, as is usual, with the criminal, scaled the scaffold and cut him down. He was taken from the mob by the police, and a surgeon sent for, who bled him and restored him to consciousness. He was immediately hanged again. This will require some beating as an instance of cold-blooded brutality.

In connection with the carrying out of the death penalty the following custom which prevailed even as recently as the beginning of the nineteenth century, is of interest, the application of the " dead man's hand." After a man had hung till death ensued the people were allowed to have his dead hand touch them, for the purpose of removing marks, wens, etc.

There is a slight difference between the law of capital punishment in Scotland and that of this country. In Scotland, in addition to treason and murder, the following crimes are punishable with death: acts of violence which, if fatal, would have been murder, *e.g.*, shooting, stabbing, strangling, throwing sulphuric acid, *i.e.*, virtually attempted murder, may be punished by death.

COURT-MARTIAL ON A NAVAL SURGEON

In the year 1818 a court-martial was held on board His Majesty's ship *Conqueror*, in St. Helena Roads, for the purpose of trying Mr. John Stokoe, a naval surgeon, with regard to his conduct with the French prisoners at St. Helena.

Early in that year the great Napoleon, then exiled on the island, was taken dangerously ill. (He died there some few years later of cancer of the stomach.) Extra medical assistance was asked for; and Admiral Plampin, commander-in-chief of the squadron at the Cape, and in the neighbouring seas, sent Mr. John Stokoe to Longwood, the residence of Napoleon, to give him what attention was possible.

In order to understand the significance of this court-martial, the political situation following the defeat of Napoleon must be considered.

After the battle of Waterloo in 1815 the fears and unrest in this country caused by the activities of Napoleon, though to a large extent removed by the defeat of the French, had by no means entirely subsided. It was felt that Napoleon, though a beaten man, was a very dangerous one. He was not, like the ex-Kaiser, a discredited and despised fugitive from his country. The Emperor had still a large and influential following, and this not only in France. There was always the possibility, even more perhaps than this, the probability, that the Napoleonic energy might show itself in a fresh outbreak of war and strife if the leader were once again a free man. Therefore extraordinary precautions were taken to ensure his safe captivity and his isolation from his fellow-creatures. An Act of Parliament was passed to regulate his imprisonment on the lonely island of St. Helena. This is placed in the middle of the Atlantic, hundreds of miles from the nearest land, and has only one small, easily guarded harbour. Longwood, the house selected for his residence, was situated on an almost inaccessible plateau, and this was guarded by a large number of troops. The island was patrolled by English warships, and no vessel but a British man-of-war was allowed to enter the harbour. Yet still the English Government were filled with nervous fears of the possibility of the escape of Napoleon. They even seriously listened to the rumours of the building of a submarine to effect his rescue. Regulations were made to prevent the access of any unauthorised persons to him; the most extraordinary precautions were taken to guard against any possibility of his again becoming a power to be feared. Sir Hudson Lowe, the Governor appointed to carry out the safeguarding of the prisoner, was probably one of the most unfit people one could imagine for such an appointment. He seemed to be lacking in every quality necessary for one holding it. He was tactless, suspicious, foolish and irritable, and all his dealings with his captive were marked by unpleasantness and quarrels.

The death of Napoleon was the cause of much perturbation. Probably no post-mortem which has ever been conducted gave rise to so much controversy as that held on the dead Emperor. The autopsy was a political event; the report on it was a political document. The Napoleonists started with the determined intention of proving that the endemic liver disease of St. Helena had caused the death of the prisoner, that he was a martyr to the environment insisted upon by the British Government. The representatives of England, on the other hand, attended the autopsy with the determination of proving this was not so, but that death was due to a disease which would have killed Napoleon wherever he had been. This tragic event—for the death of the great statesman and soldier *was* a tragedy—took place on May 5th, 1821, some six years after the Emperor's arrival. A great storm was raging over the island, trees which the Emperor had planted were uprooted, and the favourite willow by which he had been wont to rest was torn up by the wind. Sir Hudson Lowe and his officers were in attendance, momentarily expecting the news. When the death of Napoleon was notified to him, he spoke a few appropriate words with dignity and tact, but after this one decent act the usual bickering commenced. Sir Hudson ordered a post-mortem to be conducted at once, to the annoyance of the Napoleonists. The name on the coffin-plate selected by the friends of the Emperor was simply Napoleon. Lowe insisted on the addition of Buonaparte, and so the coffin remained unnamed. The body lay in state for four days, and then the funeral took place. The remains were placed by British soldiers on a car and drawn by the Emperor's own horses to a garden at the bottom of a deep ravine, chosen by Napoleon himself should burial in his own country be denied him. The grave was placed by the side of a spring shaded by willows. Lowe and his officers, military, civil, and naval, attended the funeral, and the coffin was lowered to the earth amidst salvoes of artillery and rifles The funeral was a very simple one, and thus passed a man who had played a very great part in the affairs of the world. Nearly twenty years later a French frigate took the remains of the great soldier back to his own land, where they now rest in Les Invalides in Paris. The body was laid a second time to rest, with imposing pomp, in striking contrast to the simplicity of his first burial.

The post-mortem was held the day after the death in a badly lighted room at Longwood, and was commenced at 2 p.m., lasting about four hours. The actual operation was undertaken by the physician of the Emperor, Dr. Antommarchi. There were present seven English doctors: Drs. Short, Arnott, Burton, Livingstone, Mitchell, Henry and Rutledge. In addition, three civil representatives of the English Government, and three representatives of the French at St. Helena, and three servants of Napoleon attended. It was clearly demonstrated that cancer of the stomach was present, but at the same time there was evidence of chronic inflammation of the liver. Which actually was the direct cause of death was not settled, but it was at least plain that, wherever he had been, the cancer must soon have terminated his life. Sir Hudson Lowe would not permit the least difference from the view which he officially decided to take as to the cause of death. In a letter to Lord Bathurst, Secretary of State for the Colonies, he points out that "Dr. Arnott appeared to me to have conducted himself as a perfectly upright and honest man in not encouraging the desire evinced to ascribe the disease to the liver, and showed his judgment also in having an opinion to the contrary. Dr. Short, however, thought the disease proceeded from the liver without his having ever seen the patient alive, but he feels a little ashamed, I believe, of the opinion he has expressed."

Sir A. Keith, who has made a close study of the post-mortem on Napoleon, quotes the following extract from a letter from Sir Alexander Simpson : " When my uncle, Sir James Simpson, came back from a professional visit in Berwickshire, where he had met Dr. Arnott, he was full of what Arnott had been telling him of his time in St. Helena. What specially impressed him was that Dr. Arnott had charge of the heart and other things that had been removed at the autopsy for the following night. Afraid that some of the Napoleonic retainers might come in and carry off the vessel in which they had been put at the time of the dissection, he emptied them into his wash-hand basin, covered them up with water, and lay down to sleep with loaded pistols under his pillow. He slept lightly. Hearing a splashing sound, he jumped up, expecting to see Bertrand or some one at the preparations, and found that it was only rats trying to get at the flesh. ' Fancy rats trying to make away with Napoleon's heart!' said Sir James in repeating the story."

Unless all this is considered, it will be a little difficult to understand why so much notice was taken of the conduct of Mr. Stokoe. The charges made against him were as follows. It was alleged that whilst attending Napoleon he communicated with him or his attendants on subjects not at all connected with medicine, contrary to the standing orders in force for the regulation of the conduct of His Majesty's officers at St. Helena. He was also accused of having received written communications from French prisoners, and of having answered them without previously making them known to the commander-in-chief. Another of the counts charged him with having written a bulletin of General Buonaparte's health, and with giving this bulletin to Napoleon. The bulletin was stated to contain facts relative to the health of the patient which had not come under the doctor's own observation, and which had been told to him by the General or his attendants, and yet was signed by the doctor stating that he had himself witnessed these facts. Part of the bulletin was as follows: " The more alarming symptom is that which was experienced on the night of the 16th, a recurrence of which may soon prove fatal, particularly if medical assistance is not at hand." It was alleged that he thereby intended, contrary to the character and duty of a British officer, to create a false impression that General Buonaparte was in imminent or considerable danger and that no medical assistance was at hand, whereas actually Mr. Stokoe had not witnessed any such symptoms and knew that the state of the patient was so little urgent that he had been kept waiting four hours at Longwood before he was admitted to see his patient, and that Dr. Verling was at hand and ready to attend if any emergency arose.

In addition the charges below were made against Mr. Stokoe:—

For having, contrary to his duty, communicated to General Buonaparte or his attendant information relative to certain books, letters and papers said to have been sent from Europe for the said persons, and which had been intercepted by the Governor of St. Helena ; and for having conveyed to the said General or his attendants some information respecting their money concerns, contrary to his duty, which was to afford medical advice only.

For having communicated to the General an infamous and calumnious imputation cast upon General Sir Hudson Lowe, the Governor, by Barry O'Meara, late surgeon in the Royal Navy, implying that Sir Hudson Lowe had tried to induce O'Meara to put an end to the life of Napoleon.

For having disobeyed orders of his superior officer in not returning from Longwood at the time prescribed.

For having knowingly and wilfully described General Buonaparte in the bulletin in a manner different from that in which he was designated in the Act of Parliament for the better custody of his person, and contrary to the practice of His Majesty's Government, and for having done so at the special request of General Buonaparte, although the doctor well knew that the mode of designation was a point of dispute between Buonaparte and the British Government.

For having in the whole of his conduct in the transactions mentioned evinced a disposition to thwart the regulations of Sir Hudson Lowe, and to further the views of the French prisoners, in furnishing them with false pretences for complaint.

After a very careful hearing of all the evidence, the Court found him guilty, and ordered him to be dismissed from His Majesty's service, but, in consideration of his long connection with the navy, recommended the Admiralty to put him on half-pay.

All this appears very paltry when looked at one hundred years after the event.

THE CASE OF HENRY HARRISON

THE TRIAL OF HENRY HARRISON AT THE OLD BAILEY IN APRIL, 1692, FOR THE MURDER OF DR. ANDREW CLENCHE, OF HOLBORN

THIS remarkable trial for the murder of a doctor presents such a dramatic story that I have included it in my series, though in this instance it is not a medical man who is the accused party.

Briefly the story told by the prosecution was that Harrison on the 4th of June, 1692, at 11 p.m., in Cornhill, whilst travelling in a coach, with Dr. Clenche and another man, suddenly set on the doctor and strangled him.

The clerk of the Court in his statement to the jury, after charging them to find a verdict of guilty or not guilty, pointed out to them that, in the event of this latter, they were to inquire whether the prisoner had fled to avoid the charge. If they found he had, they were to inquire what goods he possessed. The law at that time seized the belongings of a man, even if innocent, provided he had fled to avoid trial.

Counsel for the Crown at the outset accused the friends of Harrison of having conveyed away the principal witness against him, but this he denied. The charge as outlined by the prosecuting counsel was that a Mrs. Vanwicke, between whom and Harrison there was " a great kindness," had given a mortgage of her house to the doctor in consideration for money advanced, but when the time for repayment came the widow failed to carry out her obligations. The doctor therefore applied for an ejectment order, and this roused the wrath of Harrison, who threatened the doctor, saying to the widow, " Leave him to me. I'll warrant you I'll manage him.

He is a rogue and deserves to have his throat cut." About three weeks after this Harrison and another man hired a coach, and told the driver to take them to Dr. Clenche. When they arrived they sent the coachman to inform the doctor that two gentlemen wanted him to come with them to see a friend who was very ill. The coachman found the doctor in his night-gown and slippers just going to bed, but he immediately dressed himself and went to them in the coach. The coachman was ordered to drive quickly to Leadenhall Market, and when he arrived was sent to buy some poultry. This was about 11 p.m., so obviously the market was open much later than it is now. He bought the poultry, returned to his coach, and found his fares had disappeared and left a corpse behind them.

The facts as above were proved by various witnesses, and Harrison in his defence attempted to show an alibi, but those who appeared for him were of such doubtful veracity that no credence was given to their testimony.

The summing up of Lord Chief Justice Holt is such an excellent *résumé* of all the evidence, clear in all its facts, fair and concise, that I quote it as an example of what such a statement to a jury should be. Remember, we have passed from the time of the Stuarts, with its corrupt and venal judges, to that of William and Mary :—

"Gentlemen of the Jury, the prisoner at the bar, Henry Harrison, stands indicted for the wilful murder of Dr. Andrew Clenche, who was barbarously murdered on the fourth day of January last. You have heard the witnesses that have been sworn, and upon their testimony it doth appear that two persons came to Brownlow Street and in a coach, after nine o'clock at night, and sent the coachman to the doctor's house under pretence to get him to a patient, a friend of theirs, that was sick. By this contrivance they got him into their coach, which they had brought for that purpose, and then they ordered the coachman to drive to Leadenhall Street, and when they came about Holborn Bars one of them asked the coachman why he drove so slow, and bade him drive faster. When they came to Leadenhall Street then they bade him drive to the Pye Tavern without Aldgate, where one of them bade the coachman ask for one Hunt, but he not being there, one of them bade the coachman turn back, and gave sixpence to the watch to come through the gate, which was shut in the meantime; and when they came to Leadenhall Market, one of them gave the coachman three shillings and sixpence and sent him to buy a couple of fowls, which the coachman did buy and brought back to the coach, but when he came back he found the doctor in the body of the coach, leaning against the foreseat of the coach, a handkerchief being tied about his neck with a coal in it, placed upon his windpipe, which handkerchief and coal have been produced in court.

"The question is, gentlemen, whether the prisoner at the bar be guilty of this base and barbarous murder, to prove which there hath been a very long evidence given, some positive, some circumstantial. It has been proved that Dr. Clenche had some dealings with a woman named Vanwicke, and had lent her one hundred and twenty pounds, and had taken a mortgage for it. The prisoner, Mr. Harrison, was a great acquaintance, and very intimate with this woman, and did concern himself in the management of her affairs; and because Dr. Clenche did refuse to lend the woman more money, therefore he had an animosity against Dr. Clenche. The money not being paid to the doctor, as he did expect, he did call it in, and therefore this gentlewoman did oftentimes repair to Dr. Clenche's to desire further time of forebearance because she could not raise or procure the money elsewhere. That about Michelmas last, it seems, she came to a coffee-house near Warick House in Holborn, and there was Mr. Harrison, where they consulted what to do. And it was agreed that the mistress of the house and Mrs. Vanwicke should go to Dr. Clenche's, but Mr. Harrison should stay behind, for it was not thought convenient that he should go lest he should provoke the doctor. When they came to the doctor, Mrs. Vanwicke was very importunate to have more money, but the doctor would lend her no more. And when they returned to the coffee-house again, Mr. Harrison inquired what passed between the doctor and Mrs. Vanwicke. She told him that the doctor would not furnish her with any more money, although she had pressed him to do it and urged her great necessities, but advised her to go to service. 'Damn him!' says Harrison; 'does he say that a woman of your quality should go to service? He is a great rogue and deserves to have his throat cut, but let me alone; I will manage him.'

"At another place there was a discourse between Mr. Harrison and one Mr. Johnson, and that the prisoner did then speak very hard and ill words of Dr. Clenche; and that Mr. Harrison came frequently to him, and one time laid his hand upon his sword, adding some menacing words, but what they were he cannot tell; but he likewise says that at several times he did expostulate with him and told him that he would not do any good with such discourses as these were, etc. That, the mortgage money not being paid, it was thought fit that there should be a prosecution made to get possession of the mortgaged estate, and that the tenants should be forbid to pay their rents; and Mr. Harrison went to Mrs. West some days before St. Thomas' Day last, and demanded the rent of her, to which she made answer that Dr. Clenche had forbid the payment of the rent to Mrs. Vanwicke. Thereupon Mr. Harrison grew very angry and answered that Dr. Clenche was a rogue and a villain, and bid her that she should not pay him any rent. And the witness said further that the doctor, being pressed to let her have some money, refused to do it because she would spend it all upon Harrison. Then the counsel for the King called some witnesses, who gave you an account of the prisoner's shifting his lodgings the day before the murder was done. He takes a lodging at Mr. Garway's in Threadneedle

Street on the 23rd day of December, and there he continued till about the 1st of January. The 2nd of January he was at Garway's shop, and on the Sunday night he came and fetched away his things. The Monday after, being the day that the barbarous act was committed, he sent a letter to Mrs. Garway to acquaint her that he was gone out of town, but he left three half-crowns with her maid to pay for his lodging. But as to his going out of town, it was false, for he never went into the country, but took a lodging at Mr. Jones' in St. Paul's Churchyard. It is observable also that he went for a Parliament man when he lodged at Mr. Garway's and had his footmen to attend upon him, etc. There it was that he was seen to have an ordinary handkerchief and to hold it to the fire, which was taken notice of by Mrs. Jackson, the daughter of Mrs. Garway, which was not suitable, as she thought, to a Parliament man's quality, but rather fit for a seaman, for it was like the apron of the maid of the house, which hath been showed in court and compared with the handkerchief that was tied about Dr. Clenche's neck. She saith it is the same or very like that which she did see Mr. Harrison holding in his hand.

"Cartwright, the officer at the Compter, he tells you that the Sunday night, the day before the murder, Mr. Harrison came to Wood Street Compter and inquired for Mrs. Vanwicke, and that he only was in her chamber, and no other body on that side of the house but Mrs. Vanwicke, the prisoner, and this Cartwright, the keeper, who stood at the door and heard Harrison say that he would have the blood of that rogue and named Clench or Winch. Now on the Monday on which this fact was committed, he having taken a lodging at Jones his house, he came thither with a porter, who brought his portmanteau trunk about eight o'clock at night, and after he had been there a little while he went away.

"And you are told by a gentleman that lodges at the Golden Key against Fetter Lane end, that he had some acquaintance with the prisoner, that he had lent him a morning gown, and that about nine o'clock that very night he came to his lodging in a cloak, and then the gentleman asked him for his gown, and he told him that he had brought it with him. Thereupon the gentleman invites Mr. Harrison to stay and sup with him. Mr. Harrison said he could not stay, for he was engaged; he must be gone, for that a gentleman staid in the street for him to go about extraordinary business.

"The coachman tells you that near about that time two men in Fleet Street, near Fetter Lane end, hired his coach of him to go to Brownlow Street to Dr. Clenche's, but he cannot positively say that the prisoner at the bar was one of them, but he swears that he does verily believe that he was one of them.

"Being hired to go to Dr. Clenche's, he drove to the street end, but no further, because the gate at the lower end was shut up, and he could not turn his coach in the street, but he was sent by them to the doctor's to desire the doctor to come out to them, and they sat in the coach in the meantime. The doctor made haste and went to them immediately, and they drove away to Leadenhall and then to Aldgate, and they called at the Pye Tavern and inquired for one Mr. Hunt, a chyrurgeon, as I mentioned to you before; he not being there, they returned to drive through Aldgate, gave the watch sixpence and passed through the gate without any manner of notice taken, but if the watch had done their duty it might have been better discovered. But further the coachman tells you that when he came to Leadenhall Street they called to him and directed him to buy one fowl, and after that he had gone a little way from the coach they called him back and bade him take some more money and buy two fowls. So he went and bought the fowls, but when he came back the two gentlemen were gone, and he found the doctor still in the coach; and, he not stirring, he thought he had been in drink, but upon further examination and

THE CASE OF HENRY HARRISON

calling the watchman with his candle, it appeared that the doctor was strangled with a handkerchief and with a coal.

"There is one Mrs. Eleanor Ashbolt, who lives in Brownlow Street with her mother, and had been sent of an errand, and between nine and ten of the clock at night she saw the coachman in Brownlow Street and thought that these men in the coach might have put a trick upon him by going away without paying him his fare. And she says further that by the help of the lamps she did discern the face of this Harrison in the coach; he had a cloak on, with a light perriwig, and looked out of the coach and did swear at the coachman, and by this means she knew him when she saw him again to be the same man both by his face and voice. The woman, indeed, was not before the coroner, and she gives you this reason for it, because her mother was not willing she should be concerned in such a matter as this was, and what she could say was not known to Mrs. Clenche till after the second sessions, and when he was in Newgate she saw him there and declared he was the same man.

"There was another piece of evidence, viz., that of the boy's, which does not appear; he was examined before the coroner. There has been evidence given of ill practice to take him out of the way, and therefore his affidavit is read for evidence. He swears he saw two gentlemen come out of the coach when it stood in Leadenhall Street, and that, having seen the prisoner in Newgate since, he doth believe him to be the one. This, gentlemen, is the sum and substance of the evidence for the King to prove that the prisoner was one of those that committed the murder.

"You have heard likewise what the prisoner says for himself: he does undertake to prove that he was in another place, that is, that he should come into Macaffee's house . . . in Chancery Lane; and Macaffee, he tells you that there were some other company there, and that Harrison came in very cold, and that they went to cards and played one penny a corner at whist, and that he did continue there from nine till eleven o'clock; and if he was there then it is impossible that he should be guilty of this fact, for the fact was done between the same hours.

"Macaffee's wife tells you the same, and they both tell you who were there besides and who played together, and are positive that the prisoner was there.

"Baker says that he went away about half an hour after ten at night and left Harrison behind him. To confirm this evidence they have called two other witnesses, besides the drawers at the King's Head Tavern, viz., Mr. Sutton the chyrurgeon, who lives in Stone Cutter Street, and Mr. Russell. Mr. Sutton says he had been at the Horseshoe Tavern in Chancery Lane and called for half a pint of sack at the King's Head Tavern when they came by, and as they sat in the coach Mr. Harrison came by accidentally, and one of them, looking out of the coach, cries ' Harry!' or ' Harrison!' and he went to them, and they drank together another half-pint of sack. As to their meeting with Harrison and as to other passages there, Russell says the same, but as to the time of night he is not positive. And they sent one of the drawers to a house in Crown Court to inquire for somebody there.

"The drawers at the King's Head Tavern say that Mr. Sutton and Mr. Russell did call there about that time, and that they drank two half-pints of wine, and that when they were drinking a man came by with a hanging coat or cloak on and drank with them. And one of the drawers went to call somebody in Crown Court, and one of the company up with his muff and gave him a slap in the face.

"Now this is the sum and substance of the evidence you have heard on the behalf of the prisoner to induce you to believe that he was not the person that was concerned in the murder of Dr. Clenche, to which evidence an answer hath been offered, first, as to those witnesses Macaffee and his wife: divers witnesses have been produced to prove that they are people of doubtful credit;

it seems they keep a house of ill fame. Gentlemen, the people of the house are not of very good reputation; they keep a naughty and disorderly house (if you believe the witnesses); you may consider of their credit. And as to Mr. Baker: about nine years since he was convicted of an arrant cheat, which is no less than forgery, for altering the scavenger's rate for St. Giles' parish, and therefore the less credit is to be given to his evidence, for now it appears that he is a knave upon record, and the very record was produced against him, which is true, without doubt, notwithstanding his pretence of innocency. What is said by Mr. Russell and Mr. Sutton I must leave to your consideration, for they had been a-drinking, and the drawer says they were at the King's Head Tavern at eleven of the clock at night. Mr. Harrison the next day after the murder met a gentleman at Jones' coffee-house at Salisbury Court; and though he had taken a lodging at Paul's Churchyard, yet he said that he was newly come to town, and had been in Kent, and had remained there about three weeks, and that he wanted a laundress and a lodging, although he had not been out of town and had taken a lodging the day before; and then he told the witness who discoursed with him about the death of Dr. Clenche that he had formerly loved him, but said that he had been of late a barbarous rogue to a poor gentlewoman, a friend of his, and that the just judgement of God had fallen upon him for so doing, and that he would write to her to give her an account of it and advise her to write to Mrs. Clenche and tell her that she was a widow now as well as Mrs. Vanwicke; and he thought by that means to move Mrs. Clenche to pity her, being a widow as well as herself; and that whilst they were talking thus one Mr. Ravenscroft tells him that Dr. Clenche was murdered and that a bully of the town that belonged to a gentlewoman in the Compter, one Mrs. Vanwicke, was suspected, at which Mr. Harrison was much startled and said that no one was concerned with that gentlewoman but himself, and for aught he knew he might be taken up for it.

"Now what said Mr. Harrison further for himself? Why, says he, this gentlewoman is not in prison at the prosecution of Dr. Clenche, and was not so affirmed, but so reported, and whether it were so or no is no great matter. Gentlemen, you ought to consider the evidence you have heard against him and also to weigh well the evidence he hath brought for himself.

"It is most plain, if you believe the witnesses, that Mr. Harrison was concerned for this woman Vanwicke, and hath threatened Dr. Clenche, calling him rogue and rascal, and said he deserved to have his throat cut; that Harrison went under disguise for some time before the murder. You have had an account of the handkerchief, what kind of handkerchief Harrison had and what handkerchief was taken about Dr. Clenche's neck; you have seen and you have heard what evidence was given by Mr. Humston, how the prisoner was with him about nine o'clock that night and how he refused to stay and sup with Mr. Humston. If Mr. Harrison had no earnest business he might have staid with Mr. Humston better than to have gone to an alehouse in Crown Court and played at cards at one penny a piece a corner; he might have had better fare, no doubt.

"The witnesses for the prisoner say for him that he came to Macaffee's house about nine o'clock at night and staid till eleven; that is contrary to that evidence given for the King, viz., that he was in the coach at Brownlow Street end, for if he was at Macaffee's house all that time they mention, it is impossible he should be guilty. All these things are under your serious consideration. You had best go together; and if you are not satisfied upon the evidence you have heard that he is guilty, then you ought to acquit him. But if you are satisfied that he did commit this murder, then you ought to find him guilty."

The jury found him guilty, and he was then put back,

as was the custom, till the last day of the sessions, when he was sentenced to death. He died protesting his innocence.

He had been previously tried for another murder, but convicted of manslaughter only. Shortly after this trial a man named John Cook, who, it was suggested, was the other murderer of Dr. Clenche, was put on trial, but acquitted.

THE PROSECUTION OF DR. HADWEN

THE trial of Dr. Hadwen, of Gloucester, in 1924 for manslaughter was a very unhappy example of a man prosecuted on account of his unorthodox views on pathology. The opinion of the general public, shared, it is to be hoped, by the great majority of the medical profession, is emphatically that this accusation should never have been brought, and that it would never have been so had it not been for the fact that Dr. Hadwen was a well-known anti-vivisectionist and anti-vaccinationist. His triumphant acquittal caused the greatest rejoicing in the town where he practised and where he was so well known, so popular and so beloved. Probably never have such scenes been witnessed at any trial of modern times. The large and enthusiastic crowds, the impossibility of repressing the rejoicing outside and even inside the court, the popular sympathy exhibited throughout the country by the press and the public—all contributed to make the conclusion of the case most noteworthy. *Truth* expresses the general view held as to the prosecution. The following extract from its issue of November 5th, 1924, is interesting, if mortifying, reading: " The acquittal of Dr. Hadwen at Gloucester Assizes should give satisfaction to many besides the doctor himself and his personal friends. Apart from any questions of medical theory and practice that it raised, the prosecution was—if not malicious in the technical sense—inspired by sentiments which had little relation to the administration of justice. It was malicious in the sense that it emanated from animosity towards Dr. Hadwen personally and readiness to accomplish his professional downfall. The feeling that was at work may easily be seen from the striking contrast between this case and the ordinary case in which a doctor incurs the imputation of negligence or professional ignorance in his treatment of a patient.

"In the ordinary case it is notoriously difficult to obtain evidence against a medical man even in a civil action for damages, far more so when criminal negligence is imputed. The disposition of the profession is to stand by one another loyally in time of trouble, this not merely out of brotherly love, but because the credit of the profession is at stake, unless the accused has so flagrantly misconducted himself that his brethren think it more desirable to wash their hands of him. When it comes to a possible case of manslaughter, a medical coroner often sits in the judgment-seat and holds the scales of justice with a visible bias in favour of the brother whose treatment of the deceased is called in question.

"The Public Prosecutor cannot be blamed for taking up the case after the coroner had committed Dr. Hadwen on a charge of manslaughter, but I confess that the attempt which was made on behalf of the Crown to remove the trial to the Central Criminal Court against the wish of the defendant seems to me almost to suggest that the Crown lawyers had become infected with the same spirit as the Crown witnesses. The Lord Chief Justice and his colleagues refused this application. . . . Apart from all question of the animus among the witnesses for the prosecution, the indictment rested on matters of opinion respecting wholly technical questions. From these opinions Dr. Hadwen honestly dissents, and, whether he is right or wrong, a layman may well hesitate to pronounce him a criminal because he holds his own opinion and follows it in his practice."

The following is a very brief *résumé* of the events leading up to the trial: Dr. Hadwen attended a family named Burnham One of the children, Nellie, had an attack of sore throat. She was getting on quite well, and the doctor had not seen her for a few days, when he was sent for and found her suffering from pneumonia. A relative of the Burnham family persuaded the mother to send for another doctor. This was done, and Dr. Hadwen was told his services were no longer required. The child died, and an inquest was held. The first intimation Dr. Hadwen had of the death was on August 13th, when he was suddenly summoned to the coroner's court and told he ought to bring a solicitor with him, as a serious charge was to be preferred against him. The jury returned a verdict of manslaughter against Dr. Hadwen by a majority of nine to three.

The trial took place at Gloucester Assizes on October 27th, 1924, before Mr. Justice Lush. Mr. C. F. Vachell, K.C., and Mr. St. John Micklethwait appeared as counsel for the prosecution, whilst Dr. Hadwen was represented by Sir Edward Marshall Hall, K.C., and Mr. A. F. Clements.

Mr. Vachell, in opening for the Crown, said that a little girl named Nellie Burnham, ten years of age, died at Gloucester in August, 1924. She died of diphtheria and pneumonia, which followed on it. She was attended in that illness by Dr. Hadwen, who stood charged with manslaughter, because the prosecution alleged that through his inattention, gross neglect, and want of skill or knowledge, or both, he failed to detect the disease from which the child was suffering and to administer the proper remedy, and that, if he had not so grossly failed in his duty as a medical man, in all probability the child would have recovered and would have been alive now. The jury would hear from his lordship what amount of actual negligence rendered a man criminally responsible when death resulted from it. Any person, whether he is a properly qualified medical practitioner or not, who professes to deal with the life or health of others, is bound to have competent skill to perform the task which he holds himself out to perform, and bound to treat his patients with care, attention, and assiduity, and if a patient dies for want thereof, he is guilty of manslaughter.

Mr. Vachell then proceeded to review at length the evidence to be called for the prosecution, and remarked that Dr. Hadwen in this case never took a swab from the throat of the patient with a view of seeing whether the diphtheria microbe was there or not ; yet, counsel submitted, here was a case of a most suspicious nature in view of all the surrounding circumstances. There was one happening to which perhaps the defence would attach some importance ; that was on one occasion when the little girl, while the mother was away from home, came downstairs to fetch some water. He gathered that the suggestion would be made that the child caught pneumonia and that it was pneumonia which caused her death. The post-mortem proved death to be due to diphtheria and pneumonia. If the child did contract pneumonia and died from that independently of anything to do with the diphtheria, there was nothing that could be laid to the charge of Dr. Hadwen ; but the evidence he was about to call would establish the fact that the pneumonia was of that sort which followed and was a sequel to diphtheria. They knew Dr. Hadwen as a gentleman of position in the city and a justice of the peace. Still if the evidence satisfied the jury that he had been grossly negligent, little caring what attention he paid to the case, and that in consequence of that inattention the child's life had probably been sacrificed, then, much as they might regret it, it would be their duty to find him guilty. Dr. Ellis, of Gloucester, who was the doctor called in to supersede Dr. Hadwen, was very severely cross-examined by Sir Edward Marshall Hall.

I am sorry to put it to you, but you have a very strong feeling against Dr. Hadwen, have you not ?—No, I have not.

Be careful.—I am very careful.

Did you write to the *Daily Express* and the *Daily Mail* asking them to send representatives to interview you, as you could give important information with regard to

Dr. Hadwen's medical position ?—You are referring to August last year.
Yes. You did ?—Yes.
Did they both send representatives ?—I forget now. I think one of them did.
Both. Shall I bring them to court ? They are here.—No. I do not dispute it.
Was your communication to them so libellous that they never printed a word of it ?—I forget entirely.
Did either the *Daily Mail* or the *Daily Express* or the Gloucester paper print any of it ?—I do not know they did not.
Did you tell these people that Dr. Hadwen was not entitled to the qualifications that appear after his name in the books of reference ?—I told them there was a discrepancy.
In the letters you wrote to the *Express* and to the other paper did you say, " I have some very interesting information to give your representative concerning Dr. Hadwen, if he will kindly call " ?—I wrote to one of them because he specially asked me for information.
Why should you, a member of the same profession, take upon yourself to communicate to a London paper matter derogatory to one of your brother professionals in the city ?—Because he had been communicating to the local press and to the press all over the world matter derogatory to me and to everybody else in the profession.
In saying he did not believe in vaccination ?—He said more than that.
He simply said he did not believe in vaccination and you people did, and you took it upon yourself to say that that was a reflection on you personally ?—It was not a question of belief in vaccination ; it was a question of the epidemic here, and the suggestion he made was that there was no small-pox in the town : it was all chicken-pox, and that the whole epidemic had been trumped up for the benefit of the members of the profession.

THE PROSECUTION OF DR. HADWEN 315

So you thought you would communicate private information with regard to his professional status to the papers ?—I had been asked to give all the information I could.

The only witness called for the defence was Dr. Hadwen himself, who told the Court that he thought the case was one of ulcerative tonsillitis, that he had no belief in the antitoxin treatment of diphtheria, and that he would never allow a patient of his to have this remedy if he could help it.

Mr. Vachell then again addressed the jury. They would be asked, he said, to consider whether there was in this case culpable neglect, and if so, did that neglect either cause or accelerate the death of the child ? The first matter which one was bound to consider was whether the child had ever had diphtheria or not. As against all the evidence of the prosecution, they had simply the evidence of Dr. Hadwen, the most interested person in the case. His whole anxiety was naturally to escape from the charge that was made against him. Not one single medical man had been called before them to support any of the views and theories upon which the doctor had lectured so eloquently in the witness-box. That perhaps would be more important when one came to consider the merits of antitoxin than when one was dealing with this first question, as to what the child was suffering from. But Dr. Hadwen stands alone and says in effect, " You must discredit all the witnesses for the prosecution. Accept my theories on disease ; put on one side the whole weight of the medical men of this and all other countries. I do not believe them ; I have no regard for them. Accept your facts from me." Dr. Hadwen preferred not to give antitoxin. The question of antitoxin was more than a belief with the doctor: it was a religion. Dr. Hadwen had said he would not give antitoxin and would try to prevent others from giving it to his patients, and it was worthy of consideration whether the true explanation of the doctor's conduct throughout was to be found in that and was based upon it. Might it not be that the doctor was prepared to call it tonsillitis and treat it as such rather than notify the case and let it go to the isolation hospital? They would have to consider whether that was the cause of or had accelerated death. The next thing they had to consider was how far Dr. Hadwen could be said to be criminally liable for what he did. Much depended on what he actually saw. The case for the prosecution was that antitoxin ought to have been administered on his first visit. If Dr. Hadwen, in the excess of his zeal for doctrines which are believed in by but few of his fellow-practitioners, wilfully shut his eyes to the symptoms and persuaded himself to believe that this was not diphtheria, but something he might call tonsillitis, and if he were prompted in that by the knowledge that if he called it diphtheria the child would receive antitoxin treatment, that was neglect on his part of so gross a character and so tinged with feeling, that it surely came within the range of criminal neglect. If he neglected to give care to his patient and indulged in his own special whims in medical matters, that again was criminal neglect. A doctor's first care must be his patient, and not the airing and practice of his own particular views, and if there were a recognised method of dealing with a disease, and if the results as shown by statistics were greatly in favour of the use of that particular remedy, was a doctor to say, because he had acted on a general theory differing from all other medical men, that he was to allow a child to run a risk which could not exist if the child were given the antitoxin treatment by some one more orthodox than himself? Was it the sort of care that poor people were entitled to expect even if they paid only a small fee for the services of a doctor?

One thing, said counsel, in conclusion, which had done good to mankind and saved a large number of lives, was the particular serum which Dr. Hadwen chose to despise.

He had sufficient information before him to make him suspicious of diphtheria, and he ought to have taken steps which all prudent doctors did. He should have taken a swab, and the antitoxin treatment would have been applied and the child's life in all probability saved. Instead, he went on his somewhat curious views upon the whole subject of antitoxins and the whole question of bacilli and germs—views which no one had come into the box to support. He chose rather to take things into his own hands and treat the case as tonsillitis. This was something so gross and so unfair, both to the patient and the poor mother, that the jury should feel bound for the protection of public welfare to register a verdict to show that they regarded it as a crime. He had no doubt that Dr. Hadwen was sincere in his somewhat unusual beliefs, and the probability was that those beliefs made him deliberately close his eyes to the true condition of the child. If he had done his duty and exercised proper care, had examined the throat, and looked at the symptoms, and administered the antitoxin which he abhorred, the strong probability was that the child would never have died.

Sir Edward Marshall Hall then addressed the jury for the defence. He said the case for the prosecution almost entirely depended upon the evidence given by that most eminent medical man, Sir William Wilcox, for whom he (counsel) had the greatest regard. But he was not in a position, however great his eminence, to come down and say there was an absolute rule or practice by all qualified men that on the suspicion of diphtheria they must take a swab and inject antitoxin. He (counsel) submitted with the greatest confidence that it would be a terrible day for this country, for the medical practitioners as much as for the people who were their patients, if any such broad proposition of law were laid down.

The jury had to ask themselves whether Dr. Hadwen diagnosed the case as one of diphtheria, and if he did not, was it an honest diagnosis, or did he wilfully (by reason of his prejudice against the well-known fashionable diphtheria treatment) and deliberately shut his eyes to the symptoms which he otherwise ought to have seen? In his (counsel's) submission, although he was not saying it was irrelevant, it was only of collateral relevancy that it was a fact that the child was suffering from diphtheria, because if the jury were satisfied that the child was suffering from diphtheria in such an aggravated form as to be mainly responsible for its death, then they might say that it was incredible that a doctor with the experience of Dr. Hadwen should have honestly mistaken those symptoms. That was really the test of the case. Although they had the word of four medical witnesses that the child died from diphtheria, it was not conclusive against Dr. Hadwen, and it was only so far as that evidence affected Dr. Hadwen that it was of importance to the case. Dr. Hadwen had thirty-five years' experience, and he was entitled to the benefit of any reputation he had earned among his fellow-citizens in the great city where he practised, however much they disagreed with the extremity of his conclusions and ideas, and he was before them as an honest man who deserved his reputation. Dr. Hadwen said he had not diagnosed diphtheria, and that it was not diphtheria as far as he knew; but unfortunately he could not say whether that was right or wrong by reason of the unfair way in which he had been treated in the case.

He asked them to say that the girl caught pneumonia consequent on a chill got by going downstairs at night. If they thought the girl did go downstairs in her bare feet to get some water, and as a result of that contracted pneumonia from which she died, Dr. Hadwen was not guilty under any consideration. Had the jury any doubt about it? According to the statement of the mother, the child was seized with vomiting and was much worse after this. There were two facts which he (counsel) regarded as of vital importance. One was the admitted fact that the child ran the risk of incurring a chill; the other was that the type of pneumonia was the pneumonia one would expect from a chill. The jury might think that Dr. Hadwen was obstinate, that his views on medical matters were eccentric, but he hoped they would not believe the suggestion that he was the only medical man in England who was opposed to the administration of antitoxin. In this case it was admitted that Dr. Hadwen had given the brother of the little girl the best attention, and this was the weakness of the case for the prosecution. Here they had to explain away something. Dr. Hadwen said the boy never had diphtheria, but had ulcerative tonsillitis. He treated him and cured him, and treated Nellie in the same way, and would have cured her had she not contracted this chill. Was Dr. Hadwen to be charged with manslaughter and convicted because he omitted to give the child on what was the third day of illness antitoxin treatment, of which he strongly disapproved, or charged and convicted of manslaughter because he did not take a swab and call in another doctor to administer the antitoxin, or because he was said to have failed wilfully or neglectfully to diagnose diphtheria but treated the child for another disease? Where was the negligence? Mistaken diagnosis possibly, probably if they liked. If they thought Dr. Hadwen was wrong and the child was suffering from diphtheria, that was a chance which every one took when a doctor was called in. No doctor was infallible and no doctor was liable for an honest mistake. No one could say that was manslaughter.

In conclusion Sir Edward said the jury must be satisfied that the child died of diphtheria, and that this death was the result of negligent treatment by Dr. Hadwen, before they could bring in a verdict of guilty. If they were not satisfied, he was entitled to be acquitted.

Mr. Justice Lush in his summing up pointed out to the jury that they had now reached the last stage of this very serious and somewhat unusual case. They had listened to two very powerful speeches, and it was now his duty to sum up the evidence, after which it would be their duty to say what their verdict was.

"The case is undoubtedly, as I have said, a very serious one. It has consequences that extend beyond those who are personally concerned in this case. A charge of manslaughter is brought against a medical man who has for some thirty years been following his profession and practising in this city of Gloucester, and of course to him it is a matter of the utmost importance. It is a matter of great importance to the public, to the community, and, I may say, to the medical profession, because while on the one hand children and others are entitled to be, and must be, protected against criminal neglect, criminal misconduct, on the part of a medical man, it would be deplorable and disastrous if a medical man, following his profession according to the best of his judgment and acting honestly in his treatment of a patient, were to think that he had hanging over his head a weapon like this if anything should go wrong with his patient.

"Now it is of the utmost importance you should realise this fact. You are not sitting as a jury merely to criticise Dr. Hadwen's views. You are not here merely to say whether he has or has not adopted views which, in your opinion, a wise medical man ought not to adopt. The charge against him is that he caused the death of this little girl. Many cases have been tried in these courts in which a medical man has undertaken the cure of a patient and has in the course of the endeavour to cure the patient chosen to administer a dangerous drug or perform some operation in the hope that it would do good to the patient. If the drug was administered or the operation performed in such a disgraceful or careless fashion that the patient died, then there is no difficulty in saying that the doctor caused the death of the patient,

But the peculiarity of this case is this. Nobody suggests that Dr. Hadwen did anything, administered a drug or performed an operation or did anything, which caused the death of Nellie Burnham. What is said is that he was so neglectful in his diagnosis and in his treatment that the child whose life would have been saved if proper care had been used died through that neglect, and the Crown therefore has to prove this, not only that there was neglect, but that she would have had her life saved or prolonged.

"There are two quite distinct questions that you have to deal with in this case. The first is whether there was culpable neglect on the part of Dr. Hadwen; the second, if there was neglect, was the death caused by it? If you come to the conclusion that on August 1st, the day on which Dr. Hadwen first attended Nellie, there was nothing to suggest that the child was suffering from a serious condition of the throat, it seems to me that there is this difficulty in the way of the prosecution, and I want you to bear this in mind. The doctor went again on August 4th. This was six days after the commencement of the child's illness, because the child was taken ill on July 30th. We know from Sir William Wilcox and all the other doctors that unless the antitoxin is given within six days it is practically ineffective. It is practically useless to give it; and if the truth is that until August 4th Dr. Hadwen had no reason to suspect that there was anything seriously wrong with the child's throat, it seems to follow that, even if he did after August 4th neglect the child, that did not really affect the recovery of the child. It certainly did not make the withholding of the antitoxin a matter of any seriousness. I ask you to attach the greatest importance to this question. What was the condition of the patient when Dr. Hadwen first saw her? If she showed signs of diphtheria, if he then ought to have said to himself, 'Well, this is a serious case. I must give it close attention,' then you will have to ask yourselves whether he did give it the attention that the case deserved, having regard to the symptoms. Then it will become important to you to consider whether he ought or ought not to have taken a swab and administered antitoxin, which we are told is the course the ordinary careful doctor follows. But if, on the other hand, on August 1st this little girl was showing only the same symptoms which her brother had shown, if there was nothing serious in the throat, nothing to call the attention of the doctor to the fact that it might be diphtheria, then no one would think of criticising him for not taking a swab or for not administering antitoxin. Therefore you have to bear in mind the importance of that date and ask yourselves whether the Crown has proved to your reasonable satisfaction that on that 1st of August the child did show signs of a serious malady which the doctor with gross neglect refused to consider. So much for that part of the case.

"The other factor which bears upon the question whether the death was caused by neglect is the matter you have heard so much about, the pneumonia. If the pneumonia was really the secondary consequence of the diphtheria, then, if the doctor is responsible for the diphtheritic condition continuing, of course he would be equally responsible for the pneumonic condition, because it would follow as a consequence of the diphtheria. But if, on the other hand, the pneumonia was brought about by an entirely independent act, the unfortunate act on the part of the child of getting out of bed, going downstairs, walking with bare feet upon the tiled kitchen, and then going back to her bed, if, in fact, it was that which caused the pneumonia and the pneumonia caused the death, then one cannot say that neglect on the part of the doctor in the earlier days of August had anything to do with her death. Therefore you have to consider this question with reference to pneumonia from that point of view. Did the child die of pneumonia? If she did was the pneumonia the consequence of the diphtheria which the doctor ought to have discovered and treated in the early days of August, or was it the consequence of something the child unfortunately did, and for which no one can blame Dr. Hadwen? These are the two things, the important factors, for you to take into account when you come to consider the second of the two questions you have to deal with, namely, Did the neglect in fact cause death? If it did not all I can say to you is that there is an end to the case.

"Then we come to the medical evidence, and the medical evidence is important with regard to this matter of neglect particularly. In one sense it does not matter whether the child died of diphtheria or whether it never had diphtheria, but in another sense it is a matter of importance, which you cannot ignore and with which you must deal. If the child never had diphtheria, then away goes the case for the prosecution, for their case is that the doctor was guilty of wicked and culpable neglect in not recognising and treating it. The child undoubtedly had pneumonia. The doctors called by the prosecution say the pneumonia was secondary to diphtheria. If the child never had diphtheria, the pneumonia could not have been the secondary consequence, and it must probably have been from chill contracted on the day the child went downstairs. One cannot shut one's eyes to the importance of this question, Had the child diphtheria? Do not misunderstand me. It does not follow if she had that Dr. Hadwen was criminally responsible. I have dealt with the question of his neglect on the hypothesis that she had diphtheria, but if she had not, the case against him disappears. Now we come to this very singular aspect of the case. We have heard of Dr. Hadwen's views and mental attitude with regard to the generally accepted theory that diphtheria is a bacillus disease, as to the discovery of the bacillus and the discovery of its treatment by antitoxin. We have heard his views as to the correctness of that theory. As I have said before, you are not sitting here as a tribunal to criticise these views, to say whether you agree with them or whether you do not. Some people who have heard them may take a very strong view about them and I think it is legitimate to say it would be very unfortunate if any one doctor were to shut his eyes to improvements in medical treatment which are accepted by the medical profession as a whole and to say, unless he has good ground for saying so ' I prefer to follow the old-fashioned treatment; I do not believe in these discoveries.' After all, medical science is a great science, the medical profession is a very great profession, and unless a doctor is going to avail himself of the discoveries that are made from time to time by those who follow the medical profession, one is not likely to see that development of medical science and improvement in medical treatment which one hopes to see. It does not follow from that, of course, that a man who will stick to his own views is guilty of culpable and wicked neglect. A doctor is allowed by our law to practise his profession in the way which he honestly thinks is the best, and if a doctor does hold peculiar views, and honestly holds them, and works them out and follows them because in his judgment they are the best methods to apply, one cannot say that he is guilty of any misconduct or any culpable or wicked neglect, even though one may think he is sadly mistaken. But I think one can conceive a state of things in which a man can get his mind into such a state of prejudice that really his position is this, that he would rather sacrifice his patients than his prejudices. I do not say that is true of Dr. Hadwen at all. I only say it is a possible state of things, and if a man allows his mind to be so prejudiced and his judgment to be so blinded that he is unwilling to avail himself of discoveries and learn things that are being taught by the profession of which he is a member, I can understand a jury saying of such a man that he is guilty of wilful neglect. Now we come to this question: Was the child suffering from diphtheria or not? You have a very powerful body of evidence on the part of the prosecution upon that question. A swab taken gave a positive result, and the presence of the bacillus was found, and the fact that the bacillus theory is adopted and acted upon by almost every doctor in the land, the evidence that you have had with regard to the membrane that came away, and the evidence of the positive diphtheritic result that you have had with regard to the other two children makes a strong body of evidence on the part of the prosecution on this question. You have heard the evidence of Dr. Hadwen on the point, who, as I say, does hold strong views about the uselessness of this bacillus theory, and you have to ask yourselves whether the child was or was not suffering from this disease. If you come to the conclusion that she was not, of course the criticism against Dr. Hadwen falls to the ground. If you come to the conclusion that she was, it does not in the least dispose of the question, but it is then a factor which must be put into the scale, and to which proper weight must be given, but even then you are thrown back upon the question to which I have referred before, namely, Did the neglect, if it existed, cause the death of the child? May I repeat the salient points? and then I have done. The burden of proof is upon the Crown. The Crown must establish that Dr. Hadwen was guilty of culpable, wicked neglect in his treatment of the patient. They must prove that, if he had not been guilty of that neglect, he would have discovered in the ordinary course that the child was suffering from diphtheria. They must prove that the condition of the child at the time was such—I mean that the stage was so early—that by the use of antitoxin the child's life would have been, at all events, prolonged, and they must prove that he was guilty of culpable neglect, or would have been if he had discovered the cause of the malady, in not administering antitoxin : that is to say, in other words they must show that the death of the child must be laid at his door, because it was he who had undertaken the charge of the child ; that he had the means at his disposal of saving that child's life, and that he wilfully —I mean by that not intentionally, of course, but that he wickedly and with gross neglect—refused to avail himself of the means at his disposal, and refused to make himself acquainted with what the child was suffering from, and with the remedy he had at hand. If the Crown has proved all these things, then, without regard to the consequences, you will say so and find him guilty. But if the Crown has failed to prove either of them, if the Crown has failed to prove the neglect, or even if they have proved it, and they have failed to prove that that neglect caused the death, then Dr. Hadwen is entitled to a verdict of acquittal. I will ask you now to consider the evidence and tell me whether you find Dr. Hadwen guilty or not guilty."

The jury retired, and, after a few minutes' consideration, returned a verdict of not guilty. The result was greeted with prolonged applause in court, which the officials were quite unable to suppress. Thus ended a trial which served no useful purpose and which caused world-wide comments on the conduct of some of the members of the medical profession in Gloucester.

www.ingramcontent.com/pod-product-compliance
Lightning Source LLC
Chambersburg PA
CBHW020726180526
45163CB00001B/120